The Uncertain States of America Reader

THE UNCERTAIN STATES OF AMERICA READER

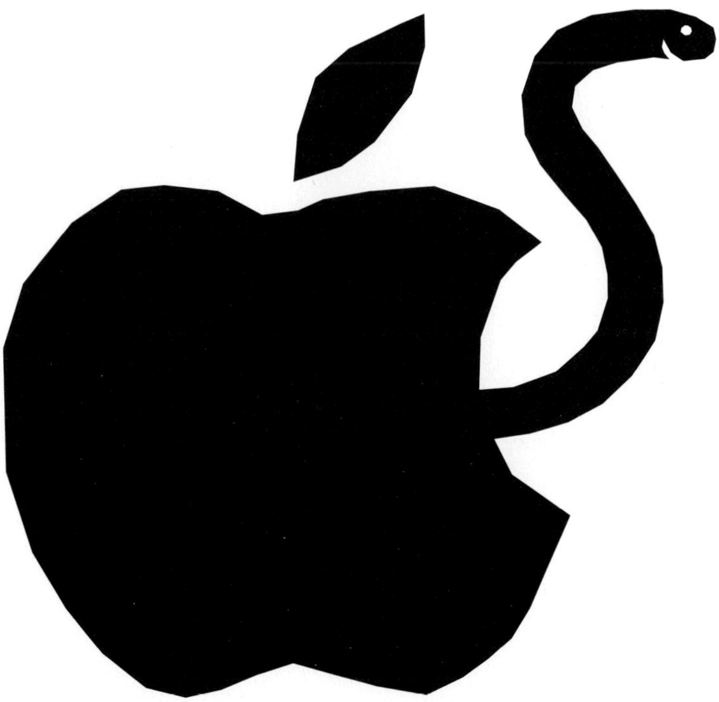

Sternberg Press
Astrup Fearnley Museum of Modern Art / Serpentine Gallery
2006

Contents

Curators' foreword

That something should be written about art is taken as self-evident. Russian philosopher Boris Groys has spelled out this unwritten law in all its might: "Images without text are embarrassing, like a naked person in a public space. At the very least they need a textual bikini in the form of an inscription with the name of the artist and the title (in the worst case this can read 'untitled')."

Since our exhibition "Uncertain States of America" already has a catalogue, the function of this additional collection of texts, compiled by Noah Horowitz and Brian Sholis, cannot be reduced to this fear of nakedness. Nor is it motivated by that hapless, and endlessly replicated, reflex to produce something new for the sake of further differentiating our "product," or for having our voices better heard. So why has it been produced? Primarily out of curiosity. We are not aware of another reader such as this and it was among the earliest side projects we discussed pursuing before this exhibition's debut in Oslo last year. Thus we offer the fruit of this long-term preoccupation. If this anthology can provide first hints at answers to the questions posed in the compiler's introduction, it has accomplished its task.

We want to thank everyone involved. This book is dedicated to the memory of Jason Rhoades (1965–2006), a friend and colleague who was unmistakeably American to the last.

Daniel Birnbaum
Gunnar B. Kvaran
Hans Ulrich Obrist

Editors' introduction

This reader, a companion volume to the "Uncertain States of America" exhibition catalogue, began in 2005 when the curators met with artists in their studios. What were the artists reading? What articles, books, reviews—and, they soon discovered, cartoons, cookbooks, memoirs, and film scripts—were influencing their practices? A comprehensive survey of these curiosities was not included in the earlier exhibition catalogue. It remained, pace Obrist, an "Unrealized Project."

Invited one year later by the curatorial team to construct such a list, we began by surveying the artists in the show and using their recommendations, many of which are included in the reading list at the back of this book, as a starting point for the selection of texts presented here. What follows is a synthesis of their nominations and our own research into significant recent writings by American artists and critics on artistic practice and cultural politics in the United States today. Keeping with the theme of this exhibition, emphasis has been placed on identifying "young," "emerging" writers, though salient pieces by a comparatively older generation and by those who reside outside of America are also included.

We hope that the following selections introduce some new writing and writers and shine a fresh light on more familiar passages. Equally, we hope that this book's reception reaches beyond those audiences who experience the exhibition first hand, and that it becomes a conduit of knowledge outside the immediate exhibition-going public.

The present volume is not a "portrait of this exhibition's artists in text" (an early, and mightily optimistic, vision). Nor is it a top-down survey of all that is novel and noteworthy in today's art world. Cognizant of this exhibition's ambitious modus operandi, to represent "a 'new' vision in American contemporary art," we realize, of course, that some may view this publication as precisely a currency-enhancing invocation of already prevalent curatorial/critical interests. And we understand that such a publication indelibly sanctifies its content, that it operates as a value filter or, as Isabelle Graw observes in these pages, a "sound bite" in order to "underline claims for art-historical importance or theoretical erudition." Yet it is our underlying hope that this reader belies such a roll call of erudite endorsements and that its contents engage readers in unanticipated manners.

It is commonplace to note that contemporary art is swaddled in a haze of words and that it is futile to attempt a synoptic overview of art discourse, so we drew simple boundaries beyond which our inquiry would not trespass, several of them congruent with those set by the "Uncertain States of America" exhibition. The two most binding examples: each piece of writing included here has been published since 2000, and each discusses contemporary art, aesthetics, politics, or the amorphous and expansive zone where these three concerns overlap. Selecting texts thus became a game, albeit one burdened by methodological complications. How to accommodate writings both by artists in "Uncertain States of America" and others critical of their programs, or, for that matter, the very presuppositions of such a traveling group show? What, we contemplated, could be an appropriate framework to muster comprehensiveness in the face of mind-boggling pluralism and attendant information overload? How to play the game? One artist's advice proved invaluable: "Comprehension and coherency are dead ringers for the longing for authority. Don't be an authority. And don't apologize for not being an authority." So we aimed for an eclectic sampling of material by writers—art historians, journalists, critics, artists, philosophers, a graphic designer-slash-lawyer, as well as a fictional character devised by an artist collective—whose contributions, we felt, gained from their placement alongside one another and from being set in relief against the project as a whole.

* * *

In recent years, many have noted how fashionable art that addresses its broader social context has become. The translation of Nicolas Bourriaud's *Relational Aesthetics* into English in 2002 and the ongoing debate about this set of essays is one prominent example of this tendency. Others pertain to the intensification of discussion about the Internet's (virtual) social power and the agency of extra-gallery/museum practices, the latter of which inspired "The Interventionists: Art in the Social Sphere," an exhibition curated by Nato Thompson and presented at Mass MoCA in the summer of 2004.

There has also been a notable upsurge of interest in the art world's supposedly mutating structural composition. For example, while new technologies may enable individuals to act and transact at a distance, there has of late been a curious intensifying of interaction among buyers, sellers, enthusiasts, and pundits at international and ever-trendy art fairs, auctions, biennials, and symposia that now demarcate the art calendar as a matter of course. These developments have not ruptured the clout of cultural epicenters like New York or London, but they have hastened the transformation of how contemporary art's specialist community of artists, dealers, curators, collectors, critics, administrators, sponsors, and policymakers do business: on the run and behind the veil of ever-more-elaborate VIP rituals. Such processes may have aided contemporary art's ascension as a lifestyle commodity, but the pragmatic need to secure financing and visibility in this competitive economy of symbolic goods and services arguably exposes it to opportunism and instrumentalization as never before. The lamented "crisis" of contemporary criticism is at least partially a result of this change: How does one distinguish among so many exquisitely manufactured and seamlessly managed products?

The writings by Jack Bankowsky, Andrea Fraser, Matthew Jesse Jackson, Miwon Kwon, Robert Morris, and Julian Stallabrass included here explore various aspects of these developments, and their reverberations are palpable elsewhere in this volume and in much of today's broader cultural discourse. Book titles such as *Art, Money, Parties* (2004) have thus come to embody the preconditions of this moment, while "Arty Party," Hal Foster's review of Bourriaud's *Relational Aesthetics* and *Postproduction* (2002) and Obrist's *Interviews: Volume I* (2003), offers not only a cogent reading of these three publications but also an instructive if (glib) synopsis of today's art world at large: "Apparently, if one model of the old avant-garde was the Party à la Lenin, today the equivalent is a party à la Lennon."

Despite appearances to the contrary, the fundamental nature of art production remains largely intact: artists still create, patrons still collect, and critics still critique. Yet some accentuations within this value chain do indeed appear to be novel (or at least more apparent): the art industry's privatization and its (at times) politically suspect diffusion into developing economies offer two prominent cases in point. Echoing Bankowsky, one might say that today's art is just *more*: more visible, more mediated, more spectacularized, more institutionalized, more scrutinized, more expensive, more profitable, and more "global." "The international Guggenheim conglomerate isn't so much 'McMuseum,'" Peter Plagens elsewhere reflects, "as it is Boeing or General Dynamics—contemporary art on a military-industrial scale."

Buttressing these developments is an attenuation of interest in specific regional activities. On one level, this is a natural byproduct of the exhibition industry's globalization, whereby biennials, project spaces, and conferences from Cuba to Korea take local socio-political contexts as points of departure. Equally, this interest in the regional appears to constitute the inevitable flip side to 1990s-era globalization hyperbole, with the now hackneyed promises of multilateral cultural exchange replaced by more nuanced readings of these processes' complexities (as epitomized in the five "platforms" of Documenta XI, 2001–02). Whatever its roots, the increasing attention focused on artistic proceedings outside of traditional Western art centers is having a formidable impact in the classroom, salesroom, and across tireless rumor mills; as in other industries, China, Russia, Eastern Europe, and the Middle East have become pivotal foci of speculation.

Counterbalancing this trend—and following in the wake of 9/11 and the 2004 re-election of George W. Bush—is the zeroing in of (primarily European) interest in American art and artists. In the past year alone, one could cite "Uncertain States of America," "USA Today" at the Royal Academy of Arts in London, "This is America: Visions of the American Dream" at the Centraal Museum in Utrecht, the Netherlands, and even "Day for Night," the 2006 Whitney Biennial (curated by Chrissie Iles and Philippe Vergne, Europeans now ensconced in American institutions).

Any cross-cultural interpretation is bound to create misunderstanding, and surely each of these exhibitions draws a limited portrait of the culture it seeks to portray. A somewhat atypical example, "The American Effect: Global Perspectives on the United States, 2000–2003," held at the Whitney Museum of American Art in 2003, exemplifies the dangers inherent in such projects. While many of the above exhibition organizers are one step removed from their subject matter—in the center looking at the periphery, or vice-versa—a two-step removal marked the organization of "The American Effect," in which an American curator, Lawrence Rinder, traveled outside of the country to find artists whose art critiqued the United States; the resultant exhibition, however, was, in the words of one reviewer, "hectoring and jejune and did little to advance the terms of that encounter."

This is undoubtedly a moment marked by a serious interest in the actions America is taking on the world stage—actions that have been described as a cause for grave concern. We do not attempt to authoritatively engage these concerns here. We do, however, think that this sampling of discourse by and about a country's visual artists leads to insights about its politics and society not gained elsewhere.

Many of the artists in this reader's eponymous exhibition would, of course, be quick to disavow explicitly political readings of their work, preferring, as Kori Newkirk recently stated during a panel discussion at Bard College's Center for Curatorial Studies, to "seduce first." He continued: "'Political' content can [simply] come in through the side door or window." The art world's definition of the term "political" remains fuzzy (as Pamela M. Lee rightly notes of its definition of "globalization" as well), but, on occasion, this thinking-through-form counters the obfuscation that now stands for contemporary American political discourse. At the very least, it gives a sense of what it is like to live in the United States today, and results in some inspired debate. We hope that this book serves not only as a valuable compendium of recent writing about contemporary art but also as inspiration to seek further understanding of these "Uncertain States."

* * *

We would like to thank Julia Peyton-Jones, Daniel Birnbaum, Gunnar B. Kvaran, and Hans Ulrich Obrist for inviting us to undertake this project and for being instrumental in its realization; Caroline Schneider of Sternberg Press for ably seeing the book into print; the artists for their consistently trenchant criticisms of and honest responses; all of the authors and publications who granted reprint permission; Charles Gute and Nicole Lanctot for their unflagging copyediting efforts; and David Reinfurt and Stuart Bailey of Dexter Sinister for their grace under pressure. Likewise we wish to thank Greg Allen, Eric C. Banks, Christopher Bedford, Tom Eccles, Bettina Funcke, Melissa Giannini, Liam Gillick, Rachel Harrison, Michael Ned Holte, Gareth James, Miriam Katz, Elizabeth Linden, Molly Nesbit, Lauren O'Neill-Butler, Amie Robinson, Scott Rothkopf, and David Velasco for their thoughtful contributions to the dialogue that produced this book.

Noah Horowitz and Brian Sholis

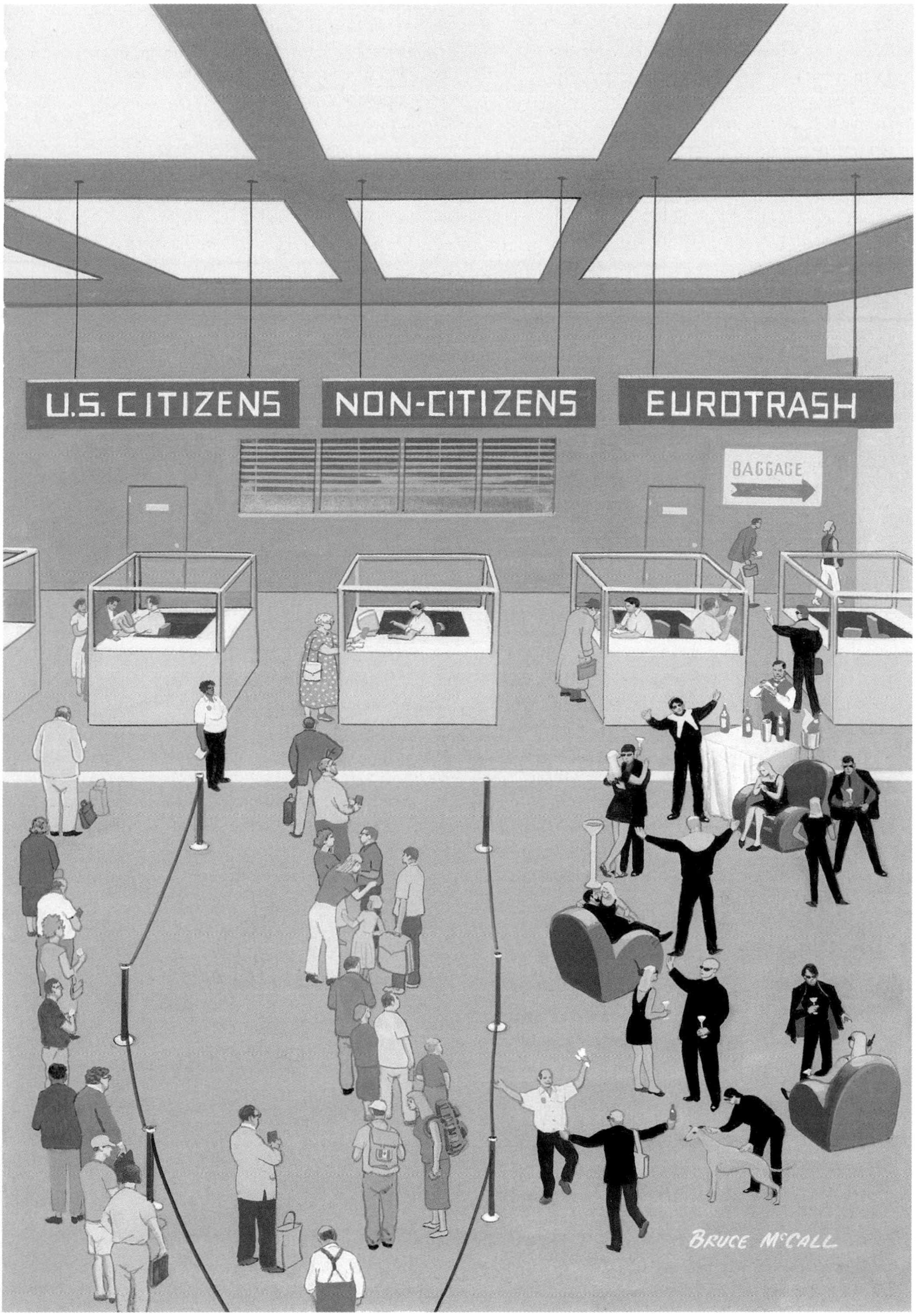

Bruce McCall, *Euro Trash*, cover of the *New Yorker*, October 14–21, 2002

John Bowe, Marisa Bowe, and Sabin Streeter, eds.

Eric Beull, Art Mover

Excerpt from *Gig: Americans Talk About Their Jobs*, New York: Three Rivers Press, 2000

I have wanted to be an artist since 1985, when I was a sophomore at a large Midwestern college and I took a painting course. I had never painted, drawn, or done anything artistic before then—except sometimes try to play a guitar—and I only started because I could not think of anything else to do in school. But I liked it from the beginning. It's one of the few things that ever really interested me. That and girls. [Laughs]

I guess I never seriously thought that I would become famous as a painter. And now, after being in New York City for ten years, and seeing how the art world works, I know for sure that fame will not happen.

The New York art world is a lot like *Peyton Place*, if you know what I mean. There are a few major players and, in a way, they decide who is hot and which artist they can push on the viewing public. It has a lot to do with money. The bigger the money behind the artist, the more famous the artist will become. And by money I mean what gallery is representing the artist and which collector has bought the artist's work. Fame happens to only a handful of people. And there is a huge gap in the art world between haves and the have-nots. You are either making big bucks or you are just a schlepper of some sort for twelve bucks an hour or less.

For a while, I thought I could teach art. I thought I could be a college professor and have a decent life, with plenty of time do my own work. But after my three years in an MFA program, I believe that the art school system is one big lie. The teachers, for the most part, are third-rate hacks, usually past their prime both as teachers and artists. The chance of a young person getting a job is very slim and I gave up on the idea of teaching a long time ago. Although it is a good way to meet young girls if you're a dirty old man.

So I am an art mover.

I get up around seven in the morning most days, sometimes slightly hungover from lack of sleep or beer, and then I get in a truck and drive around for eleven or twelve hours, sometimes more in the busy seasons, carrying big crates of art from the homes of rich people or warehouses to museums or other warehouses. The best is to drive to the Hamptons because it takes all day and you usually only do three stops, and two of those involve a milkshake at the Candy Kitchen in Bridgehampton and then the beach.

But this doesn't happen too often. Usually, we just drive to certain parts of Manhattan. We go to the same places a lot—Sotheby's, Christie's, museums, galleries, framers, and some private dealers. And warehouses. That's something that I bet people don't know: the vast majority of the world's art—including a lot of what you see in books and think of as being really famous—is just boxed up in warehouses. Look at the Museum of Modern Art, only like five percent of their collection is shown. The rest is in crates. Sometimes it reminds me of the final scene in *Citizen Kane*.

My fellow art movers are mostly artists. A few are musicians and a few are just normal guys. I like working with other artists. There is a core group of us who have been with our company for at least three years. We talk about art, usually in the negative, like how crappy a show is that we see, or else we gossip about the art world. But actually, lately, we mostly talk about the job and the stupidity of it. None of us have had any major success, although some have had one-person shows and there's a guy I know who shows with a really good gallery in the city. But so what, the market sucks right now. I mean, this guy, he's still working on the trucks. As for the rest of us, most of us realize that we will never be able to support ourselves as artists, even though everyone wishes they could.

I have moved all the big-name white male artists of this century, and I would say that most of the art we move, if we art movers see it, we don't like. It all seems very old, very stale. Most artists, once they become successful, just seem to repeat themselves. And speaking for myself as a mover, not as an artist, it pisses me off when I break my back for something that was made with no sense of craft, or is needlessly heavy, or is too big and full of self-importance. I always like art that is small and light, even if it is crappy.

A lot of the time we do not even know what it is we are moving because it's already in a crate when we arrive. But sometimes, very rarely, you see something great. Like you go to Si Newhouse's place on the East Side and see a Lucian Freud painting in the living room, which I thought was really impressive. And then—with the crates—who knows what's in there. I was once escorted by police from the airport to the Metropolitan Museum, so whatever was in those crates must have been worth something to someone.

Of course, basically everything we move is worth a lot of money. All of our private clients—you know, the individual art collectors—are rich. Very, very rich. It's hard to say what the average rich person's collection is like. Usually the more money one has, the better the art, but of course, there are always exceptions. One of the first things I did on this job was to move the entire collection of a rich idiot who made his money in shopping malls. There was a lot of kinetic sculpture, including a giant fake rock made of fiberglass, mounted on a concrete slab in the backyard. If you flipped a switch in the kitchen, the rock moved back and forth on the slab. Talk about stupid. And this rock could have paid my salary for six months. And the rich idiot wore those polyester golf pants with no belt loops. And we found a dildo in his bedroom.

Then there was this guy who had this very large suburban house full of taxidermy animals, like elephant feet and big-game heads on the wall. The whole house was filled with them and it was very odd. What made it even odder was that the house seemed like it had not been lived in for the last five years. It was really dusty and dirty. The guy'd moved to Montana, I think. But it didn't matter where he was—we carried all of his dead animals out to our temperature-controlled truck, which took them back to our warehouse, where they are now stored in a climate-controlled room for an indeterminate amount of time.

Collectors are weird. Very weird. I once went to pick up an installation piece that consisted of a long wooden table and a canoe. And inside the canoe were dried up pieces of bread that the artist had chewed up and spit out. I think this was supposed to be some sort of Zen activity that was supposed to, you know, comment on consumption in a capitalistic society, or something stupid like that. Anyway, the whole canoe was filled with these hard, mouth-sized pieces of bread and when we arrived the collector had these two Japanese teenage girls counting all the pieces. How could it possibly matter if there were two thousand six hundred or two thousand five hundred and seventy-five pieces of this dried, chewed-up bread? It was so absurd. The final count was like three thousand two hundred and sixty-three or something, which I wrote down on the paperwork. I wonder if the people at the museum counted the pieces when it arrived.

The collector of this bread did help us get the table into the too-small elevator, which was very nice. Most people just close the door on you—and that's one of the worst things about this job—art movers are treated like any other service person. Which means that we're treated like crap. For starters, we have to go into buildings through the back entrances. Next time you are on the Upper East Side try going into a doorman's building with a package. See what happens. Or try going into Joan Rivers' pad to pick up some jewelery and watch the house maid look at you like you are insane when you ask to use the bathroom. That is the thing about the really rich—you are always dealing with the assistants, the secretaries, the maid, the doorman. They are the ones who will never give you a tip, either. Why should they? It's not their Monet you just moved. However, when you do see the rich goofball with the sexy wife or girlfriend, he will probably give you a tip because he wants to show off in front of her. Especially if she is new.

And then, after the service entrances, you have to ride in the service elevators. These are some of the scariest places in the world, if you ask me. New York is full of old ones that are operated by cables. And the high-rise types are like being inside wind tunnels—try riding in one with too much weight. We had to lift this thousand-pound marble slab into the elevator of the UN apartment building because it was too long to go straight in. It took about six of us to lift it. Then, while it was leaning against the elevator wall and we were underneath it, the car started to drop erratically because of the weight. We got stuck in there for almost an hour. The whole time was spent thinking we were going to die, telling stupid jokes about disaster movies and trying not to shit in our pants. This was done for this bachelor type who had nothing but Hawaiian shirts in his closet. Family money from aluminum, I think.

The service entrances and elevators make you realize that you are part of the lower class, and I guess in that the architects have succeeded in some perverse way. I mean, you feel like a service person when you are in them—you know where you are and why you're there. It's very humiliating—as is being treated like shit by the owners and the doormen and everyone else—but it makes a certain amount of sense, architecturally. I just wish I could make every architect who designed a small elevator or a dangerous service entrance come on the truck with us for one day, so I could show them what idiots they are. I have a real distaste for architects now. Look at all the ugly buildings in New York City and remember: they are worse on the inside.

It is funny how my view of certain artists—and of the art world in general—has gone down the toilet from doing this job. I guess that I think there are just too many people making art. And most of the art just isn't very interesting. It's depressing, so I am trying to find another job right now. I really do not want to work in the art world in any capacity anymore because it does not pay enough money and because I'm just kind of sick of it.

But, you know, I have a studio at home and whenever I get the chance, I try to work. So I guess I haven't completely lost my interest in art. I don't get much time to do it, maybe once a week or so, and I have not actually painted in two years, but I have been doing these drawings that are really small. I still do it because I like the activity of making something. Although, I suppose I could do something else and be a lot more satisfied.

Julian Stallabrass

The Rules of Art Now

From *Art Incorporated: The Story of Contemporary Art*
(Oxford: Oxford University Press, 2004)

It is a basic art-world orthodoxy, echoed just about everywhere, that contemporary art is ungraspably complex and diverse. The variety of contemporary forms, techniques, and subject matter in art is indeed bewildering. The conventional media of painting, sculpture, and printmaking have been overlaid with installation and "new media," which can encompass anything from online art to computer-controlled sound environments. Artists cultivate for themselves images that range from traditional guru or shaman roles to beady-eyed, tongue-in-cheek chancer and careerist, and personas that include star-struck adolescent girls and engorged, axe-wielding psychotics. Art's concerns are also various, touching upon feminism, identity politics, mass culture, shopping, and trauma. So it should not be surprising that art's ungraspable character is a staple of art writing by critics, curators, and publicists. Maybe art's fundamental condition is to be unknowable (that concepts embodied in visual form can encompass contradiction), or such statements may be part of an ideological outlook that conceals uniformity.

There are several reasons to suspect that the conventional views conceal something. Firstly, most art is instantly recognizable both to novices and the informed, and not just because it is on display in the gallery. Secondly, total randomness is one form of total uniformity. Thirdly (in tension with the second thought), as we have seen, permissiveness is far from total, and much cultural production is systematically excluded from the contemporary art world. Fourthly, each element of art's variety is hybridized with others in a process that leads to wider uniformity. Finally, there is so much current work that (like advertising) uses visual signs in a conventional manner. So perhaps art's knowability is on the increase, alongside statements boasting its essential unknowability.

There can, of course, be no pretense to scientific objectivity in any account of art. No such analysis can be objective in the way that, say, the examination of beetles can, since any account has some influence over the very scene that it surveys. The wide influence of Greenberg's sweeping account of the development of modern art as a Hegelian progress towards formal abstraction helped stimulate Pop Art, its explicit refutation.

Since the rise of the avant-garde, only art viewed from a historical distance has appeared to have direction and coherence, while the present always seems clouded in confusion. This loss of the orientation that we appear to have when looking at current art is a long-established feeling. In fact, those writers who, for better or worse, grasped without ambiguity an impetus in the present (such as Greenberg) have been the exceptions. Perhaps the historical mode of viewing art simplifies what we see, reducing it to what is of interest to the present; but perhaps this is simply the necessary task of intellectual work in which diverse phenomena must be ordered, placed in hierarchies of importance, and much ignored or forgotten, to achieve a meaningful perspective on a scene.

It is evident through our own period, as the art of what was once thought of as the global periphery traveled to the center of art-world attention.

Art in the 1990s has sometimes been thought of as a synthesis between grandiose and spectacular 1980s art with the techniques and some of the concerns of Conceptual art. The result was to splice linguistic and conceptual play with visually impressive objects. Tobias Rehberger's *Seven Ends of the World*, to take a single example, fills a room with clusters of glass balloons that glow with different colored lights in a beautiful, slowly changing display; the lights in the balloons are renditions of local light conditions in various locations around the world, relayed over the Internet. The piece is both a technically accomplished, spectacular and appealing object, and the manifestation of an idea.

Perhaps this synthesis is the result of a negative dialectic, which has forced on art not a realization but rather a taming of Conceptualism's radical critique, in a false accommodation with what it most despised. This is certainly the meaning of an installation by veteran Conceptual artists Art and Language at the Lisson Gallery in 2002. Here they remade their famous *Index* work —originally a piece meant to encourage interaction and dialogue—as a candy-colored, functionless sculpture, juxtaposed with a nonsensical pornographic text—a reference to the antics of the "young British artists." From the point of view of the dealers, however, as Alex Alberro argues, from the very beginning Conceptualism carried with it the elements of that accommodation.

In any case, a spectrum of art lies along the line of the varying elements of this synthesis. One end—the most conventional and the most likely to be associated with unreconstructed notions of male genius—mixes the barest elements of a conceptual framework with large quantities of emotion, spirituality, or humanism to warrant the production of epic works—we might think here of Bill Viola, Anish Kapoor, or Antony Gormley, and (most recently) Matthew Barney. At the other—and this is now a far commoner practice, as we have seen—concepts drive the production of objects in materials or media that are selected to suit them. Both ends react against the pervasiveness of the mass media: the first in presenting the viewer with a sublime spectacle in which massive amounts of material or (latterly) data; in performance, the body and sometimes blood of the artist form an assurance of organic and unique presence, as against all that is copied and transmitted. At the other end, mundane elements of the environment or the media are pitched into non-instrumental play: this can be seen clearly in works that take mass-media spectacle and simply remove the spectacle, a plain example being Paul Pfeiffer's alteration of the film of the Ali-Foreman boxing match, "Rumble in the Jungle," by removing the boxers. Indeed, a defining feature of art since the end of the cold war has been this play with borrowed images, material, and media, which has whittled away at deep, serious art of genius until its practitioners, now few, appear as eccentric survivals of a previous age, while traditionalists can only wail at the blanket dominance of "Conceptualism" and "installation."

What characterizes this new production most is the movement of readymade objects (or at least readily recognized objects) and signs from one place to another, and their assemblage in novel reconfigurations. To start with some simple examples which come close to puns, take some instances of gilding: Cerith Wyn Evans's gold crash barrier elides ideas of money and control, and produces a striking hybrid object; Sylvie Fleury does the same for shopping trolleys; Paola Pivi has gilded a jet fighter and, in an added element, displayed it upside-down. Or to take another frequently used example, think of artists' treatment of that most valued of consumer objects, the car: there is Orozco's famous *La DS* (1993), a Citroën DS cut in half lengthways, a portion taken out of the middle then stuck back together to make a slimmed-down version; or Gabinete Ordo Amoris's elongated Lada taxi (three welded into one) to make a Cuban taxi-limousine, commenting prettily on the peculiarities of the rise of a nouveau riche on the island; or Damián Ortega's exploded Volkswagen, its component parts hanging like a 3-D diagram of a kit-assembly of the car on wires. (There are plenty of other examples, from Rehberger, Fleury, Charles Ray, and others.) These movable elements may be qualities as well as things: we can think of Orozco's *Oval Billiard Table* (1996), or Maurizio Cattelan's *Stadium* (1991), an elongated table football game that can be played by twenty-two people at once.

More generally, a vast range of art has been produced that contains such simple combinations of elements. To survey a large number of these is to have the (illusory) impression of an art world machine that takes elements out of their functional place in the world and recycles and recombines them, so that, taken as a whole, any combination of signs and objects will eventually be arrived at. Displacement is a key technique of advertising, like art, which must shock and amuse or at least interest the viewer; use and placement are the main elements that separate art and advertising, which otherwise remain close and engage in theft from one another.

There is a structural reason for this systematic exploration of such combinations as artists compete to find a distinctive place within the art world. Howard Singerman puts it: "The [art] student's task, like that of his works, is to take—and to mark—his or her place."[1] As more and more positions are filled, it seems as if no bringing together of elements is taboo. An extreme case is Zbigniew Libera's *Lego* (1996), a series of concentration camps built with children's building blocks, which along with other similarly provocative works about the Holocaust were displayed at the Jewish Museum in New York in a show called "Mirroring Evil" in 2002. The show was condemned in much of the mainstream press but was defended by liberal academics. Seen from the point of view of each artist's individual projects, such pieces are various, distinct, and personal, and each may have a particular meaning. Seen from the point of view of the art world as a system, they appear as the component parts of a uniform machine, which produces a large range of novel combinations that are tested against various publics for marketable meaning.

Lest Hume's point—that all human imagination is nothing more than the combination of found elements—be thought to apply here, it should be said that, in comparison with modern and even many postmodern practices, these combinations have become simpler, their elements more manifestly found, their recombination more promiscuous and arbitrary, and the meanings that they generate more fleeting and cursory. For Paul Virilio, in recent lectures published as *Art and Fear*, in contemporary art the focus on the present, the obliteration of the past, and the type of sign-swapping encouraged by digitization are closely linked. Indeed, there is a relation between the rapid play of images and the development of free trade, the erosion of barriers, historical memory, and identities in favor of the fungibility and mobility of objects, signs, and bodies.

This link with capital is generally disavowed in favor of another, more congenial reading: while in the past stylistic contradiction or inconsistency was seen by art historians as the unconscious expression of social contradictions (the locus classicus here is Meyer Schapiro's analysis of the sculptures at Souillac), now a fully conscious enactment of these inconsistencies is used to highlight an awareness of the cultural decadence of the present age. Naturally, that very awareness and its parading in works of art allow viewers to enjoy the spectacle of decadence, and assure them that mere awareness of it is sufficient to bear them a loftier plane.

This uniformity in art-making is reflected in prominent critical accounts of contemporary art in the mid-1990s, which should be no surprise, since the production of art and the writing which supports it are hardly separable. Even so, there is a sharp contrast between much academic writing on art and art criticism. Academic writing has tended to be caught up in the continued dominance of deconstruction, old Freudian and Lacanian models (widely discredited in other fields), and identity-based accounts. In one sense, this writing, which consists of apparently willful readings, abounding in poetic associations and arbitrary leaps, is a reflection of the freedom ideally found in art itself. The writer's performance is as creative as the artist's. Yet much academic art writing, too, demonstrates a hidden uniformity, produced by institutional pressures, beneath its apparently various surfaces. The particular advantage of dominant deconstructive and psychoanalytical accounts is that they can be arbitrarily applied to the most unlikely of works with predictably "critical" results: traumatic voids have even recently been discovered in the glib, slick surfaces of pieces by Sam Taylor-Wood. Once the method is learned, any material can be fed into the machine. Thus the publication quotas that are institutionally demanded of academics with little research time are met.

Those writers with more of a stake in the art world, and with wider readerships, have quite different concerns. In US art criticism during the mid-1990s there was a revival in writing about beauty, once a neglected topic, which reflected the rise of decorative and saleable art as the economy revived. In part this can be seen as a way of forgetting about issues of politics, money, difference, and elitism which pressed hard (too hard, for some) on art in the US in the late 1980s.

To get a feeling for these developments, we will look at three important US writers on art—and here we return to the predominant center for the consumption of art—who, despite their widely differing stances, share striking common characteristics: Arthur Danto, Thomas McEvilley, and Dave Hickey. All are liberal white males (so we exclude here prominent conservative complainers against the state of the arts, such as Robert Hughes and Hilton Kramer). All have wide readerships. Danto and Hickey have been associated with the revived focus on beauty in contemporary art.

Danto writes for the left-liberal magazine *The Nation* and is a very well-known philosopher and theorist of contemporary art, particularly of what he sees as the break in art production set in train by Andy Warhol. If Warhol's Brillo Pad boxes cannot be visually distinguished from actual Brillo Pad boxes, he argues, it follows that art cannot be defined in terms of its visual distinctiveness, and must instead be characterized philosophically. McEvilley is a distinguished lecturer in art history at Rice University, and has a PhD in classical philology. He is a contributing editor to *Artforum*, and has done much to promote the understanding of non-Western art. He came to wide attention with a systematic and stringent critique of the assumptions underlying the New York Museum of Modern Art's 1984 exhibition, "'Primitivism' in Twentieth Century Art," which led to a lengthy and fractious debate with the curators. Dave Hickey, professor of art criticism and theory at the University of Nevada, Las Vegas, a highly popular writer with an engaging prose style, is a recipient of the MacArthur Foundation "genius award." Each of these writers brings a set of particular and extraneous interests to art criticism, as many of the best writers on art have done: for Danto, it is philosophy; for McEvilley, anthropology and the classics; for Hickey, popular music and literature.

Danto's *After the End of Art* claims that the character of art has changed radically since the 1970s and the last gasp of the avant-garde, and is now properly post-historical. Modernist and avant-garde views were tied to an idea of historical progress—towards formal abstraction, perhaps, or the merging of art and life. For Danto, in contrast, "life really begins when the story comes to an end," and those who now expect art to progress have missed the point, which is that the final synthesis has been reached. While Danto does not mention him, this stance is close to that of Francis Fukuyama's widely publicized political views in his book *The End of History and the Last Man*, and is based on the same Hegelian contention that, while of course events continue to occur, history has come to a close; we are settled forever with a version of the system which now sustains us. Similarly, for Danto, once art had passed through the black night of the 1970s (to which he compares, with its dreadful politically engaged work, the Dark Ages), it emerged onto the sunny Elysian fields of universal permissiveness, never to leave. And in those fields, any mixing of styles or patching together of narratives is as good as any other.

We have seen that, from one point of view, this is a good description of contemporary art, and is definitely plausible. It has had considerable resonance in the art world, and figures who are much at odds with Danto in other respects echo it. For instance in his book *Design and Crime*, Hal Foster, one of the most influential and powerful academic writers about contemporary art, describes art's current "symbolic weightlessness" and its disengagement with history and even its own historically given problems:

> *One might go further: contemporary art no longer seems "contemporary," in the sense that it no longer has a privileged purchase on the present, or even "symptomatic," at least no more so than many other cultural phenomena.*[2]

Danto wants to say that contemporary art is contemporary but that it means more than merely art made now: "The contemporary is, from one perspective, a period of information disorder, a condition of perfect aesthetic entropy. But it is equally a period of quite perfect freedom."[3] That freedom was produced by the view of art that asked philosophical questions about its very conditions of existence, and was no longer tied merely to questions of how it looked. Liberated from the burden of that history, artists could make work "in whatever way they wished, for any purposes they wished, or for no purposes at all."[4] This is a fully utopian achievement, which Danto has little hesitation in comparing to Marx and Engels's vision of communism, in which people could fulfill themselves in activities of their choosing.

In *Art and Otherness*, McEvilley's account of the contemporary art world, global others coming into equal and full voice have undermined modernist certitudes and allowed postmodern diversity to flower. Bad, old universal teleological modernism (as he characterizes it, with unnuanced readings of Kant and Greenberg) has been defeated by plural, forward-looking postmodernism, through which we can glimpse possible utopian futures. The account of modernism given here (one that has more plausibility in the US, no doubt, where the figure of Greenberg still looms) is smooth and unitary, innocent of the many variations, contradictions, and disputations that it used to contain. In any case, given its passing, judgments of quality—once considered absolute—may be relativized, and in doing so we can draw on the tools of anthropology. According to McEvilley:

> *At moments of intense social ferment, art can serve to retard, disguise, or misrepresent a society's potential for change. Today, against all odds, art is performing the opposite role. Tracking the future, it senses avenues along which a new self may emerge into the light of a redefined history.*[5]

In such uncertain times, artists produce works that are necessarily dark, oracular, and ambiguous, a faithful reflection of the epoch. Part of this uncertainty is due to the emergence of multiple non-Western views, and a corresponding relativization of Western values that McEvilley sees emerging particularly from the 1980s. For McEvilley this does not mean the end of history but the end of one singular and particular view of it. The ideological totality of modernism has yielded to a glorious plurality of positions; but this is not to say that no new synthesis will emerge, only that it has not yet been glimpsed. But for the time being, that is just fine:

> *Why not let the world breathe for a while without a meta-narrative constricting it into a narrow space that is claimed as ultimate? Why not let it feel its way into the future without those totalizing, globalizing, universalizing, redemptionist myths which have so much in common with religious prophecies?*[6]

Like Danto's, this is a cheering view of the diversity of the contemporary art scene, and it gains plausibility because, while modernism was never as simple or unitary as McEvilley has it, there has been a decided and positive increase in the diversity of voices heard in the art world. In his writings about specific aesthetic milieux in Africa, McEvilley has furthered that change, and proved more sensitive to the complexities and contradictions it implies than in the broad-brush claims he made in *Art and Otherness*.

Dave Hickey, too, wants viewers to relax, enjoy art, and especially to forget about the evils of the market. His book *Air Guitar* contains a plea to allow the arts to thrive free of academic brow-creasing at what Hickey describes as that specifically US invention—a "big, beautiful art market" that simply and democratically reflects popular taste. Writing of the attitude of Las Vegas academics to their home town, he claims "they think it's all about money, which, I always agree, is the worst way of discriminating among individuals, except for all the others."[7] For the alternative to the market, bred in state funding of the arts and propagated in academia, is a civil-service-run, politically correct, theoretically defended culture, comprising "'critique of representation,' which, at its heart, is a critique of representative government—bald advocacy for a new civil service of cultural police."[8]

Hickey's well-honed rhetoric is used to bolster the notion that "democracy" is embodied in market mechanisms, so that the laws of supply and demand set the hierarchy of prices which really does reflect what people want from art. This view is loosely associated with the standard line of liberal thinking that says that you cannot have democracy without the market. It is another matter, though, to say that the market can substitute for democracy. If that is a very doubtful claim even when applied to free markets, when applied to the art market—which is highly archaic, controlled, and restricted—its foolishness is crystal clear.

For this view to appear remotely plausible, Hickey has to believe that cultural distinction does not matter, that to look at art requires no special skill or education, and that entry into the art world is a purely voluntary matter (if you want in, you are in). It is a touchingly idealist view for an art-world insider to hold, apparently innocent of the workings of social distinction, money, and power. Hickey would have us believe that

> everyone *in this culture understands the freedom and permission of art's mandate. To put it simply:* Art ain't rocket science, *and beyond a proclivity to respond and permission to do so, there are no prerequisites for looking at it.*[9]

There are certainly elements of truth to this: the arts as a profession is not defended against outsiders in the way medicine, law, or engineering are; appreciating art is definitely not rocket science, and people can understand a lot about it just from being exposed to the general run of commercial culture. However, the single biggest determinant of gallery-going is education, and this is partly because art at all levels (from academic to commercial) defines itself against mass culture. In doing so, it regularly uses complex references to art history that require specialist knowledge of its viewers. Hickey himself, far from being an ordinary Joe, spent years doing a PhD, thus leaping over the most forbidding barrier to access.

Hickey sees himself as a fan of art, just as he is a fan of rock and roll, and there should be no more need for a fan of art to trouble himself about it being a commodity than he would over the buying and selling of CDs. To counter this view, we should turn to another well-known critic who has also written much about rock—Diedrich Diederichsen. In a mordant examination of the state of contemporary art criticism, he points to the obvious difference between fan literature and art criticism. Fan literature is written for those who are likely to buy a product and helps them to decide whether to do so. As a result it is highly focused and instrumental. Nearly all the audience for art criticism, however, have no prospect of owning the works they are reading about. The writing, too—in its specialist academic and populist versions—serves quite other functions, in which judgments of quality are either not made at all, or are made only on the basis of a subjective parading of taste. Hickey's writing, of course, falls into the latter category.

Hickey has also recently curated an international show in his campaign both to reinstate beauty and popularize art and remove what he sees as an elitist concern with political and social agendas. The show, which opened in 2001, SITE Santa Fe's Fourth International Biennial, was modestly entitled "Beau Monde: Towards a Redefined Cosmopolitanism." In the catalogue, Hickey stated that since what audiences remember of exhibitions is an ambience (and not ideas), he had resolved to touch everything there with high spirits and a light heart. The warehouse space at SITE Santa Fe was transformed with gardens, a picture window, and fantastical architectural detailing, and works were disposed in appealing vistas. Orthodoxy in biennials was the supposed target for the intended redemption. Hickey claimed they had been "perversely devoted to marketing ideas of regional identity and local exceptionality in the normative language of post-minimalist artistic practice." He misunderstands what such shows are about, of course, for we have seen how they are founded on the idea of hybridity and cultural exchange, though Hickey is right about the unified language in which all this difference ends. This misunderstanding allows Hickey to recommend a cosmopolitanism in which cultural resources are mixed, and which actually plays to the main presumptions underlying the internationalism he is complaining about. The actual contrast is more straightforwardly political and becomes clear in Hickey's extraordinary claim for the show: while exhibitions that deal with cultural identity tend to be made up of art that poses problems, the art in "Beau Monde" aspires to *solve* them: "The visible resolution of cultural dissonance has its moral and intellectual consequences, its social allegories, its uses and function" (it is curious here how Hickey's normal facility with plain language deserts him, perhaps under the pressure of the absurdity of the claim).[10] The mutation of the biennial in "Beau Monde" is an instructive one. Retaining the celebration of hybridity, it switches the standard response of the work from positive to negative but to similar propaganda effect; the conventional biennial recommends multiculturalism and complains that old, conservative barriers to trade and cultural exchange hold back its progress; "Beau Monde" gloried in its current successes and the beauty they produced.

The artist Renée Green has enumerated some current art-world clichés exemplified by Hickey's writing:

> *1. Art is borderless.*
> *2. Thinking causes over-seriousness and the deflation of fun and beauty, which are equated with aesthetic pleasure.*
> *3. To think means to think too much and is in conflict with experiencing (which is thought of in binary terms and is thus associated with feeling, i.e., feeling/experiencing vs. thinking).*[11]

Hickey strangely presumes that people—and educated art audiences in particular—cannot take pleasure in a demanding work, a political work, or even a play of ideas.

All three critics, Danto, McEvilley, and Hickey, arrive via very different routes at similar destinations: that the contemporary art world is (in the infamous words of Robert Venturi and his collaborators in a book, *Learning from Las Vegas*, that is one of the main roots of postmodernism) "almost all right." Viewers of art should be content to bask in its glorious and unencompassable diversity.

We have seen that there are many reasons why that very diversity has become a prescribed uniformity. Bourdieu points to another: both the production and consumption of works that have emerged from a long tradition of ruptures with tradition carry with them a cargo of historical references, becoming simultaneously thoroughly historical and dehistoricized. They refer to a multitude of forms but truly remember none of them, nor the conditions of their creation being forgotten. History is reduced to a pure history of forms, laid out like a table from which any combination of options can be selected.

Another way of saying that there is eclecticism—an equalizing and mixing of styles and histories—and the alluring "real" of everyday life to back this up, is by claiming that the reality appealed to here is the real of money. It was put this way by Lyotard in his foundational treatise on postmodernism, and has recently been reiterated with force by Hardt and Negri, in their influential reconsideration of global governance and economics, *Empire*, where they drew out the close parallels between postmodernism and the market.

The remarkable feature of this scenario is the convergence between academic interpretations of art and those more populist writings that recommend the untroubled enjoyment of beauty. Academics, who are committed to applying Occam's Razor in reverse to any conceivable cultural problem, and critics, who strive for a reasonable, measured, and entertaining clarity, both favor fragmentation, the divided subject or psyche, the limits and bad faith of socially produced knowledge, and the sublime vertigo of the unknowable. And this at a time when art is increasingly dominated by thoroughly comprehensible tactics and techniques.

In any case, the plausibility of these views has lately taken a battering. Particularly since the events of September 11th, the rise of overt US imperialism—with its flagrant and insouciant flouting of international law—strikes against the multiculturalism and globalization exemplified in McEvilley's account. The return of a cogent opposition to capitalism, and with it vanguard art, should have been impossible if Fukuyama's and Danto's accounts were accurate. Hickey's boosting of beauty and the market looked good only as long as the economy boomed, and art consumers continued to indulge themselves with pretty objects. These factors and others, particularly the increasing divide between the technological capabilities of much new art and the actuality of its ownership and distribution, exacerbated existing tensions in the art-world system, and may continue to aggravate them further.

Notes

1. Howard Singerman, *Art Subjects: Making Artists in the American University*. Berkeley: University of California Press, 1999, 186.
2. Hal Foster, *Design and Crime (and Other Diatribes)*. London: Verso, 2002, 124.
3. Arthur C. Danto, *After the End of Art: Contemporary Art and the Pale of History*. Princeton: Princeton University Press, 1997, 12.
4. Ibid, 15.
5. Thomas McEvilley, *Art and Otherness: Crisis in Cultural Identity*. Documentext/McPherson, 1992, 12.
6. Ibid, 145.
7. Dave Hickey, *Air Guitar: Essays on Art and Democracy*. Los Angeles: Art issues Press, 1997, 21.
8. Ibid, 71.
9. Ibid, 107.
10. Dave Hickey, "Beau Monde, Upon Reflection," in Dave Hickey, ed., *Beau Monde: Toward a Redeemed Cosmopolitanism (SITE Santa Fe's Fourth International Biennial)*, 2002, 79.
11. Renée Green, "Introductory Notes of a Reader and 'A Contemporary Moment,'" in Jürgen Bock, ed., *From Work to Text: Dialogues on Practise and Criticism in Contemporary Art*, Fundaçaõ Centro Cultural de Belém, Lisbon, 2002, 248.

Johanna Burton and Isabelle Graw

When Procedures Become Market Tools

Texte zur Kunst 61, June 2006

Appropriative practices in the works of young US artists may show formal analogies with historical modes of appropriation—but there can be no doubt that both generations will not be easily fused into one art-historical agenda.

In their conversation, Isabelle Graw and New York-based art historian and critic Johanna Burton explore in which way and to which degree neo-appropriationists really work with reference to their historical precursors, which can be the role of relationships between critic and artist that are based on loyalty and friendship for the production of theoretical insight, and how the work of the art historian—permanently negotiating the art market's desire for intellectual "soundbites"—is currently faring.

IG – Though it is always dangerously reductive to pin down a methodological approach, I will nevertheless attempt to describe what I at least see as your preferences in that regard. To me it seems that your art-critical and art-historical writing combines two approaches—an insistence on the importance of "identity" or "social place" that comes from the tradition of identity politics and feminist art history, and a more subtle, non-literal and sometimes even outright formalist attention to the material specificities of artworks.

JB – When you say non-literal do you mean non-narrative?

IG – Yes—you seem to insist on the meaning of a work of art, which is not evident at first sight and is not easily reduced to a certain topic or a decipherable narration—say "oppression" or "female identity." My impression is that you are interested in a more attentive and complex reading of those art works that all too easily have been classified as feminist.

JB – Yes, I would agree to some extent with your assessment of what I do, as I think that a purely social-contextual feminism or a literal positing of content onto works can be limiting, and a turn to what you are calling "formalist" concerns actually enables a more thorough discussion of what I see as feminist concerns. I also think that the feminism that I'm interested in comes particularly from the arrival of post-structural theory in the late '70s and '80s in America, so it isn't first-generation feminism, which of course I'm interested in the legacies of, but which can tend, or is sometimes thought of as leaning towards, essentialism. By contrast, this moment in second-generation feminist theory was looking at ideas of difference and a kind of multiplicity, and a number of voices happening at once. And that tends towards this reading that you have made of my work, where you are actually looking at the object, and not just thinking about its context, but the operations of the object itself.

IG – It is certainly true that feminist art historians of the first and even second wave often did not pay much attention to artworks' aesthetic dimension, their materiality or the nature of the artistic procedures employed. But I wonder if it is at all possible to opt for an analysis of the "object itself." How could one draw a distinct line between the parameters of the object proper and its social and discursive context? Are you actually seeking to reintroduce a border between an "inside" and an "outside," thus bordering on a notion of immanence?

JB – I am not at all interested in reintroducing a line between the two things. But I am interested in pointing out that such a line is naturalized, in a sense, when discourse about social context places objects as secondary. So that kind of naturalized break I think is something that has to be addressed. There is always a supplement in the object that I think, at least in the works that I am attracted to, doesn't allow this really easy literal reading, where it can be: this equals oppression, this equals some kind of idea. This isn't about immanence; it's about complicating—rather than introducing—any border between inside and outside.

IG – Personally speaking, it was the whole complex of "appropriation" that seemed to offer a way out of this methodological impasse, as it is a concept implying a relation between what is considered "inside" and "outside" of a given art work. More precisely, the notion of appropriation may describe a relationship between the one who's appropriating, the appropriated material and the artistic procedure of appropriating. As I know you are currently writing your dissertation on that topic, and many of the artists you have written about—most prominently Wade Guyton or Kelley Walker—have taken up procedures of appropriation in their work, thereby referring back to the historical formation of the late '70s, early '80s. If understood as a relational concept, appropriation transgresses or at least questions any substantialist assumption of "immanence." What are the reasons for your interest in the whole complex of appropriation?

JB – Well, the first thing I should say is that my dissertation focuses on appropriative strategies from the late '70s through the early '80s. I am largely suspicious of most of the contemporary appropriation that's happening. Because I think that there is a wholesale appropriation. Appropriation has become the kind of sign of criticality that is easily consumed.

IG – Indeed—it has become an artistic standard and can't claim to stand for any of the claims made for it twenty-five years ago: for instance the notorious death of the author, critique of representation, resignification, etc.

JB – Exactly, and I think that partly has to do with what you are calling the procedure, which if it ever got us out of the trap of immanence has itself now become immanent in some sense—or at least it holds up some false promise of immanence. Such procedures are now thought of as having a kind of immanent *critical* promise. Which might have something to do with my interest in looking at the objects themselves more closely. It's at the moment that you can make the argument about the immanence of the object that I think such a concept of immanence has probably shifted to something else. And I think that right now, at least, the market tends to really privilege procedures—that they are seen as immanently critical, which, advertised as such, means that they probably aren't any more. And there is an incredible thirst for anything that "looks like" appropriation. Part of the reason that I am interested in a few of the young artists that are using it is that most contemporary appropriation, it seems to me, follows a kind of mode of citing the past that seems to do away with any real connection to the past, presenting a superficial patina of the past instead. I would call it the patina of politics, the patina of criticality. That in re-presenting past imagery and procedures, they also make a kind of proprietary claim to the material that they've taken. The artists I find to be using appropriation more effectively don't sit so easily with this disinterment, and the works they make seem to me to call into question the very procedures they rely on.

IG – One could even say that appropriation today has developed into a kind of referentialism, as many artists trust in the supposedly over-determined meaning or arcane attraction of the material they're appropriating …

JB – Yes, and they get applauded and acknowledged as having some kind of knowledge. Appropriation has become a style more than anything. But there are a few artists who use it differently, Wade Guyton being one that you brought up. The way he's working, and why I am interested in him, is that I feel he actually poses the question about this kind of comfort we have today with constantly circulating signs. Less than feeling comfortable, I feel like his work often professes a real anxiety, and doesn't feel that it actually belongs in the history it invokes at all. There is a kind of disconnection that happens, actually. And in creating disconnections, he allows the particularity of certain kinds of appropriated signs to actually become general, which is something I am thinking about a lot. You think you know what these signs are, but in fact they are often rendered very mute and very citational, as opposed to referential. They are very much less transparent than work by so many other artists who are just referring to things that seem very obvious and clearly legible. There is an illegibility to some of his work that I find very interesting. A kind of stubbornness that I don't think has to do with his feeling comfortable, so much as with feeling unsure about his own procedures.

IG – But isn't the material he appropriated from art books equally "meaningful" or "over-determined"? And doesn't his work rely on the implications of the particular images he's using? In that sense his sources attain the function as an ultimate legitimation for a painterly practice desperately in need of justification. I would go so far as to say that this aspect can even be discerned on the level of procedure: The appropriated material is usually filtered through mechanical printing devices, thereby giving the impression that the material has been given a new meaning and relevance. Furthermore it arrives at securing the individual signature everyone longs for.

JB – It is true that there's the expression part of it that comes weirdly through those glitches of the mechanization, but that too functions ambivalently.

IG – But to deliberately allow mistakes in the printing process is by now part of a conventional painterly repertoire combining chance and intentionality—think of Andy Warhol or Christopher Wool.

JB – You are right, but my argument for his work is that it makes visible or makes obvious all of the biggest pitfalls of the process. So that the criticism that you levy is completely legitimate, but it's also so obvious in a sense that then I wonder what can happen afterwards. Given the cultural moment that we are in, it is really hard to imagine what a "critical procedure" could look like. While I believe strongly that criticality still exists in art, we can no longer count on certain strategies as having greater proximity to it than others. Performance, for instance, doesn't seem to hold that promise in the way that it once did. Neither do mechanized procedures that divorce the hand or procedures that emphasize it. Recently, Andrea Fraser, whom I respect very much, wrote elegantly about the way institutional critique itself has become fully "institutionalized."

All of this is hardly to say that there are no critical procedures, but instead that we need to consider carefully just what we mean when we deem something critical or uncritical.

IG – But I am wondering whether appropriating over-determined imagery—for instance Kelley Walker's appropriation of pictures showing violent scenes of race riots—can under these circumstances be an option. Let's say he adds traces of brushstrokes in the form of digitally produced toothpaste—what can this mean? Are we told that brushstrokes are always highly mediated? Isn't that banal? Or is the appropriated imagery simply transferred into a painterly register? When thinking about Walker's work, I must admit a feeling of being "unchallenged." Or is there something that I simply don't get?

JB – I think my interest in Walker's work has to do precisely with this over-determined imagery. It is almost like the minimal means necessary to do something. And to me there is something worthy of note about that, in that I feel right now there is a great deal of satisfaction in terms of artists using images, whereas these are so indebted to Warhol, almost embarrassingly so, that there seems to be, in addition to expressionist brushstrokes, a really masturbatory and over-the-top oedipal dimension in Walker's work. Again I found myself interested in looking at work that doesn't take any pains to conceal its own almost ingratiated, highly anxious status to something else, and it isn't about opening up or even shutting down this idea of authorship, the way it happened in the '80s. It doesn't seem to be mimicking that strategy. Instead it seems to be doing the opposite, introducing a kind of perversity into the equation, as if the truth of the death of the author has inspired a particular kind of necrophilia.

IG – In the sense of negative aesthetics? Are we faced with an impasse?

JB – Maybe so. For me it's about trying to think through the seeming incongruity between the death of the author and this really conservative moment—worse even than the Reagan era of the '80s—that we're in right now. In much new appropriation work, there's a kind of recuperative gesture that I feel strangely reasserts originality and authenticity by proclaiming to do the opposite. It makes me really uncomfortable. This isn't a mimicking of the procedures of '80s appropriation but an aestheticization of them that amounts to something quite opposing in impulse. When I look at artwork that appears to instruct us a second time that originality and authorship have been done away with, it seems not only clichéd at this point but also dangerous. I am much more interested in work that acknowledges the '80s, say, as introducing a set of procedures that could be seen as inevitably turning against themselves, morphing out of control. These artists don't refer to '80s—or other—strategies as found objects but instead question their relevancy and complicated legacy.

IG – Even if it is true that artists like Kelley Walker or Wade Guyton question the relevance of their procedures, their work nevertheless relies on them. By defending Wade's work by referring to his attention to the pitfalls of appropriation, don't you continue to attach importance to procedure as such? I wonder if one can still claim today that procedures are that meaningful and significant. Is it still enough to focus on procedure? May we not establish other criteria?

JB – My answer is that I don't know if it is enough. I feel like part of the interest for me in continuing to follow his work, and a number of other artists who don't neatly fit in with this conversation, has to do with seeing whether it is or isn't enough. Part of the reason that I continue to be interested is that, in some senses, it doesn't feel like enough at all. Those paintings are *about* something being missing. There is not a simple satisfaction in them. But I do think this connects a little bit to what I find overlooked in, say, the work of Sherrie Levine, who was always very vehement about wanting to be involved in the market. I find she is one of the most critically intelligent and critically forceful of the appropriationists. And it is very interesting that her relation to the market—and to art itself—was one of desire. When I first learned that, I remember feeling uncomfortable.

IG – Her relationship to the work of male artists could equally be described as a kind of oedipal longing: a strong desire to belong to a canon determined by male artists.

JB – This was the second point I was going to make: nobody ever writes about her desire for these objects, the pure—oedipal maybe, but certainly covetous—desire, and her very much wanting them, to have them and to *make* them. I do think that's one thing that happens, that the objects get short shrift. In one interview Levine said something about how when people talk about her work, they often talk at the edge of the frame and move outward, they never look into the middle of it.

IG – She used to frame her early works with a very elegant passe-partout, thereby producing an even more rarefied aesthetics that finally became her signature style.

JB – It is funny because you are maybe the only other person who's interested in this part of her work, which is maybe assumed to be non-critical. But right now there seems to be, when looking back, something unplumbed about that. What does it mean to marry these two impulses? One which undoes everything, and the other that redoes it, and even makes it more fetishized, because of its undoing in the first place. It is a curious thing for me. Something to do with access, for someone like Levine, or Sherman, that is very deeply gendered, too. There is this way that I do read that as a feminist position, whether the artists themselves think about it that way or not. I don't think that it works the same way for a male artist in 2006. Someone like Guyton is also really interested in subject positions, although his work has never been written about this way. He uses really iconic, kind of funny imagery, but no one really thinks it is funny. I don't know if you've seen these paintings that he has done with these huge flames. It is almost just too dumb in a way, flaming paintings with big Us on it—the interpellative pronoun paired with a "burning" signifier!

IG – The ones he showed at Friedrich Petzel Gallery? Don't you think that there is a crucial difference between claiming a subject position by using appropriation in the '80s—which was a way for many women artists to be noticed and included in the canon—and the situation we're facing today, with a market that tends to be extremely inclusive especially when your work shows signs of belonging to what Bourdieu called the "space of the possible"?

JB – Yes, but I don't know if Guyton "appropriates" as often as people think. In those flame paintings I just mentioned there's almost no exterior reference at all. There's big dots from Photoshop, and the flames that are not taken from a recognizable source but from some book jacket that nobody ever knows, which of course has its own relevance in terms of appropriation. But then appropriation has come to be understood as so fully procedural that it seems to almost not matter what this kind of work looks like, when I talk to people about it. It seems that we can talk about the procedures without talking about the works, and that's an interesting thing, and one that I don't especially like. What I should say in full disclosure is that I am pretty anxious about our moment right now, and about my place in it. Because I feel that no matter what I write about an artist, however carefully I try to construct an argument, it almost never gets read, even though it *does* circulate —a strange situation.

IG – This makes me think about how your name was used in the recent press release of Wade Guyton's show at Friedrich Petzel.

JB – I was never asked about that.

IG – They didn't ask you if they could use it?

JB – No, it showed up.

IG – The press release quotes one sentence that basically claims that the references appearing in his work are far too general and therefore can't be attributed to any singular context. Your proposition was taken out of context and was ultimately made to function as an art-historically sanctioned form of legitimization.

JB – The question of "public relations" is difficult for me in many ways because I started writing about this work, and I will continue to do so, as far as I'm concerned, because I am interested in the work and being involved in a dialogue about it. When you are sitting in front of the computer in a kind of intellectual exercise of trying to think through a problem, you hope you are offering possibilities to a reader and to yourself. But it gets excerpted as a single sentence that sounds like a pronouncement, which I am not making at all. This is really a crystallized example of what happens, but more and more I am noticing that there is this kind of split: on the one hand, there's the matter of doing art history, where you're safely relegated to the past, and you don't have to go out and engage in the quick schedule of the monthly show, that's so directly linked to the market. It doesn't really matter for the market if you write about Cézanne; Cézanne collectors are going to keep collecting his work. But new thinking on Cézanne and his context is important, and people do agree on the value of that, though because it doesn't exactly translate to market value, the attribution of intellectual value is much cleaner. With Guyton, on the other hand, what I write gets circulated, and you end up having this really strange feeling about trying to offer questions or propositions, and it being transformed into advertising, though I think things are a lot less simple than this.

IG – Intellectual capital is needed for the transformation of cultural capital into economic capital. But the situation is complicated: On the one hand art critics don't have the power to immediately affect the processes of value formation, for instance on the so called secondary market. We might raise doubt about the relevance of Neo Rauch paintings but this wouldn't lead to a diminished market value. On the other hand, art critical propositions are used like "sound bites" in order to underline claims for art-historical importance or theoretical erudition.

JB – If you doubt the work that means that there's some tension inherent in it. That makes the writing better I think, because it poses an argument around the work. I find the best writing tends to acknowledge, rather than smooth out, such tensions. I've written about a number of artists, but what I've really focused my attention on, in the last four or five years, are the artists that I actually love the most. And what I realized is the artists that I love the most tend to not actually be "central" at least in a market sense. Figures like Joan Jonas, who has been working for decades and who is experiencing a renaissance in terms of recognition and historical importance. And certainly people are starting to get to know much more about the work she's done during her life, but there's no real drive in terms of a central primary or secondary market for sure. Even Sherrie Levine I think continues in some degree to evade the market in this way. I went to her last show a couple of times. Nearly everybody I talked to asked: "Why is she still doing this?" It was really interesting to me that while interest in her has increased exponentially, because interest in the phenomena of appropriation has increased, many people still really don't like her work or don't like what they see as this gesture that she was—and still is—involved in. I am just really interested in knowing how she has managed to continue practicing in a way that sticks in people's craws at a moment when almost nothing seems able to.

IG – As you said, there currently is a constantly increasing rediscovery of certain appropriation artists. It started with the revalorization of Richard Prince, who had fallen out of favor for a while, and is now reaching record prices on the secondary market and found a culmination in the judgment of, for example, Troy Brauntuch, who disappeared for a long time and is now represented by a gallery in New York. It seems as if every dealer needs at least one "authentic" first-generation appropriation artist. It's interesting that you insist on writing about artists who have not been channelled through this incredibly intense value-making machine. On the other hand you were asked to write a catalogue text for the current Whitney Biennial and also to contribute an essay to the catalogue of the current exhibition in Zurich, which groups four male artists—Seth Price, Josh Smith, Kelley Walker and Wade Guyton—in a kind of neo-formalist male bonding.

JB – The catalogue isn't out yet. But, this is a great question because in a way I am constantly re-assessing my interest in appropriation in a general and more historical sense, and then there is the question of which of the younger artists I am interested in and why. And this is a group of artists that I am interested in. I've kind of garnered critiques over the last year and a half, but I wonder how you would go about these things too, when you stand very much behind certain practices—as I do with all of these artists to some degree. The way I try to go about things, when I decide to write, is to put some internal pressure on an artist's practice—and my own!—although I have to admit I'm not always sure what that means, or if I'm successful at it. The only analogy that I have is that I'm from Reno, Nevada, originally. I knew I wanted to be in dialogue with people. And I knew I wanted to talk about art. So for many many years I educated myself through art magazines and books and went to the local college, and got really interested in the dialogues. What I realized is that after all these years of feeling outside institutions, and thinking that I had an interesting set of things to say about it, it didn't get me any closer to it. And there really wasn't anyone to discuss ideas with, except my partner at the time, so we decided to pack our bags and move to New York, and now there is a substantial handful of people I talk to all the time, which is extremely satisfying. So I had to go right into the middle, and now here I am studying at an ivy-league school and writing for what are arguably the most market-driven magazines while simultaneously being totally immersed in the academy. But now I get to be in the conversation —in a few conversations, in fact. And there's a real ambivalence for me about that. Because it's that old dumb cliché about the outsider and the insider—which do you choose? When you're outside, you think you see things really clearly, and once you've been invited in, can you still exert the power or the pressure that drove you to get there in the first place? I can't really answer that. This is the long way of getting to the Whitney Biennial catalogue. The commission for that text was very loose but was basically to write an entire essay on young—I wasn't told hot, but that's the implication of the Biennial of course—artists who are using appropriation, and talk about the tactics of appropriation today. And of course one would assume this should be a salutary essay. You generally aren't commissioned to write badly about the artists.

IG – The same holds true for Zurich. You couldn't have written a non-apologetic text, could you?

JB – No, but I am playing with these expectations; for the Biennial catalogue I didn't write about any of the artists in the show, even Kelley Walker, who was of course in it. Instead, I wrote about older procedures, for instance in the work of Jasper Johns and Levine. And I talked about what it meant for those to be radical procedures. I don't know if it ends up being an interesting text or a really romantic one. Maybe it's both.

IG – I detected a certain refusal on your part to play the role of a promoter for all these artists. But you also seem to insist on a certain degree of loyalty to certain artists whose work you closely followed. Is it possible to raise doubts about their procedures and the weight that is put on them while remaining loyal to them? And do these doubts end up feeding the value-making process as well?

JB – I am loyal in the sense that—whereas people tend to sign on with you when you're hot and interesting, and then they're on to the next thing —I am wanting to have a longstanding dialogue about ideas with a certain number of people that I established relationships with in the first place because of the art and because of shared ideas and questions. That's the way these friendships came to be in the first place. And loyal only in the sense that when there is doubt, we actually do express it and talk about it and use it as means to do more interesting work. And I've actually been having this conversation a lot with a friend of mine, Bettina Funcke—what does it mean to be asked to write a critical text by an artist, one that's clearly going to be in a catalogue, in which you actually have certain tough questions you want to ask about the practice? How does that operate? I think that can be an interesting way of trying to go about things.

Andrea Fraser

From the Critique of Institutions to an Institution of Critique

Artforum, vol. 44, no. 1, September 2005

Nearly forty years after their first appearance, the practices now associated with "institutional critique" have for many come to seem, well, institutionalized. Last spring alone, Daniel Buren returned with a major installation to the Guggenheim Museum (which famously censored both his and Hans Haacke's work in 1971); Buren and Olafur Eliasson discussed the problem of "the institution" in these pages; and the LA County Museum of Art hosted a conference called "Institutional Critique and After." More symposia planned for the Getty and the College Art Association's annual conference, along with a special issue of *Texte zur Kunst*, may very well see the further reduction of institutional critique to its acronym: IC. Ick.

In the context of museum exhibitions and art-history symposia such as these, one increasingly finds institutional critique accorded the unquestioning respect often granted artistic phenomena that have achieved a certain historical status. That recognition, however, quickly becomes an occasion to dismiss the critical claims associated with it, as resentment of its perceived exclusivity and high-handedness rushes to the surface. How can artists who have become art-historical institutions themselves claim to critique the institution of art? Michael Kimmelman provided a ready example of such skepticism in his critical *New York Times* review of Buren's Guggenheim show. While the "critique of the institution of the museum" and the "commodity status of art" were "counterestablishment ideas when, like Mr. Buren, they emerged forty or so years ago," Kimmelman contends, Buren is now an "official artist of France, a role that does not seem to trouble some of his once-radical fans. Nor, apparently, does the fact that his brand of institutional analysis … invariably depends on the largesse of institutions like the Guggenheim." Kimmelman goes on to compare Buren unfavorably to Christo and Jeanne-Claude, who "operate, for the most part, outside traditional institutions, with fiscal independence, in a public sphere beyond the legislative control of art experts."[1]

Further doubts about the historic and present-day efficacy of institutional critique arise with laments over how bad things have become in an art world in which MoMA opens its new temporary-exhibition galleries with a corporate collection, and art hedge funds sell shares of single paintings. In these discussions, one finds a certain nostalgia for institutional critique as a now-anachronistic artifact of an era before the corporate mega-museum and the 24/7 global art market, a time when artists could still conceivably take up a critical position against or outside the institution. Today, the argument goes, there no longer is an outside. How, then, can we imagine, much less accomplish, a critique of art institutions when museum and market have grown into an all-encompassing apparatus of cultural reification? Now, when we need it most, institutional critique is dead, a victim of its success or failure, swallowed up by the institution it stood against.

But assessments of the institutionalization of institutional critique and charges of its obsolescence in an era of mega-museums and global markets founder on a basic misconception of what institutional critique is, at least in light of the practices that have come to define it. They necessitate a reexamination of its history and aims, and a restatement of its urgent stakes in the present.

I recently discovered that none of the half-dozen people often considered the "founders" of "institutional critique" claim to use the term. I first used it in print in a 1985 essay on Louise Lawler, "In and Out of Place," when I ran off the now-familiar list of Michael Asher, Marcel Broodthaers, Daniel Buren, and Hans Haacke, adding that, "while very different, all these artists engage(d) in institutional critique."[2]

I probably first encountered that list of names coupled with the term "institution" in Benjamin H.D. Buchloh's 1982 essay "Allegorical Procedures," where he describes "Buren's and Asher's analysis of the historical place and function of aesthetic constructs within institutions, or Haacke's and Broodthaers's operations revealing the material conditions of those institutions as ideological."[3] The essay continues with references to "institutionalized language," "institutional frameworks," "institutional exhibition topics," and describes one of the "essential features of Modernism" as the "impulse to criticize itself from within, to question its institutionalization." But the term "institutional critique" never appears.

By 1985, I had also read Peter Bürger's *Theory of the Avant-Garde*, which was published in Germany in 1974 and finally appeared in English translation in 1984. One of Bürger's central theses is that "with the historical avant-garde movements, the social subsystem that is art enters the stage of self-criticism. Dadaism ... no longer criticizes schools that preceded it, but criticizes art as an institution, and the course its development took in bourgeois society."[4]

Having studied with Buchloh as well as Craig Owens, who edited my essay on Lawler, I think it's quite possible that one of them let "institutional critique" slip out. It's also possible that their students in the mid-'80s at the School of Visual Arts and the Whitney Independent Study Program (where Haacke and Martha Rosler also lectured)—including Gregg Bordowitz, Joshua Decter, Mark Dion, and me—just started using the term as a shorthand for "the critique of institutions" in our after-class debates. Not having found an earlier published appearance of the term, it is curious to consider that the established canon we thought we were receiving may have just been forming at the time. It could even be that our very reception of ten- or fifteen-year-old works, reprinted texts, and tardy translations (by the likes of Douglas Crimp, Asher, Buren, Haacke, Rosler, Buchloh, and Bürger), and our perception of those works and texts as canonical, was a central moment in the process of institutional critique's so-called institutionalization. And so I find myself enmeshed in the contradictions and complicities, ambitions and ambivalence that institutional critique is often accused of, caught between the self-flattering possibility that I was the first person to put the term in print, and the critically shameful prospect of having played a role in the reduction of certain radical practices to a pithy catchphrase, packaged for co-optation.

If, indeed, the term "institutional critique" emerged as shorthand for "the critique of institutions," today that catchphrase has been even further reduced by restrictive interpretations of its constituent parts: "institution" and "critique." The practice of institutional critique is generally defined by its apparent object, "the institution," which is, in turn, taken to refer primarily to established, organized sites for the presentation of art. As the flyer for the symposium at LACMA put it, institutional critique is art that exposes "the structures and logic of museums and art galleries." "Critique" appears even less specific than "institution," vacillating between a rather timid "exposing," "reflecting," or "revealing," on the one hand, and visions of the revolutionary overthrow of the existing museological order on the other, with the institutional critic as a guerrilla fighter engaging in acts of subversion and sabotage, breaking through walls and floors and doors, provoking censorship, bringing down the powers that be. In either case, "art" and "artist" generally figure as antagonistically opposed to an "institution" that incorporates, co-opts, commodifies, and otherwise misappropriates once-radical—and uninstitutionalized—practices.

These representations can admittedly be found in the texts of critics associated with institutional critique. However, the idea that institutional critique opposes art to institution, or supposes that radical artistic practices can or ever did exist outside of the institution of art before being "institutionalized" by museums, is contradicted at every turn by the writings and work of Asher, Broodthaers, Buren, and Haacke. From Broodthaers's announcement of his first gallery exhibition in 1964—which he begins by confiding that "the idea of inventing something insincere finally crossed my mind" and then informing us that his dealer will "take thirty percent"[5]—the critique of the apparatus that distributes, presents, and collects art has been inseparable from a critique of artistic practice itself. As Buren put it in "The Function of the Museum" in 1970, if "the Museum makes its 'mark,' imposes its 'frame' ... on everything that is exhibited in it, in a deep and indelible way," it does so easily because "*everything that the Museum shows is only considered and produced in view of being set in it.*"[6] In "The Function of the Studio" from the following year, he couldn't be more clear, arguing that the "analysis of the art system must inevitably be carried on" by investigating *both* the studio and the museum "as customs, the ossifying customs of art."[7]

Indeed, the critique most consistently in evidence in the post-studio work of Buren and Asher is aimed at artistic practice itself (a point that may not have been lost on other artists in the Sixth Guggenheim International Exhibition, since it was they, not the museum officials or trustees, who demanded the removal of Buren's work in 1971). As their writings make clear, the institutionalization of art in museums or its commodification in galleries cannot be conceived of as the co-optation or misappropriation of studio art, whose portable form predestines it to a life of circulation and exchange, market and museological incorporation. Their rigorously site-specific interventions developed as a means not only to reflect on these and other institutional conditions but also to resist the very forms of appropriation on which they reflect. As transitory, these works further acknowledge the historical specificity of any critical intervention, whose effectiveness will always be limited to a particular time and place. Broodthaers, however, was the supreme master of performing critical obsolescence in his gestures of melancholic complicity. Just three years after founding the *Musée d'Art Moderne, Département des Aigles* in his Brussels studio in 1968, he put his "museum fiction" up for sale, "for reasons of bankruptcy," in a prospectus that served as a wrapper for the catalogue of the Cologne Art Fair—with a limited edition sold through Galerie Michael Werner. Finally, the most explicit statement of the elemental role of artists in the institution of art may have been made by Haacke. "'Artists,'" he wrote in 1974, "as much as their supporters and their enemies, no matter of what ideological coloration, are unwitting partners … . They participate jointly in the maintenance and/or development of the ideological make-up of their society. They work within that frame, set the frame and are being framed."[8]

From 1969 on, a conception of the "institution of art" begins to emerge that includes not just the museum, nor even only the sites of production, distribution, and reception of art, but the entire field of art as a social universe. In the works of artists associated with institutional critique, it came to encompass all the sites in which art is shown—from museums and galleries to corporate offices and collectors' homes, and even public space when art is installed there. It also includes the sites of the production of art, studio as well as office, and the sites of the production of art discourse: art magazines, catalogues, art columns in the popular press, symposia, and lectures. And it also includes the sites of the production of the producers of art and art discourse: studio-art, art-history, and, now, curatorial-studies programs. And finally, as Rosler put it in the title of her seminal 1979 essay, it also includes all the "lookers, buyers, dealers and makers" themselves.

This conception of "institution" can be seen most clearly in the work of Haacke, who came to institutional critique through a turn from physical and environmental systems in the 1960s to social systems, starting with his gallery-visitor polls of 1969–73. Beyond the most encompassing list of substantive spaces, places, people, and things, the "institution" engaged by Haacke can best be defined as the network of social and economic relationships between them. Like his *Condensation Cube*, 1963–65, and his *MOMA-Poll*, 1970, the gallery and museum figure less as objects of critique themselves than as containers in which the largely abstract and invisible forces and relations that traverse particular social spaces can be made visible.[9]

Moving from a substantive understanding of "the institution" as specific places, organizations, and individuals to a conception of it as a social field, the question of what is inside and what is outside becomes much more complex. Engaging those boundaries has been a consistent concern of artists associated with institutional critique. Beginning in 1969 with a *travail in situ* at Wide White Space in Antwerp, Buren realized many works that bridged interior and exterior, artistic and non-artistic sites, revealing how the perception of the same material, the same sign, can change radically depending on where it is viewed.

However, it was Asher who may have realized with the greatest precision Buren's early understanding that even a concept, as soon as it "is announced, and especially when it is 'exhibited as art' … becomes an *ideal-object*, which brings us once again to art."[10] With his *Installation Münster (Caravan)*,

Asher demonstrated that the institutionalization of art *as art* depends not on its location in the physical frame of an institution, but in conceptual or perceptual frames. First presented in the 1977 edition of Skulptur Projekte in Münster, the work consisted of a rented recreational trailer, or caravan, parked in different parts of the city each week during the exhibition. At the museum serving as a reference point for the show, visitors could find information about where the caravan could be viewed *in situ* that week. At the site itself, however, nothing indicated that the caravan was art or had any connection to the exhibition. To causal passersby, it was nothing but a caravan.

Asher took Duchamp one step further. Art is not art because it is signed by an artist or shown in a museum or any other "institutional" site. Art is art when it exists for discourses and practices that recognize it as art, value and evaluate it as art, and consume it as art, whether as object, gesture, representation, or only idea. The institution of art is not something external to any work of art but the irreducible condition of its existence as art. No matter how public in placement, immaterial, transitory, relational, everyday, or even invisible, what is announced and perceived as art is always already institutionalized, simply because it exists within the perception of participants in the field of art as art, a perception not necessarily aesthetic but fundamentally social in its determination.

What Asher thus demonstrated is that the institution of art is not only "institutionalized" in organizations like museums and objectified in art objects. It is also internalized and embodied in people. It is internalized in the competencies, conceptual models, and modes of perception that allow us to produce, write about, and understand art, or simply to recognize art as art, whether as artists, critics, curators, art historians, dealers, collectors, or museum visitors. And above all, it exists in the interests, aspirations, and criteria of value that orient our actions and define our sense of worth. These competencies and dispositions determine our own institutionalization as members of the field of art. They make up what Pierre Bourdieu called *habitus*: the "social made body," the institution made mind.

There is, of course, an "outside" of the institution, but it has no fixed, substantive characteristics. It is only what, at any given moment, does not exist as an object of artistic discourses and practices. But just as art cannot exist outside the field of art, we cannot exist outside the field of art, at least not as artists, critics, curators, etc. And what we do outside the field, to the extent that it remains outside, can have no effect within it. So if there is no outside for us, it is not because the institution is perfectly closed, or exists as an apparatus in a "totally administered society," or has grown all-encompassing in size and scope. It is because the institution is inside of us, and we can't get outside of ourselves.

Has institutional critique been institutionalized? Institutional critique has *always* been institutionalized. It could only have emerged *within* and, like all art, can only function *within* the institution of art. The insistence of institutional critique on the inescapability of institutional determination may, in fact, be what distinguishes it most precisely from other legacies of the historical avant-garde. It may be unique among those legacies in its recognition of the failure of avant-garde movements and the consequences of that failure; that is, not the destruction of the institution of art, but its explosion beyond the traditional boundaries of specifically artistic objects and aesthetic criteria. The institutionalization of Duchamp's negation of artistic competence with the readymade transformed that negation into a supreme affirmation of the omnipotence of the artistic gaze and its limitless incorporative power. It opened the way for the artistic conceptualization—and commodification—of everything. As Bürger could already write in 1974, "If an artist today signs a stove pipe and exhibits it, that artist certainly does not denounce the art market but adapts to it. Such adaptation does not eradicate the idea of individual creativity, it affirms it, and the reason is the failure of the avant-gard[e]."[11]

It is artists—as much as museums or the market—who, in their very efforts to escape the institution of art, have driven its expansion. With each attempt to evade the limits of institutional determination, to embrace an outside, to redefine art or reintegrate it into everyday life, to reach "everyday" people and work in the "real" world, we expand our frame and bring more of the world into it. But we never escape it.

Of course, that frame has also been transformed in the process. The question is how? Discussions of that transformation have tended to revolve around oppositions like inside and outside, public and private, elitism and populism. But when these arguments are used to assign political value to substantive conditions, they often fail to account for the underlying distributions of power that are reproduced even as conditions change, and they thus end up serving to legitimate that reproduction. To give the most obvious example, the enormous expansion of museum audiences, celebrated under the banner of populism, has proceeded hand in hand with the continuous rise of entrance fees, excluding more and more lower-income visitors, and the creation of new forms of elite participation with increasingly differentiated hierarchies of membership, viewings, and galas, the exclusivity of which is broadly advertised in fashion magazines and society pages. Far from becoming less elitist, ever-more-popular museums have become vehicles for the mass-marketing of elite tastes and practices that, while perhaps less rarified in terms of the aesthetic competencies they demand, are ever more rarified economically as prices rise. All of which also increases the demand for the products and services of art professionals.

However, the fact that we are trapped in our field does not mean that we have no effect on, and are not affected by, what takes place beyond its boundaries. Once again, Haacke may have been the first to understand and represent the full extent of the interplay between what is inside and outside the field of art. While Asher and Buren examined how an object or sign is transformed as it traverses physical and conceptual boundaries, Haacke engaged the "institution" as a network of social and economic relationships, making visible the complicities among the apparently opposed spheres of art, the state, and corporations. It may be Haacke, above all, who evokes characterizations of the institutional critic as an heroic challenger, fearlessly speaking truth to power—and justifiably so, as his work has been subject to vandalism, censorship, and parliamentary showdowns. However, anyone familiar with his work should recognize that, far from trying to tear down the museum, Haacke's project has been an attempt to *defend* the institution of art from instrumentalization by political and economic interests.

That the art world, now a global multibillion-dollar industry, is not part of the "real world" is one of the most absurd fictions of art discourse. The current market boom, to mention only the most obvious example, is a direct product of neoliberal economic policies. It belongs, first of all, to the luxury consumption boom that has gone along with growing income disparities and concentrations of wealth—the beneficiaries of Bush's tax cuts are our patrons—and, secondly, to the same economic forces that have created the global real-estate bubble: lack of confidence in the stock market due to falling prices and corporate accounting scandals, lack of confidence in the bond market due to the rising national debt, low interest rates, and regressive tax cuts. And the art market is not the only art-world site where the growing economic disparities of our society are reproduced. They can also be seen in what are now only nominally "nonprofit" organizations like universities—where MFA programs rely on cheap adjunct labor—and museums, where anti-union policies have produced compensation ratios between the highest- and lowest-paid employees that now surpass forty to one.

Representations of the "art world" as wholly distinct from the "real world," like representations of the "institution" as discrete and separate from "us," serve specific functions in art discourse. They maintain an imaginary distance between the social and economic interests we invest in through our activities and the euphemized artistic, intellectual, and even political "interests" (or disinterests) that provide those activities with content and justify their existence. And with these representations, we also reproduce the mythologies of volunteerist freedom and creative omnipotence that have made art and artists such attractive emblems for neoliberalism's entrepreneurial, "ownership-society" optimism. That such optimism has found perfect artistic expression in neo-Fluxus practices like relational aesthetics, which are now in perpetual vogue, demonstrates the degree to which what Bürger called the avant-garde's aim to integrate "art into life praxis" has evolved into a highly ideological form of escapism. But this is not just about ideology. We are not only symbols of the rewards of the current regime: In this art market, we are its direct material beneficiaries.

Every time we speak of the "institution" as other than "us," we disavow our role in the creation and perpetuation of its conditions. We avoid responsibility for, or action against, the everyday complicities, compromises, and censorship—above all, self-censorship—which are driven by our own interests in the field and the benefits we derive from it. It's not a question of inside or outside, or the number and scale of various organized sites for the production, presentation, and distribution of art. It's not a question of being against the institution: We are the institution. It's a question of what kind of institution we are, what kind of values we institutionalize, what forms of practice we reward, and what kinds of rewards we aspire to. Because the institution of art is internalized, embodied, and performed by individuals, these are the questions that institutional critique demands we ask, above all, of ourselves.

Finally, it is this self-questioning—more than a thematic like "the institution," no matter how broadly conceived—that defines institutional critique as a practice. If, as Bürger put it, the self-criticism of the historical avant-garde intended "the abolition of autonomous art" and its integration "into the praxis of life," it failed in both its aims and strategies.[12]

However, the very institutionalization that marked this failure became the condition of institutional critique. Recognizing that failure and its consequences, institutional critique turned from the increasingly bad-faith efforts of neo-avant-gardes at dismantling or escaping the institution of art and aimed instead to *defend* the very institution that the institutionalization of the avant-garde's "self-criticism" had created the potential for: an institution *of* critique. And it may be this very institutionalization that allows institutional critique to judge the institution of art against the critical claims of its legitimizing discourses, against its self-representation as a site of resistance and contestation, and against its mythologies of radicality and symbolic revolution.

Notes

1. Michael Kimmelman, "Tall French Visitor Takes up Residence in the Guggenheim," *New York Times*, March 25, 2005.

2. Andrea Fraser, "In and Out of Place," *Art in America*, June 1985, 124.

3. Benjamin H.D. Buchloh, "Allegorical Procedures: Appropriation and Montage in Contemporary Art," *Artforum*, Sept. 1982, 48.

4. Peter Bürger, *Theory of the Avant-Garde*, trans. Michael Shaw (Minneapolis: University of Minnesota Press, 1984), 22.

5. Broodthaers quoted in Benjamin H.D. Buchloh, "Open Letters, Industrial Poems," *October* 42 (Fall 1987): 71.

6. Daniel Buren, "The Function of the Museum," in *Museums by Artists*, ed. AA Bronson and Peggy Gale (Toronto: Art Metropole, 1983), 58.

7. Daniel Buren, "The Function of the Studio," in *Museums by Artists*, 61.

8. Hans Haacke, "All the Art That's Fit to Show," in *Museums by Artists*, 152.

9. In this, Haacke's work parallels the theory of art as a social field developed by Pierre Bourdieu.

10. Daniel Buren, "Beware!" *Studio International*, March 1970, 101.

11. Bürger, *Theory of the Avant-Garde*, 52–53.

12. Ibid., 54.

Pamela M. Lee

Boundary Issues: The Art World Under the Sign of Globalism

Artforum, vol. 42, no. 3, November 2003

You could call it a pathology of self-definition. Either that or a severe case of "boundary issues." For close to ten years now, that ambient phenomenon known as the art world has been hit by what amounts to an identity crisis, more often than not figured under the sign of globalization. Flip through the catalogues and magazines, survey the principal actors and bit players, track the ever-proliferating biennials—from São Paulo to Shanghai to Istanbul—and witness the art world's struggle to rethink its audiences and range of influence, its norms and procedures. But just how precisely has the art world addressed the conditions of "multiplicity, diversity, and contradiction"—the defining characteristics of the contemporary experience, according to Francesco Bonami—coextensive with the processes of globalization? There is the lurking suspicion shared by many longstanding art-world participants that "the Global" has simply assumed the throne formerly held by likes of the Postmodern, the Multicultural, the Simulacra, and the *informe* (and not unlike the operations of formlessness, globalization's neoliberal consequences may prove thoroughly abject).

I would argue that the way the art world conceives of itself determines its treatment of globalization. Indeed, the conventional understanding of the term "art world" betrays a set of prejudices under threat by the very global conditions the contemporary art world seeks to represent. In common parlance, the "art world" signifies a society of individuals and institutions—a social, cultural, and economic world organized around museums, galleries, and the art press and the legions of artists, critics, collectors, curators, and audiences who have truck with such sites. The image of this world is typically one of gala openings and social privilege—at once a specialized community and the locations that community would occupy (the New York art world, for example, or the gallery scene in Los Angeles)—and decidedly Eurocentric in its orientation. So it makes perfect sense that the art world thus conceived would seem stricken by both geopolitical anxiety *and* a peculiar giddiness about the current state of global affairs. For one thing, as demonstrated by the numerous high-profile exhibitions on the topic, the art world now appears embroiled in a turf war, in which its official institu-tions (namely, museums, those loci of art-historical knowledge) are imagined to defend their proprietary interests from global "outsiders" and their curatorial incursions. By the same token, something of a colonial logic underwrites the expansion of the art world's traditional borders, as if the art world itself were gleefully following globalization's imperial mandate.

We can hardly avoid using "art world" in the everyday sense of the term—it's simply too convenient, too deeply embedded in our vocabulary—

but a brief look into its provenance as a philosophical term of art might be instructive in analyzing the current struggle to effectively engage the global problematic. Perhaps the most influential postwar articulation was formulated by Arthur C. Danto in 1964. Taking Warhol's Brillo boxes as his case study, Danto's essay "The Artworld" asked after the first principle of philosophical aesthetics: What separates a work of art from non-art, the readymade from the commodity? The art object, he argued, must exist in an "atmosphere of interpretation" with other artworks, which would in turn serve as comparative vehicles of interpretation. As he put it, "To see something as art requires something the eye cannot decry—an atmosphere of artistic theory, a knowledge of history of art: an artworld." Danto argued that an object is granted the status of art if it can be conceptually linked to objects already deemed art; and a theoretical claim—an aesthetic theory—was required to justify that linkage. "There is no art without those who speak the language of the artworld," Danto reasoned. "The artworld stands to the real world in something like the relationship in which the City of God stands to the Earthly City." The art world, this Augustinian analogy implies, is a theoretical paradigm; and what comes to count as art today must necessarily find its "place" in that divine city. Like all good paradigms, however, the art world must be able to accommodate new languages and ideas in a perpetual state of conceptual readiness. "The world has to be ready for certain things," Danto wrote nearly forty years ago, "the artworld no less than the real one."

Danto's approach proves useful in parsing the global problematic, as it underscores the need for a theoretical paradigm equal to the task of accommodating the vast changes witnessed in the art world and artistic production at large over the course of the past decade. But whether the art world is a theoretical atmosphere or an institutional elite (complete with the secret handshakes that grant membership into its society), the question remains: What happens to the art world when the world itself is progressively aestheticized under the regime of global spectacle? And, further, what happens if the art world's institutional context has expanded beyond measure, in excess of the nationally inscribed institutions of the "official" art world (i.e., Europe and the United States)? On the surface of things, the institutional art world claims no separation at all from the global "outside"; the language of crisis and contradiction underwriting our current transnational frenzy suggests that exactly the opposite is the case. Moreover, the ways in which the art world has generally represented issues around globalization—as in last summer's Venice Biennale or in the Whitney Museum of American Art's "The American Effect"—suggest that a troubling distance between the art world and the global order still remains.

No doubt a big part of the art world's problem in treating the global issue revolves not only around defining globalization itself but around evaluating the political consequences that stem from its procedures. Fredric Jameson usefully, if broadly, defined globalization as "the sense of an immense enlargement of world communication, as well as of the horizon of a world market," speaking to the postwar integration of communicative, economic, and geographical forces and oft-made claims about the collapse of traditional conceptions of space and time with the emergent geopolitical order. The art world's account of the term "globalization," however, suffers from a certain fuzziness relative to its own practices. To be sure, the words "globalization," "globality," "the global" and "globalism" (the "ism" here connoting either an ethos, an aesthetics, or a kind of period style—take your pick) bear the peculiar distinction of being both ubiquitous and amorphous: ubiquitous because inescapable to any semi-informed world citizen and yet amorphous because subject to infinite shape-shifting, especially in the mainstream press. Of course, the student of the global knows full well that globalization does mean many things, bound up at once in the rhetoric of galloping free markets and in the lingering specter of Marx, simultaneously producing homogenization (read: Americanization) and radical hybridity. What's more, the fallout of such processes has sparked ferocious debate concerning globalization's political ends —whether or not it serves progressive or reactionary purposes. Where exactly *should* we stand vis-à-vis a New World Order that gives rise to the Battle in Seattle and to the so-called War on Terror? To the "multitude" and the Nike army alike? The lack of consensus around globalization's terms and implications is arguably what endows it with both its acutely anxious charge and its capacity to be generalized to the point of meaninglessness. Like the art world's treatment of postmodernism two decades earlier, the semantic stalemate around globalization is typically resolved by conceding to the plurality of its definitions. And that's part of the problem as well: In the art world's weakest iterations of the topic, it all seems like so much old-school pluralism, the bad dream of the postmodern that Hal Foster long ago characterized in terms of the world market. "The pluralist position," he presciently wrote, "plays right into the ideology of the 'free market.'" Globalization, to follow this model, translates into "the far-flung from all over," an "anything goes" approach to recent art in which floating buzzwords "conflict," "tension," and "contradiction" may be enough to move some less than compelling product.

Typically, the ways in which the art world has addressed the global question rest with the logic of representation. Representation assumes several meanings in this context: It pertains, first, to the institutional visibility of the discourse around globalism, the degree to which museums, galleries, critics, artists, and cultural consumers feel the need to pay attention to the topic, and, second, to the diversity of artists, locations, and cultural perspectives increasingly included in the art world's discourse. It goes without saying that this is no small thing, neither the opening of the art world to artists typically shut out from it (i.e., artists from Asia, Africa, Latin America appearing in biennials located in Johannesburg, Tirana, and Havana) nor the instrumental role played by curators and critics in that very opening. For those once embroiled in the culture wars, such institutional arrangements in response to global demands for representation may recall the struggles over identity politics that marked the late '80s and early '90s. And what the multiculturalism episode taught us, for better or for worse, is that such gains are not only hard-won but also deeply precarious.

But by far the sort of "globalist" representation most easily assimilated by the art world is the imagery of globalization. Lately we've seen our fair share of the aesthetics of passports and Coca-Cola: At the Venice Biennale alone we witnessed Santiago Sierra's Spanish Pavilion, accessible only to Spanish citizens with the documentation to prove it, and Kader Attia's vending machine that dispenses passports and soft drinks alike. If objects such as these represent articles of faith for the art world's global acolytes, the image of the airport (and systems of transportation in general) has become their summa. What better means to convey the expediency of markets, the freedom (or trauma) of placelessness, and the cultures of immigration and tourism than the alien space of the airport terminal? The kinds of pairings that result from this iconography doubtlessly underscore the business of "conflict" and "contradiction" emblematic of the global question, but too often, the superficial emphasis on image and theme comes at the expense of critical readings of the work. Shots of cargo containers by the Milanese artists' collective Multiplicity propose quite different things from an Allan Sekula series involving the same. You can lump together a picture of a tarmac by Andreas Gursky with a Martha Rosler photo of an airport lounge, but the comparison will be spurious at best, the kind of category error art historians rightfully brush off as "pseudomorphology."

The art world, in other words, has responded to contemporary geopolitics largely through representations of the global and its thematics. Its approach is a kind of *globalism*, what I earlier referred to as an aesthetic or "period style." But this tack offers a relatively limited picture of the sociopolitical situation, reflecting an art world that still sees itself as distinct from the "real" world "outside" it, analogous, say, to the way that a figure is positioned in relation to its ground. Apart from the nods we dutifully make to expanding networks of communication and the broad recognition that globalization may change the way we go about our art history, we must keep in mind that globalization is as much a process as a thing and that the "atmosphere of theory" which Danto identified as the "artworld" may move us closer to thinking critically about our relationship to those processes. Case in point: Consider how we all contend with the banality of the airport (aside from its glossy image in the iris prints that regularly turn up at galleries). By now, any number of people have noted that citizenship in the art world is measured by the number of frequent-flier miles one chalks up in the service of the business. A few months ago, I conversed with a well-known artist about his extensive international travel; and the staggering number of miles he sheepishly volunteered confirmed this thesis without his being familiar with it. The point, basic though it may be, is that activities constitutive of the art world's horizon are indivisible from the activities of globalization itself. What we treat as a given to our métier is, in fact, immanent to the processes we usually associate with the emerging transnational order.

And if it's a theory of immanence we're looking for, we might take a page from the most cherished manifesto of the antiglobalization movement, Antonio Negri and Michael Hardt's *Empire* (2000). Let's admit these are strange days when a book that makes ample reference to Spinoza, Machiavelli, Deleuze, and Duns Scotus accrues a kind of pop-culture stardom. Strange, too, is Negri's celebrity in art-world circles, given the book's relative quiet on the subject of art (the one art-historical reference in the book's 478 pages is—appropriately enough—Serge Guilbaut's canonical *How New York Stole the Idea of Modern Art* [1983]). Nevertheless, Negri's art-world acclaim was much in evidence at Documenta 11—for which he had contributed, with Hardt, an essay to one of its "platforms" on democracy—no less than at last summer's Venice Biennale, where the phantom presence of *Empire* was all-pervasive (and hardly a stone's throw from Padua, where the autonomist movement with which Negri was associated in the '70s committed some of its most violent acts). Should we take the book's energetic rhetoric of multitudes and counter-Empire seriously, however, we need acknowledge the particular language of immanence it borrows from Spinoza and Deleuze. A theory of immanence stresses the here and now against the dialectical or transcendent; as it is thought through the logic of globalization, it suggests that there is no longer any global "outside," no Archimedean point from which to survey the workings of globalization with cool, critical distance. It bears saying that numerous critics have challenged Negri and Hardt on this point, but for the immediate purposes of discussing the art world, the plane of immanence finds metaphorical expression in a telling (and in this context, uncanny) turn of phrase. On the coming of counter-Empire, Hardt and Negri write, "This is the founding moment of an earthly city that is strong and distinct from any divine city."

One is loath (or at least seriously reluctant) to equate the workings of the art world with the multitude or the earthly city (and while some of us may well be self-identified cultural laborers or even simply workers, far too many others would seem to rule by sovereign decree). Regardless, the unintended reversal of Danto's Augustinian metaphor forces us to confront our methodological shortcomings on the global question, bringing the art world down to earth, so to speak. Indeed, our most urgent challenge is to account more critically for the way the art world has internalized the conditions of the global as its daily habitus: its institutional, political, and economic imperatives as well as its artistic and critical ones. And we need to productively rethink the "art world" as itself a mode of immanent global production, not just as a passive mirror reflecting the sweeping geopolitical changes thought to remain outside of it. Let me repeat Danto's words as an injunction to our own practices as artists, critics, curators, historians, and audience members: "The world has to be ready for certain things, the artworld no less than the real one." This "atmosphere compounded of artistic theories" must be ready for the day when the art world's traditional borders are indivisible from those of the global order we are inclined merely to portray.

Miwon Kwon

Itinerant Artists

Excerpt from *One Place After Another: Site-Specific Art and Locational Identity*, Cambridge, MA: The MIT Press, 2002

The increasing institutional interest in current site-oriented practices that mobilize the site as a discursive narrative is demanding an intensive physical mobilization of the artist to create works in various cities throughout the cosmopolitan art world. Typically, an artist (no longer a studio-bound object maker; primarily working now on call) is invited by an art institution to produce a work specifically configured for the framework provided by the institution (in some cases the artist may solicit the institution with a proposal). Subsequently, the artist enters into a contractual agreement with the host institution for the commission. There follow repeated visits to or extended stays at the site; research into the particularities of the exhibition itself (its thematic structure, social relevance, other artists in the show); and many meetings with curators, educators, and administrative support staff, who may all end up "collaborating" with the artist to produce the work. The project will likely be time-consuming and in the end will have engaged the "site" in a multitude of ways, and the documentation of the project will take on another life within the art world's publicity circuit, which will in turn alert another institution to suggest another commission.

Thus, if the artist is successful, he or she travels constantly as a freelancer, often working on more than one site-specific project at a time, globetrotting as a guest, tourist, adventurer, temporary in-house critic, or pseudo-ethnographer[1] to São Paulo, Paris, Munich, London, Chicago, Seoul, New York, Amsterdam, Los Angeles, and so on.[2] Generally, the in situ configuration of a project that emerges out of such a situation is temporary, ostensibly unsuitable for re-presentation anywhere else without altering its meaning, partly because the commission is defined by a unique set of geographical and temporal circumstances and partly because the project is dependent on unpredictable and unprogrammable on-site relations. But such conditions, despite appearances to the contrary, do not circumvent or even complicate the problem of commodification, because there is a strange reversal now by which the artist comes to approximate the "work," instead of the other way around as is commonly assumed (that is, art work as surrogate of the artist). Perhaps because of the absence of the artist from the physical manifestation of the work, the presence of the artist has become an absolute prerequisite for the execution/presentation of site-oriented projects. It is now the *performative* aspect of an artist's characteristic mode of operation (even when working in collaboration) that is repeated and circulated as a new art commodity, with the artist him/herself functioning as the primary vehicle for its verification, repetition, and circulation.[3]

For example, after a yearlong engagement with the Maryland Historical Society, Fred Wilson finalized his site-specific project *Mining the Museum* (1992) as a temporary reorganization of the institution's permanent collection. As a timely convergence of institutional museum critique and multicultural identity politics, *Mining the Museum* drew many new visitors to the Society, and the project received high praise from both the art world and the popular press.[4] Subsequently, Wilson performed a similar archival excavation/intervention at the Seattle Art Museum in 1993, a project also defined by the museum's permanent collection.[5] Although the shift from Baltimore to Seattle, from a historical society to an art museum, introduced new variables and challenges, the Seattle project established a repetitive pattern between the artist and the hosting institution, reflecting what has become a familiar museological practice—the commissioning of artists to rehang permanent collections.[6] The fact that Wilson's project in Seattle fell short of the Baltimore success may be evidence of how ongoing repetition of such commissions can render methodologies of critique rote and generic. They can easily become extensions of the museum's own self-promotional apparatus, while the artist becomes a commodity with a special purchase on "criticality." As Isabelle Graw has noted, "the result can be an absurd situation in which the commissioning institution (the museum or gallery) turns to an artist as a person who has the legitimacy to point out the contradictions and irregularities of which they themselves disapprove." And for artists, "subversion in the service of one's own convictions finds easy transition into subversion for hire; 'criticism turns into spectacle.'"[7]

To say, however, that this changeover represents the commodification of the artist is not completely accurate, because it is not the figure of the artist per se, as a personality or a celebrity (à la Warhol), that is produced/consumed in an exchange with the institution. What the current pattern points to, in fact, is the extent to which the very nature of the commodity as a cipher of production and labor relations is no longer bound to the realm of manufacturing (of things) but defined in relation to the service and management industries.[8] The artist as an overspecialized aesthetic object maker has been anachronistic for a long time already. What they *provide* now, rather than *produce*, are aesthetic, often "critical-aesthetic," services. Andrea Fraser's 1994–1995 project in which she contracted herself out to the EA-Generali Foundation in Vienna (an art association established by companies belonging to the EA-Generali insurance group) as an artist/consultant to provide "interpretive" and "interventionary" services to the foundation, is a uniquely self-conscious playing out of this shift.[9] Through this and prior performance pieces, Fraser highlights the changing conditions of artistic production and reception in terms of both the content and the structure of the project.

Thus, if Richard Serra could once distill the nature of artistic activities down to their elemental physical actions (to drop, to split, to roll, to fold, to cut, etc.),[10] the situation now demands a different set of verbs: to negotiate, to coordinate, to compromise, to research, to promote, to organize, to interview. This shift was forecast in Conceptual art's adoption of what Benjamin H.D. Buchloh has described as the "aesthetics of administration."[11] The salient point here is how quickly this aesthetics of administration, developed in the 1960s and 1970s, has converted to the administration of aesthetics in the 1980s and 1990s. Generally speaking, the artist used to be a maker of aesthetic objects; now he/she is a facilitator, educator, coordinator, and bureaucrat. Additionally, as artists have adopted managerial functions of art institutions (curatorial, educational, archival) as an integral part of their creative process, managers of art within art institutions (curators, educations, public program directors), who often take their cues from these artists, now see themselves as authorial figures in their own right.[12]

Concurrent with, or because of, these methodological and procedural changes, there is a reemergence of the centrality of the artist as the progenitor of meaning. This is true even when authorship is deferred to others in collaborations, or when the institutional framework is self-consciously integrated into the work, or when an artist problematizes his/her own authorial role. On the one hand, this "return of the author" results from the thematization of discursive sites, which engenders a misrecognition of them as natural extensions of the artist's identity, and the legitimacy of the work's critique is measured by the proximity of the artist's personal association (converted to expertise) with a particular place, history, discourse, identity, etc. (converted to content). On the other hand, because the signifying chain of site-oriented art is constructed foremost by the movement and decision of the artist,[13] the (critical) elaboration of the project inevitably unfolds around the artist. That is, the intricate orchestration of literal and discursive sites that make up a nomadic narrative *requires* the artist as a narrator-protagonist. In some cases, this renewed focus on the artist in the name of authorial self-reflexivity leads to a hermetic implosion of (auto)biographical and subjective indulgences.

This being so, one of the narrative trajectories of all site-oriented projects is consistently aligned with the artist's prior projects executed in other places, generating what might be called another "site"—the exhibition history of an artist, his/her vitae. The tension between the intensive mobilization of the artist and the recentralization of meaning around him/her is addressed in Renée Green's 1993 *World Tour*, a group reinstallation of four site-specific projects produced in disparate parts of the world over a period of three years.[14] By bringing several distinct projects together, *World Tour* sought to reflect on the problematic conditions of present-day site specificity, such as the ethnographic predicament of artists who are frequently imported by foreign institutions and cities as expert/exotic visitors. *World Tour* also attempted to imagine a productive convergence between specificity and mobility, in which a project created under one set of circumstances might be redeployed in another without losing its impact—or, better, might find new meaning and gain critical sharpness through recontextualizations.[15] But these concerns were not readily available to viewers of *World Tour*, whose interpretive reaction was to see the artist as the primary link between the projects. Indeed, the effort to resituate the individual site-oriented projects as a conceptually coherent ensemble eclipsed the specificity of each and forced a relational dynamic between discrete projects. Consequently, especially for an audience unfamiliar with Green's practice, the overriding narrative of *World Tour* became Green's creative process as an artist in and through the four installations. And in this sense, the project functioned institutionally as a fairly conventional retrospective.

Just as shifts in the structural organization of cultural production alter the form of the art commodity (as service) and the authority of the artist (as primary narrator and protagonist), values like originality, authenticity, and singularity are also reworked in site-oriented art—evacuated from the art work and attributed to the site—reinforcing a general cultural valorization of places as the locus of authentic experience and coherent sense of historical and personal identity.[16] An instructive example of this phenomenon is "Places with a Past," a 1991 site-specific exhibition organized by independent curator Mary Jane Jacob, which took the city of Charleston, South Carolina, as not only its backdrop but "the bridge between the works of art and the audience."[17] In addition to breaking the rules of the art establishment, the exhibition wanted to further a dialogue between art and the socio-historical dimension of the place.[18] According to Jacob, "Charleston proved to be fertile ground" for the investigation of issues concerning "gender, race, cultural identity, considerations of difference ... subjects much in the vanguard of criticism and art-making ... The actuality of the situation, the fabric of the time and place of Charleston, offered an incredibly rich and meaningful context for the making and siting of publicly visible and physically prominent installations that rang true in [the artists'] approach to these ideas."[19]

While site-specific art is still described as refuting originality and authenticity as intrinsic qualities of the art object or the artist, these qualities are readily relocated from the art work to the place of its presentation—only to return to the art work now that it has become integral to the site. Admittedly, according to Jacob, "locations ... contribute a specific identity to the shows staged by injecting into the experience the uniqueness of the place."[20] Conversely, if the social, historical, and geographical specificity of Charleston offered artists a unique opportunity to create unrepeatable works (and by extension an unrepeatable exhibition), then the programmatic implementations of site-specific art in projects like "Places with a Past" ultimately utilize art to promote Charleston as a unique place. What is prized most of all in site-specific art is still the singularity and authenticity that the presence of the artist seems to guarantee, not only in terms of the presumed unrepeatability of the work but in the way the presence of the artist also endows places with a "unique" distinction.

Certainly, site-specific art can lead to the unearthing of repressed histories, help provide greater visibility to marginalized groups and issues, and initiate the re(dis)covery of "minor" places so far ignored by the dominant culture. But inasmuch as the current socioeconomic order thrives on the (artificial) production and (mass) consumption of difference (for difference sake), the siting of art in "real" places can also be a means to *extract* the social and historical dimensions of these places in order to variously serve the thematic drive of an artist, satisfy institutional demographic profiles, or fulfill the fiscal needs of a city. It is within this framework, in which art serves to generate a sense of authenticity and uniqueness of place for quasi-promotional agendas, that I understand the goals of city-based international art programs like "Sculpture. Projects in Münster 1997." According to its co-curator Klaus Bussmann,

> *The fundamental idea behind the exhibitions was to create a dialogue between artists, the town and the public, in other words, to encourage the artists to create projects that dealt with conditions in the town, its architecture, urban planning, its history and the social structure of society in the town ... Invitations to artists from all over the world to come to Münster for the sculpture project, to enter into a debate*

> *with the town, have established a tradition which will not only be continued in the year 1997 but beyond this will become something specific to Münster: a town not only as an "open-air museum for modern art" but also as a place for a natural confrontation between history and contemporary art ... The aim of the exhibition "Sculpture. Projects in Münster" is to make the town of Münster comprehensible as a complex, historically formed structure exactly in those places that make it stand out from other towns and cities.*[21]

Significantly, the appropriation of site-specific art for the valorization of urban identities comes at a time of a fundamental cultural shift in which architecture and urban planning, formerly the primary media for expressing a vision of the city, are displaced by other media more intimate with marketing and advertising. In the words of urban theorist Kevin Robins, "As cities have become ever more equivalent and urban identities increasingly 'thin,' ... it has become necessary to employ advertising and marketing agencies to manufacture such distinctions. It is a question of distinction in a world beyond difference."[22] Site specificity in this context finds new importance because it supplies distinction of place and uniqueness of locational identity, highly seductive qualities in the promotion of towns and cities within the competitive restructuring of the global economic hierarchy. Thus, site specificity remains inexorably tied to a process that renders the particularity and identity of various cities a matter of product differentiation. Indeed, the exhibition catalogue for "Places with a Past" was a "tasteful" tourist promotion, pitching the city of Charleston as a unique, "artistic," and meaningful place (to visit).[23] Under the pretext of their articulation or resuscitation, site-specific art can be mobilized to expedite the erasure of differences via the commodification and sterilization of places.

The yoking together of the myth of the artist as a privileged source of originality with the customary belief in places as ready reservoirs of unique identity belies the compensatory nature of such a move. For this collapse of the artist and the site reveals an anxious cultural desire to assuage the sense of loss and vacancy that pervades both sides of this equation. In this sense, Craig Owens was perhaps correct to characterize site specificity as a melancholic discourse and practice,[24] as was Thierry de Duve in claiming that "sculpture in the last 20 years is an attempt to reconstruct the notion of site from the standpoint of having acknowledged its disappearance."[25]

Notes

1. See Hal Foster, "The Artist as Ethnographer," in *The Return of the Real: The Avant-Garde at the End of the Century* (Cambridge: MIT Press, 1996), on the complex exchange between art and anthropology in recent art.

2. Not exactly the portable studio or Marcel Duchamp's *Boîte-en-valise* (1941) but a descendant nonetheless. A productionist reading of modern art has focused on the model of the alienated and fragmentary labor of the assembly line worker as producer of objects. What I am proposing here is a consideration of another neglected model of labor, that of the itinerant salesman who, rather than being bound to a stationary point in the space of production, must travel extensively for the dissemination, distribution, and promotion of commodities.

3. The current modes of site-oriented practices can be mapped along an alternative genealogy of performance art. Consider, for example, Vito Acconci's comments on performance art as a publicity-oriented, contract-based practice: "On the one hand, performance imposed the unsaleable onto the store that the gallery is. On the other hand, performance built that store up and confirmed the market-system: It increased the gallery's sales by acting as window-dressing and by providing publicity ... There was one way I loved to say the word

'performance,' one meaning of the world [sic] 'performance' I was committed to: 'Performance' in the sense of performing a contract—you promised you would do something, now you have to carry that promise out, bring that promise through to completion." Vito Acconci, "Performance After the Fact," *New Observations* 95 (May–June 1993): 29. Thanks to Frazer Ward for directing my attention to this text. For a recent consideration of site-specific art from the point of view of performance, see Nick Kaye, *Site-Specific Art: Performance, Place, and Documentation* (London: Routledge, 2000).

4. By strategically introducing objects from the material history of African Americans and Native Americans (until then buried in the Society's storage) into existing displays of refined cultural artifacts, Wilson exposed the extent to which the histories of these "minority" cultures have consistently been repressed in the dominant narrative of the history of the United States. The matter-of-fact juxtaposition of, for example, slave shackles from before the Civil War and elaborately decorated silver tea services from the same period, presented with equal distinction under the category of "Metal Works," provided disturbing visual evidence of the violent legacy of slavery and racism in this country. The project also served as a local critique of the Maryland Historical Society itself—Society's own holdings used to point up the prejudicial and exclusive nature of "definitive" museological histories written in the form of the institution's exhibitions and publications. For details on this project, see Lisa Corrin, ed., *Mining the Museum* (New York: New Press, 1994).

5. See Fred Wilson's interview with Martha Buskirk in *October* 70 (Fall 1994): 109–112.

6. In the name of interdisciplinarity, and in an effort to rejuvenate permanent collection exhibitions, several museums have also engaged high-profile philosophers, cultural theorists, sociologists, and other intellectuals from nonart fields for curatorial commissions. See, for instance, Jacques Derrida's curatorial project at the Louvre presented in the Hall Napoléon from October 26, 1990, to January 21, 1991, published as *Mémoires d'aveugle: L'autoportrait et autres ruines* (Paris: Editions de la Réunion des musées nationaux, 1990).

7. Isabelle Graw, "Field Work," *Flash Art* (November/December 1990): 137. Her observation here is in relation to Hans Haacke's practice but is relevant as a general statement concerning the current status of institutional critique. See also Frazer Ward, "The Haunted Museum: Institutional Critique and Publicity," *October* 73 (Summer 1995): 71–90.

8. See J. I. Gershuny and I.D. Miles, *The New Service Economy* (New York: Praeger, 1983); and Saskia Sassen, *The Global City: New York, London, Tokyo* (Princeton: Princeton University Press, 1991).

9. It should be noted that the artist herself initiated the project by offering such services through her "Prospectus for Corporations." See Fraser's *Report* (Vienna: EA-Generali Foundation, 1995). For a more general consideration of artistic practice as cultural service provision, see Andrea Fraser, "What's Intangible, Transitory, Mediating, Participatory, and Rendered in the Public Sphere?," *October* 80 (Spring 1997): 111–116. Proceedings of working-group discussions organized by Fraser and Helmut Draxler in 1993 around the theme of services, to which Fraser's text provides an introduction, are also of interest and appear in the same issue of *October*. See also Beatrice von Bismark, Diethelm Stoller, and Ulf Wuggenig, eds., *Games, Fights, Collaborations* (Stuttgart: Cantz Verlag, 1996).

10. Richard Serra, "Verb List, 1967–68," in *Writings Interviews* (Chicago: University of Chicago Press, 1994), 3.

11. Benjamin H.D. Buchloh, "Conceptual Art 1962–1969: From the Aesthetics of Administration to the Critique of Institutions," *October* 55 (Winter 1991): 105–143.

12. For instance, the "Views from Abroad" exhibition series at the Whitney Museum, which foregrounds "artistic" visions of European curators, is structured very much like site-specific commissions of artists that focus on museum permanent collections as described above. The first two exhibitions in the series featured the "visions" of Rudi Fuchs of the Stedelijk Museum, Amsterdam (June 29–October 1, 1995), and Jean-Christophe Ammann of the Museum für Moderne Kunst, Frankfurt am Main (October 18, 1996–January 5, 1997). These exhibitions traveled to the curators' respective home institutions after their run in New York City.

13. According to James Meyer, a site-oriented practice based on a functional notion of a site "traces the *artist's* movements through and around the institution" and "reflect[s] the specific interests, educations, and formal decisions of the producer"; and "in the process of deferral, a signifying chain that traverses physical and discursive borders," the functional site "incorporates the body of the artist" (emphasis added). See Meyer, "The Functional Site," in *Platzwechsel*, exh. cat. (Zurich: Kunsthalle Zurich, 1995), 29, 33, 31, 35.

14. The installation consisted of *Bequest*, commissioned by the Worcester Art Museum in Massachusetts in 1991; *Import/Export Funk Office*, originally shown at the Christian Nagel Gallery in Cologne in 1992 and then reinstalled at the 1993 Biennial at the Whitney Museum of American Art; *Mise en Scène*, first presented

in 1992 in Clisson, France; and *Idyll Pursuits*, produced for a group exhibition in 1991 in Caracas, Venezuela. As a whole, *World Tour* was exhibited at the Museum of Contemporary Art, Los Angeles, in 1993, then traveled to the Dallas Museum of Art later that same year. See Russell Ferguson, ed., *World Tour*, exh. cat. (Los Angeles: Museum of Contemporary Art, 1993).

15. This is a project not exclusive to Green. Silvia Kolbowski, for instance, has proposed the coupling of generic sites and specific transferability in projects such as "Enlarged from the Catalogue: *The United States of America*" (1988). See the project annotations and Johanne Lamoureux's essay, "The Open Window Case: New Displays for an Old Western Paradigm," in *Silvia Kolbowski: XI Projects* (New York: Border Editions, 1993) 34–51, 6–15. There is a correspondence between Kolbowski's idea and Mel Bochner's remarks cited elsewhere in the book.

16. The faith in the authenticity of place is evident in a wide range of disciplines. In urban studies, see Dolores Hayden, *The Power of Place: Urban Landscapes as Public History* (Cambridge: MIT Press, 1995). In cultural geography, see Michael Hough, *Out of Place: Restoring Identity to the Regional Landscape* (New Haven: Yale University Pres, 1990). In philosophy, see Edward Casey, *The Fate of Place: A Philosophical History* (Berkeley: University of California Press, 1997). In relation to public art, see Ronald Lee Fleming and Renata von Tscharner, *PlaceMakers: Creating Public Art That Tells You Where You Are* (Boston, San Diego, and New York: Harcourt Brace Jovanovich, 1981). See also Lucy Lippard, *The Lure of the Local: The Sense of Place in a Multicultural Society* (New York: New Press, 1997). See chapter 6 for more on this issue.

17. *Places with a Past: New Site-Specific Art at Charleston's Spoleto Festival*, exh. cat. (New York: Rizzoli, 1991), 19. The exhibition took place May 24–August 4, 1991, with site-specific works by eighteen artists, including Ann Hamilton, Christian Boltanksi, Cindy Sherman, David Hammons, Lorna Simpson and Alva Rogers, Kate Ericson and Mel Ziegler, and Ronald Jones.

18. Precedents for "Places with a Past," in which the city as a whole becomes the exhibition site, include the Spoleto Festival in Italy (1962), "Skulptur Projekte" in Münster, Germany (1987), "The New Urban Landscape" in New York City (1988), and "Die Endlichkeit der Freiheit" in Berlin (1990).

19. Mary Jane Jacob, in *Places with a Past*, 17.

20. Ibid., 15.

21. Undated press release of 1997. Thus, programs like "Places with a Past" and "Sculpture. Projects" share a similar investment in generating a sense of uniqueness and authenticity for their respective places of presentation. As such endeavors to engage art in the nurturing of specificities of locational difference gather momentum, there is a greater urgency in distinguishing between the *cultivation* of art and places and their *appropriation* for the promotion of cities as cultural commodities.

22. Kevin Robins, "Prisoners of the City: Whatever Can a Postmodern City Be?," in Erica Carter, James Donald, and Judith Squires, eds., *Space and Place: Theories of Identity and Location* (London: Lawrence & Wishart, 1993), 306.

23. Cultural critic Sharon Zukin has noted, "It seemed to be official policy [by the 1990s] that making a place for art in the city went along with establishing a marketable identity for the city as a whole." See Sharon Zukin, *The Culture of Cities* (Cambridge: Blackwell Publishers, 1995), 23.

24. Addressing Robert Smithson's *Spiral Jetty* and the *Partially Buried Woodshed*, Craig Owens has made an important connection between melancholia and the redemptive logic of site specificity in "The Allegorical Impulse: Toward a Theory of Postmodernism," *October* 12 (Spring 1980): 67–86.

25. Thierry de Duve, "Ex Situ," *Art & Design* 8, no. 5–6 (May–June 1993): 25.

Matthew Jesse Jackson

Managing the Avant-Garde

New Left Review 32, March–April 2005

Stroll around Moscow, and soon enough you will come face to face with the post-Soviet avant-garde: Volkswagens emblazoned with the bold, quasi-constructivist logo of the Avant-Garde Bank, a corporate-finance outfit set up in 1994. Apparently, the legacy of Soviet modernism taps into a Muscovite social imaginary where commerce, Constructivism, finance and revolution have become entirely comfortable bedfellows. For Russia's new business class, Pavel Mansurov's 1920s design undoubtedly evokes a pleasing mixture of domestic cultural prestige and risk-taking audacity.

Outside Russia, the visual and rhetorical productions of the Soviet avant-garde have been invoked widely in the arena of business administration. Management texts such as Tom Peters's *Thriving on Chaos: Handbook for a Management Revolution* and Michael Hammer and James Champy's *Re-Engineering the Corporation: A Manifesto for Business Revolution* have celebrated the transformation of the revolutionary political project into the jargon of neoliberal managerial strategy.[1] In their calls for organized anarchy and workplace insurrection, these writers have forged a crucial zone of corporate avant-gardism—one that surreptitiously conflates the libertarian, *soixante-huitard* sense of "revolution" as permanent, ludic change with the ordered socialization of art propounded by Constructivism—within the global economy. As the management theorist Ève Chiapello writes, "Part of economic life is beginning to resemble the hitherto unique experience of the artistic sector … . One can no longer posit the existence of an art world whose functioning would be the complete opposite of the economic world."[2]

Andrew Ross describes the terrain in *No-Collar: The Humane Workplace and Its Hidden Costs*, an account of the turbulent dot-com boom and bust.[3] Ross tracks the fortunes of the New York Internet start-up Razorfish, whose star employee is a part-time rave DJ named Shel Kimen. A mid-level company manager, Kimen identifies herself as "an anti-corporate female from punk culture," a "troublemaker" and "rule breaker." She describes her coordination of idiosyncratic office events as a "subversive form of corporate performance art." By fostering such administrative antinomianism, Kimen's avant-garde managerial style not only contrasts with customary images of the corporate executive, it also attempts to evoke the iconoclasm of the modernist temperament. More specifically, it calls to mind the interstitial subjectivity of the Soviet avant-gardist, forever poised between revolt and self-abnegation. As such, Vladimir Mayakovsky's career as a poet, artist, playwright and composer of advertising copy may provide a model for the activities outlined by Chiapello and Ross. Mayakovsky's self-identification as "factory-worker of verse" led him to submit willingly (sometimes enthusiastically) to the art of performance management. In poems of the 1920s such as "Bureaucratish," "Lost in Conference," and "A Factory of Bureaucrats," the poet lampooned

Soviet managers, yet he never disavowed his earlier odes to cultural administration, such as "Order No. 2 to the Army of Art":

While we dawdle
in search of fundamental answers,
all things shout:
"Give us new forms!"

My proposal: What if we considered Mayakovsky not only as socialism's poet-martyr, but also as an early avatar of *The Man in the Gray Flannel Suit*? To do so might allow us to reconsider the transformations that proceed historically from industrial Taylorism, through the "humanized" Skidmore, Owings & Merrill office, to the countercultural workspace of the go-go 1990s.[4] That is, what if we understood Mayakovsky's career not only through the prism of revolutionary romanticism, but also as a prototype for the multitasking *Organization Man* (or Woman) of the twenty-first century? Perhaps Mayakovsky's repulsion/attraction towards administration could then be reconceived as an early chapter in the last century's contest between "artists and managers"—one that has been increasingly resolved by a tendency to merge, or even trade places, as the arts become more commercialized while business recuperates their discarded mythology of creative individualism.[5]

In retrospect, perhaps it is only logical that the artists identified by Hal Foster and Benjamin H.D. Buchloh as the foremost representatives of the postwar "neo-avant-garde" often played the roles of managers. Marcel Broodthaers's museum-like installations, Yves Klein's merchandizing of "zones of immaterial pictorial sensibility," George Maciunas's archiving, packaging, and promotion of the Fluxus brand, Andrea Fraser's performances as roving museum contractor: all showcase the skills of the enterprising project coordinator.[6] Over the past forty years, we have increasingly seen artists act as business managers while corporate managers have assumed the Mayakovskyan pose of the engagé artist, placing his or her energies at the service of the system.

Management and cybernetics

With these observations in mind, I want to return to Russia, to the Moscow of the Krushchev era, to the moment when "unofficial art" first appeared in the USSR. Among "unofficial" artists, those working outside the state system, Ilya Kabakov occupied an improbable position: he created unofficial pieces in his spare time, yet by 1965 had become a full member of the graphics section of the powerful Union of Soviet Artists. Due to his status, even following his emigration to the West in 1988, where he was hailed as a "dissident artist," Kabakov shrugged off such comments, saying, "I was not a dissident. I did not fight with anything or anybody. The word does not apply to me."[7]

For over three decades, Kabakov illustrated children's books and popular science magazines by day, while producing unofficial art by night. An important source of assignments was the journal *Znanie—Sila* (Knowledge Is Power), under the influence of the artist Yuri Sobolev. Much like its 1930s counterpart, *USSR in Construction*, the pages of *Znanie—Sila* provided an official outlet for artists and designers who worked on the periphery of socialist realist orthodoxy. The journal's pages were saturated not only with correct ideology, but also with the rampant technophilia of the Soviet 1960s, particularly the period's enthusiasm for the new science of *kibernetika*. As the historian of Soviet science Loren Graham observes, "One can find no other moment in Soviet history when a particular development in science caught the imagination of Soviet writers to the degree to which cybernetics did."[8]

Pioneered by the American mathematician Norbert Wiener in the late 1940s, cybernetics analyzed the entropic forces that accompany the transmission of information.[9] According to cybernetic theory, attentive observation of the "feedback" generated by human communication and the concomitant design of responsive control mechanisms encourage a robust, well-organized society. At first, Soviet scholars discounted cybernetics, arguing that the human mind resisted machinic systematization. However, with Krushchev's launch of the "scientific-technological revolution" in 1961, cybernetics served as a testing ground for the burgeoning Soviet knowledge industry.[10] Soon, mathematicians, engineers, sociologists, and biologists were encouraged to apply the "lessons of cybernetics" in their work.[11]

Kabakov was not immune to these forces. The cybernetic fascination with the "feedback loop" and *upravlenie* ("control" or "management") were foundational for Kabakov's conceptual art. Rejecting unofficial art's devotion to pre-Soviet notions of "artistic genius" and "spiritual truth," Kabakov writes that his art, "born in the age of structuralism and information, stopped believing in the validity of each of these discoveries, and saw the similarity and equivalence of all these various truths."[12] Around this time, Kabakov first encountered the works of Vladimir Tatlin, Kazimir Malevich, El Lissitzky, Varvara Stepanova and Aleksandr Rodchenko. Displayed as they were in the Moscow apartment collection of George Costakis, or in one-night exhibitions organized by the scholar-collector Nikolai Khardziev at the State Mayakovsky Museum, the avant-garde's utopian projects, to Kabakov's dismay, functioned less as dialectical investigations of art's materiality, than as idiomatic décor for tea-drinking and conversation. Eventually, Kabakov would take matters into his own hands, updating the Constructivist impulse by bringing his art into dialogue with his daytime activities—thus highlighting the gulf between the exalted artist/scientist/engineer of the heroic years and the artist/bureaucrat of late Soviet culture.

Moscow Conceptualism

In an extensive series of drawings produced in the late 1960s and early 1970s, Kabakov seized upon his official illustrations, transcribing them into the dissected, desiccated forms of the artist's unofficial labor. With these works, Kabakov performed the roles of two independent yet distinct artistic personae: the illustrator/employee who drew for wages, and the artist/manager who analyzed the employee's illustrations as a conceptual gesture. Kabakov elaborated on these practices, straddling the private and the professional, through his collaborations with the Moscow Conceptual Circle (which included the philosopher Boris Groys and the author Vladimir Sorokin, among others).[13] The artist describes this period as a pivotal moment of transition: "In Russia our small circle was surrounded by art—official and unofficial. We wanted to be involved in non-art."[14]

Kabakov first produced "non-art" by constructing oversized *albomy* (albums): handmade boxes brimming with sheets of gray and white paper that featured minimal, hand-lettered texts, documents and nondescript drawings. The albums reflected on Kabakov's official production as an illustrator through the medium of his unofficial practice. On designated evenings in his studio, Kabakov would place an album on a stand before a group of invited guests, then ploddingly move page after page, reading the texts slowly and emphatically. Often the material in the albums spoke obliquely to Kabakov's activities as an illustrator, but as often as not the pages would be nearly blank. Like homemade structural films, Kabakov's "non-art" shifted interpretive desire away from the self-sufficient art object towards the problematized materiality of a support resignified by the artist's minimalist performance.

Such album-viewings were accompanied by Kabakov's participation in the performance events of Collective Actions. The group's moving force was Andrei Monastyrskii, the professional librarian and editor. Every few months, Monastyrskii would invite his friends to participate in a "collective action." For example, guests might endure a long ride on a commuter train to an outlying Moscow suburb, followed by a protracted wait in the cold. Finally, the invitees would carry out an "action" that might consist of walking across a snow-covered field to glimpse a banal activity performed by Monastyrskii and his cohorts. Later, the observers and participants would be invited by Monastyrskii to discuss the action and these conversations would be recorded and transcribed. Through this process, Monastyrskii, the professional archivist, amassed an imposing collection of photographs, audio recordings, and typewritten files, an essentially homeopathic undertaking in which unofficial culture's entropic forces of isolation, anomie and neglect were observed and managed.

Making a virtue of necessity, Moscow Conceptualism positioned art-making not as a professional endeavor organized around galleries and museums (little of the Conceptualists' work was ever sold). Instead, Conceptualism existed as rigorously archived marginalia attached to the texts of Soviet life and labor. By exercising self-surveillance, by subjecting each other to control and manipulation, by critically appropriating their official, professional roles, these artists developed an art practice grounded in management, analysis and the feedback loop, a hybrid genre of collaborative performance and behavioral research that nurtured a critical underground culture on the fringes of Soviet bureaucracy.[15]

These practices came to an abrupt halt when Sotheby's held Moscow's first auction of "Soviet Contemporary Art" in 1988. As the gavel hammered, the Conceptualists watched their intimate art world careen into *the* art world of bids and bargains. Since the auction, most of the unofficial artists have emigrated. Eventually settling in New York, Kabakov achieved renown for his museum and gallery installations, an art form he had barely explored while living in the USSR. Today, Kabakov relates to the international art world much as he treated the Soviet bureaucracy before it: he ascertains what is expected of him and then tries to provide it. He quickly concluded that Western art professionals had little interest in the idiolect of an aging, Soviet Conceptual artist and his underground friends. Thus Kabakov remade himself as an extravagant storyteller who portrayed communal Soviet life in the exotic new medium of installation art. As for Kabakov the exiled Moscow Conceptualist, he has engaged in a much more complex performance piece within the international art scene: if he was once committed to an art that contemplated its status as "non-art," Kabakov has since become an artist who contemplates his status as a "non-artist."

Palace of projects

One site for the unfolding of this performance has been the Kokerei Zollverein, a government-sponsored art space lodged in a former coking plant in Essen. Kabakov has proposed the construction of a gigantic, permanent art installation on the Kokerei's grounds—a new genre the artist calls the "Super-Complex."[16] The scope of Kabakov's project is daunting: it entails a Defense Department-like budget and a deadline for completion worth of NASA. So far, the artist and his wife, Emilia Kabakov, have successfully completed one permanent installation on the Kokerei's grounds, *The Palace of Projects*.[17] Modeled on Tatlin's *Monument to the Third International*, the Kabakovs' "Palace" consists of an illuminated, semi-transparent wood-and-fiber spiral shelter which showcases a maze of "projects" supposedly proposed by undistinguished Soviet citizens whose plans vary from the well-meaning and harmless to the bizarre and destructive.

Each project features several common elements: a table and chair; a written description of the author and the project; a 3-D model; and a stated goal to improve some aspect of the world. Thus a project proposed by a Mr. Solmatkin, entitled "How to Change Oneself?," argues that to be a better person one should wear a harness with angel's wings for several hours each day. Another, "Dig Canals Through the Entire Country," presented by a Mr. Stozharov, contends that since it is Saint-Simonian building schemes which bring true happiness, compulsory canal-digging would undoubtedly make the nation's populace much happier. There is also a piece called "My Book of Projects," signed by the artist Ilya Kabakov, who writes:

> *The elimination of utopianism, alas, is yet another form of utopianism. The creation of projects, project thinking, the formulation of all kinds of utopias is immanently inherent in us, our consciousness, and furthermore, it remains as a stimulus and as a basis for any of our actions as long as we remain human beings.*[18]

The maquettes for the Super-Complex present a neo-Constructivist "Utopian City," an image of modernization as it *could have been*. According to Kabakov's designs, the one-time coke production towers would serve as vast spaces of cultural nostalgia in which recordings of Wagner and Tchaikovsky would play twenty-four hours a day. Another warehouse would present an obsessive archive of Kabakov's own life and work, documenting both his experiences in the USSR and his fifteen-year project to become an ethnographically correct Russian installation artist. Visitors to the plant would traverse narrow walkways above the ground from one building to the next. They would encounter no designer gift shops, no seductive dining establishments, no high-tech displays. The installations would tread a fine line between intimidation and education. Kabakov's Super-Complex would induce the spectator to imagine an alternative art history in which the cultural and industrial forms of the nineteenth century did not leave us with Clement Greenberg's "avant-garde and kitsch," or Andy Warhol's "avant-garde kitsch," but rather with a "kitsch avant-garde," a pedagogical utopianism dedicated to vernacular project-making and project managing.

Art laboratory

By contrast, the Kokerei's administration has outlined its own plans to develop the plant as a marquee space for contemporary art, under the purported vision of Rem Koolhaas.[19] This Kokerei promises to be a post-industrial workshop, where prominent architects, designers, and artists display their creations side by side. The administrators envision a mecca for artists, cultural tourists, and local progressives. Significantly, the experience of viewing the actually existing complex is hard to describe. Improbable encounters abound. In the summer of 2002, the plant featured a swimming pool constructed from industrial leftovers by the artist-designers Dirk Paschke and Daniel Milohnic; Silke Wagner's self-consciously generic, living room–like video installation; two tigers named Ketty and Assam, procured by Ayse Erkmen; a funky bar; and a cavernous performance space where DJs freestyled on "Party the Campus Day." The Kokerei's sprawling, episodic panoply of corporeal intensities and fragmented spaces already encourages modes of engagement altogether different from the reading and evaluating performed inside *The Palace of Projects*. The visitor watches videos, skirts the tigers, lounges by the pool, grooves to the DJs, consumes a cocktail by the bar.

In this emphasis on multifaceted leisure, the Kokerei appears to follow the lead of the institution *Artforum* has described as "the last great alternative art space," the Palais de Tokyo in Paris.[20] Under the direction of Nicolas Bourriaud and Jérôme Sans, the Palais presents itself as an "experimental laboratory for contemporary art."[21] In this investigative spirit, it has recently published a compendium of art-world responses to the question, *What Do You Expect from an Art Institute in the Twenty-First Century?*[22] To sample the reactions from a range of leading curators, gallery directors, artists, designers, and critics from New York, San Francisco and elsewhere: "Art institutions in the 21st century need to be at the forefront of cultural change"; "An institution that is animal-like, a chameleon that changes with every moment"; "An institution should transform into a flexible structure" that is "constantly adaptable, ready for change"; "a de-institutionalized institution"; "the opposite of an institution"; one that would resist "all static implications of the word 'institution.'" The responses, in short, overwhelming invoke the virtues of "change" and favor an institution that zealously denies its institutional status. Sure enough, the Palais de Tokyo facilitates casual flows from commerce to entertainment to art viewing and back again, with the three activities admixed in intoxicating ways.

In their enthusiasm for institutional flexibility, the Palais and the Kokerei reproduce in the very microstructures of art's reception the instability and unpredictability celebrated in the pages of the management literature of global capitalism. Perhaps the most popular management text over the past several years has been Spencer Johnson's *Who Moved My Cheese?*[23] It has remained on the *New York Times* best-seller list for over five years, has sold fourteen million hardcover copies, and has been translated into over a dozen languages. Most important, scores of multinational corporations have endorsed it as an essential tool for efficient "change management." The book's threadbare storyline focuses on the travails of two human-like creatures as they journey through a labyrinth looking for "Cheese." Inexplicably, the characters discover that whenever they find "Cheese," it disappears: someone always moves it. After numerous mishaps, they grasp the moral of Johnson's story: "Change Happens," "Anticipate Change," "Monitor Change," "Enjoy Change," "Be Ready to Change Quickly and Enjoy It Again and Again."

Clearly, Johnson's winsome fable targets short-contract white-collar workers and other victims of the "flexibilization" of the global corporate labor force, rather than the well-ensconced art-world professionals of the Ruhr, Paris or Los Angeles. On the other hand, is it far-fetched to view the "new art space" as a subtler manifestation of the same managerial impulse that lies behind *Who Moved My Cheese?* In their sensual interactivity and nearly boundless flexibility, the Kokerei or the Palais de Tokyo spur an acceptance of the art space's functional indeterminacy and increasingly ambiguous purpose. "Flexible structures" and "de-institutionalized institutions" make not only for accessible, commercialized art spaces, but—as Andrew Ross contends—for smoothly operating workplaces as well.

Monument to the non-artist

As the Palais's questionnaire demonstrates, the present generation of art-world professionals has developed an eye for "institutional branding" on par with that of the management seminar. The museum's infatuation with superstar architectural design, as well as the growing prominence of curators and administrators at the expense of critics and academics, are hallmarks of this phenomenon.[24] Power in the art world is shifting away from the tenured stasis of academia to cultural actors plugged directly into the entrepreneurial sector. And with this transformation, subversive "anti-institutional" institutional changeability has become the defining mandate of the neoliberal world order.[25]

Having matured in a cultural field dominated by cybernetic managerial fantasies and Soviet arts administration—an environment in which artists were negligibly important save as pawns within the state's bureaucratic machinery—Kabakov has a keen ear for the doublespeak of the neo-managerial art space. In its own way, Kabakov's Super-Complex aims to be the final project of the Soviet avant-garde, a truly Mayakovskyan gesture of revolutionary megalomania. The Super-Complex would be a liberated zone where the diktats of cultural managers would be rendered redundant and ridiculous. Kabakov knows that his expectations are naïve; however, he wants Kokerei to be—whatever the dangers of self-parody—a boldly intransigent, user-unfriendly monument to the non-artist, rather than yet another exercise in Effective Cultural Management. As Adorno wrote, "Whoever makes critical and unflinchingly conscious use of the means of administration and its institutions is still in a position to realize something which would be different from merely administrated culture."[26] Perhaps Kabakov will make good on Adorno's promise.

Notes

1. Tom Peters, *Thriving on Chaos: Handbook for a Management Revolution*, New York 1987, and Michael Hammer and James Champy, *Re-Engineering the Corporation: A Manifesto for Business Revolution*, New York 1993.

2. Ève Chiapello, *Artistes versus managers: le management culturel face à la critique artiste*, Paris 1998, p. 220.

3. Andrew Ross, *No-Collar: The Humane Workplace and Its Hidden Costs*, New York 2003, pp. 103–8.

4. For an overview of design and management in the postwar United States, see Reinhold Martin, *The Organizational Complex: Architecture, Media, and Corporate Space*, Cambridge, MA 2003.

5. The avant-garde and business administration are considered in Luc Boltanski and Ève Chiapello, *The New Spirit of Capitalism*, London 2005; see also the essays in the exhibition catalogue *Work Ethic*, University Park, PA 2003. For Sebastian Budgen's review of Boltanski and Chiapello, see *NLR* 1,

January–February 2000, pp. 149–56.

6. See Hal Foster, *The Return of the Real: The Avant-Garde at the End of the Century*, Cambridge, MA 1996, and Benjamin Buchloh, *Neo-Avantgarde and Culture Industry: Essays on European and American Art from 1955 to 1975*, Cambridge, MA 2000.

7. "Interview with Ilya Kabakov" in Renée Baigell and Matthew Baigell, eds, *Soviet Dissident Artists: Interviews After Perestroika*, New Brunswick, NJ 1995, p. 142.

8. See Loren Graham, "Cybernetics," in George Fischer, ed., *Science and Ideology in Soviet Society*, New York 1967, pp. 3–18; see also Graham, *Science, Philosophy, and Human Behavior in the Soviet Union*, New York 1987.

9. Norbert Wiener, *Cybernetics; or, Control and Communication in the Animal and the Machine*, New York 1948 and *The Human Use of Human Beings: Cybernetics and Society*, Boston 1950; see also the treatment of art, society and cybernetics in Pamela Lee, *Chronophobia: On Time in the Art of the 1960s*, Cambridge, MA 2004.

10. Wiener's books were published in Russian translation in 1958, two years before he visited the USSR, as cited by Graham, *Science, Philosophy and Human Behavior*, p. 280. For an exhaustive account of cybernetics in the USSR, see Slava Gerovitch, *From Newspeak to Cyberspeak: A History of Soviet Cybernetics*, Cambridge, MA 2002.

11. Graham writes, "It was quite common in the Soviet Union in the early sixties to find articles on the application of cybernetics in such surprising fields as musicology and the fisheries industry, although frequently such expositions involved distortions of the meaning of the term 'cybernetics'"; *Science, Philosophy and Human Behavior*, p. 271.

12. Kabakov, "Modernism and Post-Modernism," unpublished manuscript, 1991, p. 1.

13. For a critical history of Moscow Conceptualism, see Ekaterina Dyogot, *Russkoe iskusstvo xx veka*, Moscow 2000. Soon to appear in English translation.

14. Ilya Kabakov in "'With Russia on Your Back': A Conversation Between Ilya Kabakov and Boris Groys," *Parkett* 34 (1992), p. 36.

15. Sven Lütticken provides a useful interpretive framework for such underground communities in "Secrecy and Publicity: Reactivating the Avant-Garde," *NLR* 17, September–October 2002.

16. Ilya and Emilia Kabakov, *Die Utopische Stadt und andere Projekte/The Utopian City and Other Projects*, Bielefield 2004.

17. Ilya and Emilia Kabakov, *Dvorets Proektov/Der Palast der Projekte/The Palace of Projects*, Essen 2001.

18. See Kabakov and Kabakov, *Dvorets Proektov*, p. 191. The Palace's projects recall Fredric Jameson's discussion of utopian miniaturization of "The Politics of Utopia," *NLR* 25, January–February 2004, in particular pp. 40–1.

19. Interview with Marita Pfeiffer, press contact, Kokerei Zollverein, Essen, July 2002.

20. Lisa Liebmann, "Top Ten List," *Artforum*, vol. 41, no. 4 (December 2002), p. 108.

21. For background on the Palais, see the analyses of contemporary curatorial practices in Nicolas Bourriaud, *Esthétique relationelle*, Dijon 1998, and *Postproduction*, New York 2002.

22. *Qu'attendez-vous d'une institution artistique du 21e siècle?*, Paris 2001.

23. Spencer Johnson, *Who Moved My Cheese?*, New York 1998. Further information is available at www.whomovedmycheese.com. For more background, see Doug Henwood, *After the New Economy*, New York 2003, as well as Thomas Frank, *One Market Under God: Extreme Capitalism, Market Populism and the End of Economic Democracy*, New York 2000.

24. Hal Foster considers these developments in *Design and Crime: and Other Diatribes*, London and New York 2002.

25. The emblematic figure in this process is the Guggenheim Foundation's motorcycle-riding, cigar-chomping director, Thomas Krens. Not only has Krens dramatically expanded the Guggenheim's empire, he invented the artworld's most fashionable persona: the roguish cultural manager. See Heinrich Klotz, "Thomas Krens und das Guggenheim," in Hilmar Hoffmann, ed., *Das Guggenheim Prinzip*, Cologne 1999, pp. 42–55.

26. Theodor Adorno, "Culture and Administration," trans. Wes Blomster, in *The Culture Industry: Selected Essays on Mass Culture*, London and New York 2002, p. 131.

Jack Bankowsky

Tent Community: On Art Fair Art

Artforum, vol. 44, no. 2, October 2005

Art fairs may not be new, but these days they are certainly *more*: more frequent, more crowded, more lucrative. With Miami and London joining Basel and New York as obligatory circuit stops, with artists decrying the constant pressure from dealers for fresh work, and with dealers bemoaning the drain on quality stock (never mind the toll of constant caravanning on the flagship operations back home), bristling under the big top has become an art-world way of life. Last season, indefatigable Chelsea cheerleader Jerry Saltz professed to sitting out the Miami and Frieze fairs "because these events make me feel existentially adrift." A bit, in this particular case, like the head Heather boycotting her prom because the whole thing gives her a bad feeling, but, suspicions of disingenuousness aside, one knows what he means.

Maybe artists are simply made of sterner stuff than newspaper critics. I can't say for sure, but while our sidelined scribe was nursing his battered sensibilities, artists—artists of a certain sort, anyway—were not only making the scene, they were literally commandeering the booths. I'll stop short of heralding the great age of "Art Fair Art" (a toxic proposition, by most lights), but if you braved any of the recent fairs, you've guessed where this is going.

At Art Basel this past summer, Rirkrit Tiravanija, a newcomer to the new genre (if not to its contextualist spirit), bricked up the entrance to the otherwise-empty booth of Berlin dealer Neugerriemschneider, inscribing one cobble with a flourish of noncompliance: NE TRAVAILLEZ JAMAIS. Adapted for Basel from a 2001 gallery exhibition, Tiravanija's theatrical work stoppage was but one of a fresh crop of responses to the concentrated context of the fair. Eight months earlier, at the second installment of London's Frieze Art Fair, the Wrong Gallery (that near-simulacral organization whose home base consists of two glass doors in Chelsea and very little else) joined forces with Noritoshi Hirakawa to serve up an even more cold-blooded take on the art fair's ecology: In plain view of the exposition's dining concession, a hired model, hefty tome in hand, sat guard beside a recently minted bowel movement, ready to field questions regarding the dietary habits that yielded her mercifully tidy production. Call it the severe strain of Art Fair Art. I'm starting, after all, with the sensational over the substantial, but the double point I mean to make holds generally: While such maneuvers have nothing to do with the manageably marketable object, neither can Art Fair Artists be said to be squeamish when it comes to the touchy codependency of art and commerce, or the PR game they play like a hand of cards.

Artists, of course, have a way of pressuring the protocols that constrain—and sustain—their vocation, and so, at a moment when the art fair has achieved an unprecedented centrality in the marketing of contemporary art, it is not so surprising to find the "talent" nipping at the hand that feeds it. In this respect, Art Fair Art owes a good deal to a century of contextual experiment —from the readymade right through to the dematerial feints of Conceptualism and its offshoots in the present (namely institutional critique). Yet if in the context of this studious lineage Art Fair Art comes on a bit like a bull in a china shop, it is because the dominant gene in its artistic DNA comes courtesy of more mercurial parentage: I am talking, of course, about that great enabler/disabler of art today, Andy Warhol, but also about such dark-horse publicity whores as Yves Klein and Salvador Dalí. From AFA forerunner works like Guillame Bijl's 1994 booth-as-lighting-fixture-emporium to John Armleder's long-running, self-manned mini-stall at Art Basel, Art Fair Art has always been at least as enthralled with the shop window as it is skeptical of its tyranny. This, before my reader gives up on me, is the place for an apology: No shortage of lame art (and worse criticism) has been propped up on the overburdened pillars of the Warholian academy. The sublime Warholian sellout is easy to grasp but tougher to master (just ask Mark Kostabi!). The fact of the matter is that while it's an after-Andy truism that the art system (of which the fair is simply the moment's rawest, rudest manifestation) can be "performed" as opposed to passively exploited (e.g., "regular" art) or actively analyzed (e.g., "institutional critique")—there are inspired "performances" and there are rote and merely one-dimensional ones.

Compare, for instance, Tiravanija's too-tidy tour de force with the mad and massive sleeper Anthony Burdin staged in Michele Maccarone's booth at Frieze last year. To Tiravanija's credit, there is something pure and brave (and expensive!) about closing up shop or, at any rate, turning an entire booth over to one elegant act of refusal. Yet to the Burdin camp, the stunt could only have appeared a slicker rehash of the L.A. artist's earlier effort. Shut down by fair authorities when the volume of Burdin's master mixing proved unpalatable to neighboring merchants, Maccarone's padlocked pen served as a bunkered base for the "recording artist" throughout the exposition's duration, a coil of razor wire strung atop the enclosure's temporary walls in a fuck-you flourish. Both refusals count, of course, as much as coy come-ons as rebuffs. But where Tiravanija's more absolute (but ultimately more familiar) move left his customers to circulate and schmooze—or simply move on—Burdin's "Keep Out!" clubhouse was a ruse to make us want in. And inside is where he redeemed the AFA genre from the hovering charge of superficiality. If Burdin's parrying with the collecting class—and the art-fair public more generally—stands apart, it is because his attention-grabbing ploy remained first and foremost a portal onto a broader culture (he would say "industry"—recording industry) in which his investment is anything but glib.

Far from ending where it began—in a line of frustrated shoppers banging at the makeshift gate—Burdin's "performance" triangulated the proceedings, engaging the fairgoer on three related fronts: First, there was the circumstance of the barricaded booth (and the buzz it generated); second, the last-minute live show of Burdin's signature "recording art," which fair administrators added to the special events docket as reparations for shutting him down (more buzz); and last but certainly not least, there were the intimate acts of seduction that the artist/dealer duo performed during private audiences with newly won fans like me. The Burdin "trap" was as much a masterstroke of managed publicity as Tiravanija's tomb, but one with a wildfire improvisatory edge. If Burdin's signature plea that all is "performed" and everything a "performance" (including my own managed tête-à-tête in the darkened booth) is, on the one hand, no more than a commonplace of life as much as of art, when adopted in earnest it suggests an impossible wager—and an ethical imperative—with ramifications in practice both dangerous and exhilarating. Once inside the booth (and PR loop), the cat-and-mouse game that began in front of the boarded-up stall took on an urgency and intricacy that laid to rest any initial suspicions that the gesture was merely smug. One by one, the artist collared his captive fans and forced them down the rabbit hole into a strange new wonderland that begins with his covers of his own covers of rock anthems and then spirals out in a viral rhythm of sampling and rebranding that re-enchants the contracts and conventions by which artists produce and ply their wares. It is a spiral that includes the fair (as any art that makes its way through the machine of culture these days in some way must) but—and this is key—is not limited to it.

The news (and bad news, I suppose, for the apologists of solipsistic pen-and-ink fantasies and School of Tuymans oils, or whatever other back-to-art-basics merchandise fills the stalls these days) is that Art Fair Art (and, more important, the post-Pop performative efforts of which it is a subset) evinces, contra the bad-boy bum rap, a measure of complexity and contradiction. If one protests too much, it is because this complexity, where it does occur, is all too readily discarded with the bad-boy bathwater. And yet one wants it both ways. One wants, that is, to make a case for the conceptual traction of this art and for the tonic scumminess of the bathwater, itself the very lifeblood that courses through Art Fair Art's veins. What I respect about Art Fair Art and what may finally set it off from so-called institutional critique (of which it is a subset, near neighbor, or antagonist, depending how you parse things) is that it is predicated on the realization that art, particularly art that presumes to stand in some critical—or better, simply revealing—relationship to the institutions to which it is bound, cannot exist at a supposedly purifying distance from the point-of-purchase universe. Where critical hand-wringing over the evils of the fair has done little more than serve up a few crowd-pleasing indictments of that old bogeyman "the market," the Art Fair Artist penetrates commerce's inner sanctum, "performs" the fair by donning the guise of the carnival shill, and in so doing defamiliarizes the fair by making the usual mercantile, critical, and social exchanges strange and even (who would have thunk it!) magical. Poor choice of words perhaps: Capital (AFA's greatest subject, as it was Warhol's) is nothing if not bewitching, though, it must be said, some artists make the chimeras dance.

"As we are only documenting these works, we have not even tried to install this work here at the fair," chanted a pair of perfectly enchanting children as I entered the booth belonging to the Wrong Gallery at the inaugural Frieze fair back in 2003. Titled *This Is Right*, the demonstration was the work of AFA old master Tino Sehgal, who trained as a dancer and economist, his apologists love to remind us—as if it were a badge of integrity in the flimsy world of art. The baby dealers bounced about the booth, fulfilling their unlikely charge by helpfully offering dimensions, edition size, price, etc., for five different works available for sale. But as one reached for a camera to capture this refreshing version of the art of the deal, the youthful merchants collapsed to the floor yelling, "We don't think it is appropriate to take pictures of our work!" Conceptual art, perhaps, but, in its crisp theatrics and surplus charm, somehow unlike any I'd ever seen before.

Sehgal loves a fair. Well, he never said that, but, as early champion Jens Hoffman noted, he is at least as fascinated by the fair's mercantile machinations as he is repulsed by its commercial imperative. Thus, it's telling that Sehgal bristles against his critique-minded apologists who, in a more purposive version of knee-jerk antimarket sentimentalism, carry on as if the market were indeed an evil from which one could simply exempt oneself. If, for instance, Sehgal uses a word such as "deproduces" (with all its Marxian flavor) to characterize the ephemeral enunciations that constitute his practice (he leaves behind no objects, permits no documentation, and only sells his work by verbal contract in the presence of a notary), he nonetheless chafes under the pressure of efforts to bring his art in line with the antimarket idealism of historical Conceptualism. In fact, he is ever careful to pair the term "deproduces" with something like its dialectical counter "produces," his placeholder for the new spaces his gestures may—and often do—open up. The point for Sehgal, as for Burdin, is to work the market, not to disappear it.

But if for Burdin all is "performance," Sehgal refuses the term as a designation for his scripted interventions, wary as he is of the necessarily domesticating undertow that attends an art-historical tag like "performance art." If surface differences between the artists abound—if Seghal, for instance, is more conventionally bookish than Burdin, his art more tidily in line with the Conceptual pedigree—a closer look at the pair reveals a shared purpose.

My point is not to polemicize against the institutional critique to which Sehgal's debt is obvious and real (the "them" to my AFA "us" has to do not with the "critique" but rather the "institution" it has itself become). Rather, I mean to claim for Art Fair Art (and the broader post-Pop performative impulse of which it is a part) a more incisive purchase on what it entails to play the game—in this case, the fair, with its concentrated audience and PR particulars—as opposed to retreating to the sanctity and safety of the ivory tower. Sehgal, like any Art Fair Artist worth the price of a VIP preview ticket, goes for the rudest wound. It's telling that rather than setting his sights on those sitting ducks, the gallery and the museum, he has tackled not just the fair but that newer "institution," the peripatetic freelance curator. In this respect, he is, it seems plain, a step ahead of the well-meaning IC academy. Here Sehgal is improbably allied with institutional-critique spokesperson Andrea Fraser. Another strong artist who's not afraid to get down and dirty with her context, she makes her best work precisely when testing the polite protocols of the critical clique over which she presides. A recent piece in which the artist copulates with a collector has occasioned all manner of hand-wringing among her apologists, many of whom undoubtedly feel she's gone and spoiled everything with her "tacky" stunt.

When I told one longtime Sehgal supporter of my article's conceit, he quickly retorted that, for Sehgal, "Art Fair Art was finished," a sentiment that the artist later refused to endorse as a general truth, though he did concede it had run its course as far as his own work is concerned. Oh for the high-period of Art Fair Art! There was Sehgal, of course, and Burdin's bunkered recording rituals, and Piotr Uklanski's ballsy tag BOLTANSKI/ POLANSKI/UKLANSKI graffitied across the back wall of Gavin Brown's booth (did the flowering of the Leipzig School precede or follow the Warsaw Renaissance? this ethnic triumvirate seemed to tease). Through the murky lens of our current belatedness, even relatively tepid examples of the genre come with a patina of priority, whether Roman Ondák's artificially created queues in London last year; Pawel Althamer's personal pup tent attached to the Frieze big top in Regent's Park; or Vanessa Beecroft's mise-en-scène featuring a cast of a nude woman made "to be placed on the desk of a powerful man," in this case a booth-bound hired model.

Can it be that the glory days of this still-youthful genre are really already behind us? This month, the third installment of Frieze, mother fair of the AFA movement, will offer a fresh opportunity to assess the state of the art. The Wrong Gallery (aka Maurizio Cattelan, Massimiliano Gioni, and Ali Subotnick) will once again bring their three-ring schtick to London at the behest of the fair's organizers. As officially appointed commissioning agents instrumental in nurturing the AFA renaissance, the trio has orchestrated a multiyear meta-Art Fair Art "performance," which, when taken in toto, may well constitute the Rokeby Venus of the genre. If their presentation of Hirakawa's exalted dump was a tad too—yuck!—easy, the tale of their invented family as creative cell and ubiquitous behind-the-scenes puppeteers is the real mirror of our tent community.

Cattelan, as his ubiquity and reach suggest, has learned Warhol's lessons well. The Andy I have in mind is not the painter of icons, but the Andy of the extra-white-cube prestidigitations, or, more to the point, the Andy who managed the delicate ecology that enabled him to accommodate both the paintings and the business art machinations under one indelible brand, claiming in the process his whole world for his capacious art. By fair time this month, the second edition of the *Wrong Times*, a self-published broadsheet, will be circulating in the aisles of the Regent's Park tent, but Cattelan's branding triumph does not end at the fair turnstiles: A concern that goes by the bad pun Cerealart will shortly offer a mini Wrong Gallery for home use via the web (whoever purchases the "toy," explains gallery principal Subotnick, "becomes a Wrong dealer"). And, in a business-art coup that should secure Cattelan's status as the Richard Branson of the Passerby set, London's Tate Modern is letting the opportunistic virus loose among its esteemed holdings. Early in the coming year, the museum plans to transplant the Wrong Gallery's original glass door from Chelsea to a wall on the third floor where it will reopen for business (art) with an exhibition program involving invited artists and, perhaps, work from the Tate collection. In a testament to Cattelan's Svengali-like might, the museum's in-house coordinator Ann Coxton has sportingly assumed the title of Gallery Janitor, ceding curatorial control to Cattelan and crew.

The ABC's of art in the post-Warholian, postperformative present are simple: The success of Cattelan's one-in-every-home routine depends on a reciprocity (I almost said "dialectic") between the broad proliferation of extra-art activities and the museum-ready icons that provide the freewheeling brand a graphic and institutional identity. Like Andy, Cattelan never forgets a simple, structural truth (and I mean this without cynicism): The whole viral apparatus hangs on a picture hook—on a couple of wooden bars stretched up with canvas and stamped with a soup can—or, in his own case, on a stack of taxidermied beasts or an army of waxwork Mini-Mes. The much-discussed spike in his auction prices was only the extravagant payoff of this well-managed system, and, as such, the best joke on the need for an object to hang the art on, for an "oeuvre," in short, to hold the whole evil empire in poise.

Lame art (and worse criticism)? Except when it works: Cattelan has clones (like Warhol's Factory minions, cuter than he); Cattelan has a magazine —or two or three (*Permanent Food* and, with Gioni and Subotnick, the *Wrong Times* and *Charley*); Cattelan is friends with the enemy (the art fair!); and Cattelan even has his own gallery (Wrong), which, it would seem to follow, makes him a dealer, or rather, in keeping with his admittedly unorthodox operation, an anti-, non-, or metadealer. Here one arrives at another AFA lesson: Once art is business and business art, the dealer as silent partner becomes—contra the taboo—an active collaborator, as, for instance, Jeffrey Deitch's persistent AFA instigations make plain, and Maccarone's full-dress burlesque of the Kelly-bag class makes poetry. (You have glimpsed her, I trust, working the aisles: Archetypal telephone screamer, glued to her cell, she sports, yes, a Kelly bag.) Artist John Armleder's self-manned mini-booth at Art Basel claims precedence here as a slow-burn masterpiece of AFA's Janus-faced artist/dealer symbiosis. For as long as anyone can remember, he has set up camp in a tiny stall on an outer ring of booths. There, year after year, the courtly figure with the single braid pours champagne to celebrate the work of decidedly unblue-chip talents in this decidedly blue-chip context, holding up a low-budget mirror to the big-budget market.

In true business-art high style, today's artist/dealers and dealer/artists are fully complicit with the entrepreneurs who operate the fair, providing a validating service in the form of a new breed of "special" projects available only at the fair, thus insuring the attendance of not just shoppers but that market-wary middleman, the critic. Such projects have their roots in the booth-specific presentations that began to proliferate back at the Gramercy Art Fair (the Deitch-curated "Florine Stettheimer Collapsed Time Salon," for example, or Thomas Hirschhorn's foil-tentacled Swiss army knife), though I would stop short of classifying these earlier efforts as Art Fair Art, which, if true to form, must do more than simply use the fair as a stage. It must make the fair—its mechanisms and machinations—the subtext, if not the central plotline, of its play. Taking this value-adding strategy to new heights, Sam Keller, director of the fair of fairs, Art Basel, is nudging his Art Unlimited section even further in the fair-exclusive direction. Formerly a graveyard for objects too cumbersome for cash-and-carry sales, Unlimited's application-only, top-dollar floor space is now allocated and organized by a (real!) curator, turning a once-dead museum attached to the live fair into a living museum, a museum that shows, you guessed it, Art Fair Art. Last summer's Unlimited announcement card even featured a dour (read black-and-white) photographic teaser for Marina Abramović's *vanitas* burlesque—a performance in which the prone, naked artist spent three hours embracing a human skeleton on a raised platform at the entrance to the champagne-addled vernissage, all within earshot of uniformed percussionists strumming a giant Doug Aitken sculpture-*cum*-xylophone. A humanized version of the Hirakawa potty project, Abramović's stunt remains, to my mind, a billboard one-liner sans the complexity I have been militating for. It may have been compelling as theater, but it lacked the viral connections that emerged, for instance, from Burdin's staging of both his passage through the fair and the rhythm of sampling and rebranding that motors his larger project, just as it missed the depth of infiltration (of the fair and art system more generally) reflected in Cattelan's hall of mirrors.

Either all art today is Art Fair Art, as a colleague recently teased, or there is no such thing as Art Fair Art in the first place. Both are true, I will gladly own, as my purpose has never been, beyond the fun of striking a movement-making posture, to suggest that Art Fair Art is more than a local hiccup in the larger tendency of performing the present, which I do believe to be among the most serious currents in contemporary art. My investment in this new nonmovement, in short, runs no deeper than the unsentimental exploits of those artists who engage the fair as an inevitable part of their world. They pass through the fair and make art out of both it and—in a Möbius twist—its place in their own ascension into brand namedom. This is a passage that, in unusual cases, and on account of the depth and truth of what these artists perform, accrues a ritual urgency, recharming and remythifying our relationship to the world —including harsh climes like the fair—which is to say, they make it real.

Chris Kraus

Whole

Video Green: Los Angeles Art and the Triumph of Nothingness
New York and Los Angeles: Semiotext(e), 2004

Tanglewood, MA
September 16, 2002

Julie Becker
2852 Berkeley Avenue
Los Angeles, CA 90026

Dear Julie,

On September 11 (the anniversary of) I was in this ashram in Tanglewood Massachusetts, and I'm not even going to tell you what put me there, the fit of despair, the endless crying, the pull in my heart towards going all the way into that blackness, which would be death, or wanting to die... all I can say is that Alexandra Kollontai, the Russian revolutionary who wrote *Red Love* (her manifesto of the multiple human relationships of sexuality friendship and love that might be possible in a revolutionary society) had a very brave project and it isn't her fault that it failed. I was exhausted.

Immediately after arriving I began to feel better, it was a strange and beautiful culture being practiced there. The path to the lake was wide and well worn but enclosed on both sides by all kinds of foliage: chokeberries and I don't know the other names, but yellow and purple and red. I felt extremely protected. Everything was held in place, the lake by the hills, the hills by the white strands of cloud in the sky, and I began to feel whole. The "hole" being filled by the "whole."

The yoga they practice here at Kripalu is based on presence, acceptance and love. They say that Everything Matters. They call it Intentional Living. You can feel it by the way they smile at the check-in desk and open the door. Or the swathes of white and pink cosmos they've planted up on the hill. Or the utterly rational way they've deployed technology within their 20,000 square foot physical plant towards the greatest efficiency, comfort and pleasure. Money is effortless here, the result of an affirmation. Some of the ones I'm learning to say are, "Money rushes to me because I am a master at multiplying its abundance" AND "A full love surrounds me" AND "Financial success comes easily to me" ... And seeing that there are so many expensive new cars in the ashram parking lot with New Age bumper stickers, maybe it's working—although I must say it's in their total exclusion of relativity (i.e., their banality) that the affirmations begin to lose me ...

There are hardly any rules here in the ashram except for the absence of cellphones and sexualized clothing. There is even an area designated for smoking, except this area isn't marked or disclosed. You have to declare yourself to the front desk staff as a smoker and then they will tell you, but I didn't do that. I tried to find it myself, unsuccessfully. Still, I was curious how this culture deals with taboos. Because it seemed to me, the Designated Smoking Area on the "east hill" above the ashram would be like the boneyard outside the Marquis de Sade's Chateau … the back end of the institution, the place where they throw all the used-up dead girls, the place that everyone knows of but nobody wants to go to.

A couple of weeks ago when you were preparing your show for Greene Naftali, I asked you, What does it mean to be Whole? You answered, *That's a good question*. Because you'd been preparing this show called "Whole" for nearly four years and you were starting to realize it would never be finished. It was becoming an endeavor as gorgeous and doomed as *Red Love*, or the San Francisco sculptor Jay DeFeo's enormous white plaster rose that grew like a tapeworm inside her apartment until it threatened to take down the whole building … or else, even jill johnston's early art writing in *Lesbian Nation*, which she later recanted, and here I am possibly imitating—

You said: "There's always an attempt to be whole. Everyone in the universe has spent time trying to become whole through religious means, from sitting in a church to yoga to swimming, and everybody is trying to get more energy and become whole."

But you couldn't do it. You'd started to realize that the real project of Whole would be "an endless exposing of parts and not ever reaching a whole," you said that, and then you added, "so I have tried to share that, that human process," but when I asked you if being Whole is like being dead, you complained, "But I haven't even had coffee yet!"

The show you mounted this month at Greene Naftali was a part of the Whole. We both agreed that showing these parts over time was the only way you could do it. Because in fact, we agreed, it's sort of a quantum tautology to think you can capture the [W]hole without falling into it … And this gets close to something like madness, a state both of us know.

In the videotape you made, called *Whole Film 2002*, you cut a square hole in the floor of your living room-studio and hoisted a model of the California Federal Bank building down through it on pulleys into the basement … The CalFed Bank was the building you saw then, looking outside the window, when you were still in the Echo Park house that became the site of this project called *Whole*. When you moved in, the house was owned by the bank, and then later it wasn't. During the three years you lived there, the place changed hands several times, it kept being bought and sold. Except no one knew what to do with it, because Echo Park hadn't gentrified yet and the real estate market was flat. The house was really a shack falling into the ground, there was constant flooding. No one fixed the place up, but the actual land wasn't worth enough yet to bother tearing it down. The lot hadn't reached its maximum value yet.

I think we were talking, later, about the mystical power of money: the way the US dollar bill is engraved with 27 masonic symbols. The bills change hands many times every day but nobody knows what they mean … You made a drawing then, called *Playful Embellishment*, with the Eye of the dollar bill pyramid blinking in front of the CalFed building, all brightened with candles and glitter.

Anyway, before you moved in, when the bank took it over, a gay man with AIDS was living in the basement apartment downstairs. It was really only a room built over cement. The man had been a stained-glass maker, but when he died nobody came to reclaim his stuff. The bank let you use downstairs for free in exchange for clearing it out, and this stuff became part of the Whole.

The walls of this room were covered in cheap pine paneling, and the basement became the metaphysical-conceptual lab for the yet-to-be-fully realized *Whole*. You found it strange to be living on top of this stuff, it was like something was brewing down there beyond your control. But really things were happening *outside* the house, the buying and selling, the change in the market, as well. There was a Tiki Bar built into the wall, one of those single-roofed things that they use to sell poolside drinks. It seemed to be holding the whole place up. As you once told me, the Bar (which you later rebuilt and called the Mysterious Object Bar) is the underside of the belly of *Whole*.

The bar, as it appears in your installation, contains certain disturbances at the "bottom" of a house that is decaying at its very foundations and has been tied up in lawsuits for years. Is the bar an alchemical center for the production of negative energy? Obviously your work *alludes to the social fact of gentrification and its attendant displacement*, as they'd say in art criticism, *while probing the psychic underside of what we call "real estate"* … the troubled lives of actual property occupants, whose troubles are only compounded by official papers and documents.

In your videotape, the camera hovers around a sign hanging on the pine-paneled wall left behind by the previous tenant. The sign is a riff on the kind of inspirational slogans hung all over the ashram (that say things like YOU ARE PERFECT IN YOUR IMPERFECTION) but his sign said IF YOU CAN KEEP YOUR HEAD IN ALL THIS CONFUSION YOU JUST DON'T UNDERSTAND THE SITUATION … and I was struck by his use of the word "situation," the way it's a noun and a verb … as you as a sculptor, i.e., a visual thinker, must have been, because it seems that part of the project of *Whole* is to willfully resituate things. In *Whole Film* 2002, the camera holds on a piece of the urban landscape, i.e. the bank, as seen through your living-room window. And then it cuts to the model you've built of the bank, which is small enough to be hoisted down into the hole … The actual bank itself is full of holes. It has those porthole windows designed to make a large building look like a plane in the hi-tech imagination of the 1950s, when commerce, like god, took off like a jet.

The landscape seen through the window was blurry and smeared.

At the ashram this week, I kept thinking about Alice when she fell down through the hole, or Ariadne, how she didn't forget to tie a string to her wrist when she left for the land of the dead. Mexican radio music blasting on the video soundtrack, the frequency of the pirate radio station someone runs near your house, the way that music enters the wires whenever we talk on the phone ... Eleanor Antin quoting Baudelaire in her installation *Minetta Lane—A Ghost Story* (1994): *The city changes faster than the human heart.*

At the ashram they always light candles at the heart of the circle when they gather to meditate. Everyone wept for the 3000 dead on September 11, because these are dead we can imagine best, they are triggers of grief, and you said, *What attempt to move forward isn't an attempt to become Whole?*

Love,
Chris

David Barringer

American Mutt Barks in the Yard

Excerpt from *Emigre* #68, 2005

Dear Emigre,

I hope you discover redeeming value in this rude bulk of a submission. I offer it for publication in Emigre. *I can imagine it literally nowhere else. The best I can say on its behalf is that I am no longer the same designer I was when I began writing it three weeks ago.* Emigre *65 & 66 triggered an imaginative gatling gun, and I am exhausted and grateful that the shooting is over.*

Entitled "American Mutt Barks in the Yard," the essay is 34,490 words long. It is ambitious and reckless and impassioned. During its composition, I did not intend it as a concerted response to the laments in your publication over the lack of cross-disciplinary/extra-disciplinary writing on graphic-design theory. Now that the composition is over (maybe), I still do not know if it represents at all what anyone had in mind. Maybe, after all this, it is still only a start.

I hope that the essay earns your interest beyond the first personal and poetic sections; the majority consists of critical thinking, vividly expressed. I understand that your time is precious and that my essay presumes to take up a good deal of it. I thank you for your consideration.

Sincerely,
David Barringer

* * *

Definition

To be self-taught is to:
– never trust the teacher & so never mistake the lesson for the final word
– be always humble in the skin of one's knowledge & modest in the suit of one's skill
– toil in the shadow of self-doubt, for the teacher lacks the authority to confer a passing grade on the pupil.

Observation

Obsessions are not economically rational.

What do I think I'm doing

Art is an expression of hope. In other words, a delusion, a denial of what is likely, a willing disregard of probabilities. Reckless defiance. An assertion of self against the odds.

Q: What artists inspire you the most?
A: The dead ones. They inspire me to work faster.

Opportunism

So I have a day job; also, I work in the off hours, doing projects I want to do but don't yet know how to do, thus expanding the zones in which I am dull or dangerous. No one ever said The Job was the be all, end all, and if they did, they were trying to hire you. If they said you're the only one who can do this particular job, they were flattering your ego in lieu of raising your salary. Meritocracy is dead. Have you heard this, too? All you need to get and keep a job is a level of competency and a feel for bluff. To move ahead, to rise, well, that's the altitude at which the lungs of merit fail. Careerism has nothing to do with excellence in a craft or transcendence in an art; it has everything to do with notoriety in a society or subset thereof. The politics of opportunism. The bloodluck of nepotism. The pressurized cabin of privilege. The cruel math of cronyism. It is here, languishing in a stagnant cubicle, that the thirtysomething idealist appreciates the original sin committed in college: it would have been far better to have forgone attentiveness to grades and stood up, walked over to the son of the CEO, the daughter of the trustee, the nephew of the judge, and shook hands. Was it such a long way, looking back, to go from here to affinity? And isn't the price of inaction too steep? Look around you. It's never too late. Join a club. Play golf. Put on a false face, pretend to care, and say hello.

Secret work

Meanwhile, I have saved myself the heartbreak and taken it as given that my job, by definition, will never satisfy me. I don't surrender. I don't check my self-respect at the door. A jellyfish from eight to six I am not. I am the same person by day as by night, after all, and Batman can apply Bruce Wayne's newly acquired know-how as usefully as Bruce Wayne can apply Batman's. Ideally, each informs the other, like neighbors exchanging recipes and gossip.

The secret work I have in mind is not a spiteful indulgence that dodges the question of how to improve one's practice of design. It is, plainly stated, work you love to do, and you get to do it with as few strings attached as possible. Besides, your off-hours muscles need not remain a secret. Bruce Wayne can wear tight shirts and fight crime, too, on his own terms. It's just that everybody knows Batman is free to kick ass for only two people: Lady Justice and himself. Secret work, working off-hours, working for yourself—however you want to word it fit the circumstances to your needs—is liberating in the best sense I can think of: the personal sense. Without the hands of the free, there is no home of the brave.

I deploy the superhero analogy to temper the designer's old bipolar personality type, the servant/rebel. We all know, by now, that graphic designers, like lawyers, like others in the service industries, are organ grinder's monkeys dancing for coin, not knights of the realm lancing for honor. To rejoice, without reservation, in one's servant status is to embrace a slave mentality, a masochism as rewarded in the cubicle, I suppose, as on the pew or oarsman's bench. Truth is a stinky lotion, but you don't have to rub it in.

Instead, I am reasonable in my expectations of the fit of my heart into the vise of my job. Look beyond the glass walls for love, my friend. Every day is a day for secret work you can put your secret heart into and make something big and grand and noble. Or else something small and personal and dignified. You're miserable most of the time anyway. Try this, the secret work we do outside the zoo. After hours, when the animals roam free, we owe no one the wages of our domesticity. Exit cage left, and you'll find the cost of entry into the world of secrets and deception is nearly as low as the cost of your free time.

Good hard work

Energy? Check. Furious will? Check. Ramming your head into the wall over and over again? On it. And while you brush the brick dust from your noodle, ask yourself how does it hurt, why does it hurt, and will it hurt differently next time? Quantify and qualify the hurt's dynamics, its context and meaning, to wit: *life is pain*; *suffering is the story of our times*; *I'm a bloody idiot*. Good hard work will sweep the crusted scabs of analysis out of your skullcase, leaving you headroom to concentrate on nothing but the urgency of your eye-level task. You'll love what work does for you. The lack of it will drive you mad. You'll become addicted to it. You'll have to; only an addict would keep at it like this, you crazy bastard. I salute you.

Explicative iteration of the previous
—Janus, god of theory

There exists the human tendency to theorize and concoct rules of cause and effect, to generalize from experience, to abstract from the anecdote, incidentally one of our greatest strengths, this capacity granting us perspective and thus the power to overcome the superstition of local coincidence and apprehend the world in proportion. This same human capacity for abstraction and generalization can also be put to more devious uses by those in whose interest it is to do so, e.g. business and government appropriating prognostications as reassuring distractions, firing off jargon-filled nonsense in order to invite critics to accept deference as inevitable. Witness the inexplicable degree of our deference to prognosticators like Alan Greenspan, Donald Rumsfeld, Bill Gates, and, well, hell, remember all the "experts" mooing blissfully during the bubble of the Nineties? Theories back then converged and were sung sweetly through our collective throat. It's an uncomplicated example of complacent herd mentality, and this danger haunts every context, economic, political, academic, and otherwise. Theories can be better than this, obviously, competing in the critical arenas of journals and conferences, opposing theories launched at each other in primitive dialectical showdowns like jury-rigged robots in those robo-battles you see on cable where victory is often circumstance-dependent. But the point is authority anywhere is susceptible to thinking too well of itself; and we, too well of it. And the troubling thing about *this*—the abdication of our skepticism in favor of knowing self-congratulation—is that *we know this & concede anyway*. So, anyway…

Angels of mercy

Are you lost? Or are you unwilling to admit cowardice in the muscle of your heart? When the economic calculations are made, weighing opportunistic careerism against good, ethical, soulful work, you are a prophet: you know which way your scales will tip. Ah, well. Self-preservation is an instinct of the apes whose genetic hides we have not fully shrugged off. Life advances not on the moving sidewalks of theoretical strategies, but on the messy improvisations of the vine-to-vine swing that we call a case-by-case basis. Maybe an easier crisis will come your way, one in which hypocrisy will feel as natural as a wool sweater and a judgment call will have nothing more at stake than money. Mortals can always try again (up to a point). In the meantime, be a patriot. Go shopping. Behold the wings of angels at the mall. In the feathers of sales tags will you find the map of your destiny revealed. It will have a magnetic strip on it.

Vicarious experience

Speaking of the greater social good, I suspect we are bored by the nostrum that art has no social utility; it has meaning and, occasionally, consequence. While it won't mow the lawn, it will allow us to experience the world from the perspective of the teenager mowing it. Graphic design might depict any of this: the mower, the manufacturer, the grass, the fertilizer, the teenager, the digital audio player, the homeowners, the lurking landscapers, the suburb, the gas station, the city planners, the county, the state of nature, the world of apathy. In choosing perspective and defining a worldview, you must make critical judgments. If you choose one perspective, you are rejecting all others. On what basis? According to what principles? On whose behalf? To what end?

Read a novel, and you will experience the world from another's point of view. This vicarious experience makes for excitement and enlightenment, sympathy and empathy, diversion and compassion, all of which can be counted soundly on the side of Social Goods. Literature's instrumental benefits (what readers get out of it) are not what motivate authors to create. Authors tend to resort to hyperbole and analogy to describe their inspiration: they give birth, channel gods, set planets in orbit. They are moved by mysterious forces, possessed by muses, driven by demons. Nevertheless, authors must also make critical judgments: *from whose point of view will I write, and whose story will I tell?* Once made, these decisions require commitment. That's why it's so critical for these decisions to be fueled by passion and piloted by good judgment—or else the rocket, failing escape velocity, will tumble to Earth.

Artists and writers are not immune to the desire to please and are not above pandering, preaching and selling out. The boundary between artists and designers—artists build sand castles while designers surrender to the undertow of business—has never been clear; in fact, the spectrum is well served by the beach analogy in that one never can be sure where the beach ends and the ocean begins. Artists are commissioned; novelists are hired to ghostwrite autobiographies of industry leaders; and Cassandre originals fetch sums envious to fine artists toiling away in factory lofts. Not to mention that an artist and designer are often one and the same person, the transformations accomplished with nothing more epic than the skirt-hoisting updraft of a financial translation (=DESIGNER) or the sleeve-rolling hunker-down of a Saturday at home

(=ARTIST). The critical judgment of a graphic designer, therefore, may be helpfully considered to be analogous to that of an artist or author. One peculiar hazard for graphic designers, however, is that by appropriating a worldview, they might, by means of that commercial appropriation, unfang the critique contained within it. It is a risk artists and authors, perhaps to their detriment, don't worry about as instinctively as designers.

Designers, on the other hand, cannot let themselves off the hook by claiming the powers and refusing the responsibilities, by saying *I'm as good as any artist* one day and *the client made me do this crap* the next. You have to put your choices where your cursors are. Choices define you: your priorities, loyalties, hopes. Abstention is impossible. You must make judgments. Where does curiosity hold your eye? Whose perspective do you want your audience to vicariously experience, and why? What story do you want to tell?

Notice I didn't say "what story *should* be told" or "what story *hasn't yet* been told." I said, "What story do YOU WANT to tell?" The "you" and the "want" are key words here, emphasizing your personality and desire, rather than (a) ethical obligation, (b) duty to compensate for gaps in the social narrative, or (c) a commitment to the client that trumps all else (that's an excuse for a failure of imagination). We're talking about *desire* desire, not whim, fancy, impulse or preference—we're talking about guts and grit, who you love, why you fight, how you live your life, not what color shirt goes with sullen denial. If you lack passion for your work, if all you have to run in are someone else's floppy clown shoes, then it will show in your sorry performance. Better to stumble on your own than to finish an indentured third.

Better to fail in your work than to work for your failure.

Dissent

In dissent, someone might point out that criteria already exist; designers throughout history have been defining and naming them, employing them and discussing their efficacy. In reply, I would argue that these criteria, too, are judgments of another past, codifications of the observations of successful and failed experiments throughout the history of art and design. And while designers may rediscover these criteria, defining the operations of their own creative imaginations in similar terms, that doesn't mean the self-consciousness of a designer's experience is any less personal. Because consciousness in general exists doesn't mean that I experience self-consciousness in a general way. Likewise, I experience the process of discovering and defining my working criteria as painfully particular. I am predated but not preempted by others.

The good mind

A good mind depends upon the capacity to think coherently and not the habit to worship the image. A good mind contains respect for fact and empathy for people, distrust of authority and the courage to argue. A good mind is vigilant against abuses of power, the signs of corruption, the wages of deceit and the wizard behind the curtain. A good mind delights in the joys of discovery, the unscripted conclusions of experiment. A good mind values history, not myth; import, not ideology; narrative, not montage; argument, not superstition; character, not stereotype; and language, not icon. All this may mean that we are asking of ourselves as designers what we ask of our writers, artists, lawyers, and, most broadly, all of us as active citizens: to think, speak, and argue as if we mattered.

Word vs. image

This emphasis on argument, narrative and language would seem to betray the bias of the writer and lawyer I am. But more so, I think (perhaps defensively) that this emphasis is predetermined when the designer's frustration is with the inadequacy of image as substitution for the complex nature of genuine thought. Narrative in literature has been deconstructed to reveal the artificiality of linear composition as well as the posturings of authority. But image is no automatic improvement when the goal is to strip away falsehood, deception, and posturing to honor honesty, ambiguity, and ambivalence. As media theorists have been murmuring since the Vietnam war, the image, as produced and consumed, is even better suited to achieve the devious ends to which iconography is aimed. Today the visual dominates, and it seems as if image and icon have usurped the role of narrative and argument. It is against this usurpation of discourse that I sling my critical stones. Does this simply mean graphic designers should use more text?

Bernadette Corporation

Preface

and

Jane, Susan, Murielle

Excerpt from *Reena Spaulings*,
New York and Los Angeles: Semiotext(e), 2004

If you look at a city, there's no way to see it. One person can never see a city. You can miss it, hate it, or realize that it's taken something from you, but you can't go somewhere and look at it and just see it empirically. It has to be informed, imagined, by many people at a time. It's an everyday group hallucination. This novel is modeled on that phenomenon. 150 writers, professional and amateur, have contributed to it, not using the mutually blind exquisite corpse method, and not using the "may I have this dance" method where writers take turns being the author, but using the old Hollywood screenwriting system whereby a studio boss had at his disposal a "stable" of writers working simultaneously to crank out a single blockbuster, each assigned specific functions within the overall scheme. The result is generic and perfect. And Reena herself benefits from it by being more of a material entity, a being, than a character—her thoughts and actions are not spanned by any author's mind. Who pulls her strings?

Mama! An author is a routine, which makes for good conversation whenever that routine climbs down from the windswept seclusion that walks and breathes centuries of the word. Fourteen meetings with the publisher it took for this author to become convinced that *Reena Spaulings* was fit for print. Thirty-six bleary-eyed howling dinners of beer and cocaine just to prove that Reena was the product of sweat and tears and frustration. All this drilling, convincing, testing, baiting proves that not only is an author a person who writes, but also a role that is negotiated and trained by those who choose the books one can read today. Becoming an author is a process of subjectivation, and so is becoming a soldier, becoming a cashier, becoming a potted plant.

Like the authors, the New York City depicted herein finds itself constantly exposed to the urges of "communism"—that is, to a chosen indifference to private property, a putting-in-common of the methods and means of urban life and language. Communism, it seems to say, is the only thing we share today, besides our extreme separation. Between the lines is a desire for the not normal situation, a wartime desire not for peace but for a better, fresher war that would produce the not normal situation. In everybody, even an underwear model.

Sometimes, hoping to generate a timely product for young readers today, we couldn't help but produce something unwanted, unexpected instead. *Reena Spaulings* is not the *On the Road* or *The Great Gatsby* of these times, which is to say that these times do not need or want those kinds of books. If the Novel, today, has lost much of its seductive power and its necessity, perhaps we can fill it with something else. This is a novel that could also have been a magazine. It's a book written by images, about images, to be read by other images, which is to say it is uninhibited and realist. Its primary content is the desire to do two things at once: to take something back and to get rid of ourselves. It took us less than three years to write. An impossible book we are now letting go of, so that Reena Spaulings can assume her final pose—along with Tristram Shandy, Edgar Huntly, Effi Briest, Silas Marner, Madame Bovary, Daisy Miller, Moby Dick, and all the others—that of literature.

* * *

An imposing limousine, stretched to accommodate upwards of thirty people, and pulled by six black horses, was traveling down the west side of Central Park. The carriage was of a design that had become well known on the streets of the city after having been made popular through a music video. It consisted of a frame onto which had been dropped a series of four identical interlinking carved bodies. The repetition of these bodies was a deliberate attempt to streamline the vehicle and deliver the impression of a sumptuous and powerful volume. There were eight wheels and eight doors. The mudguards and supports were so overloaded with highly artistic carved ornaments that their technical function was barely discernible. The shell-shaped compartments appeared to float above the wildly turbulent ornamentation. Despite the proliferation of decoration, the vehicle was actually quite dynamic, its scalloped curves also part of what propelled it forward. It was stained black as the horses that pulled it, and along its sides were painted panels depicting Arcadian scenes from the four seasons. Clearly designed for joyriding, but unlike the optimistic décor of the new mass culture encountered in the city's great travel terminuses, this single stretched and encrusted vehicle suggested rather a terminal case of singularity, a kind of overgrowth of personality that left the pleasure principle that inspired it crippled and weak and in pain.

Wooden doors began to bang open and shut and feet hit the pavements. Half-full glasses of liqueur smashed on the sidewalk, and as you expected a flock of bodyguards snaked out first before the limo discharged its more toxic, more potent contents proper, its genital material, its little beauties. The celebrities rubbed their eyes in the sun. Some were already wearing their shades. Their voices sounded thin and very far away.

"When I was small, I thought I was a horse," said Maris. She went over to one of the long black horses and patted its neck. Then she leaned her face towards the shiny coat as if scenting her young self. You could see she was really wasted. Meanwhile, Donald Trump, A-Rod, and Vincent Gallo were glowing beside her. They were wrapped in flag-like embroidered drapes, drinking beer on the street, and so drunk it looked as if they were a mass of alcohol holding itself together in the shape of men. Reena emerged last, the healthiest germ, spermatozoon, and started toward the park, pulling the others along in her wake.

Wow. This is it? The tent is tightly packed, with a stage inside and all kinds of banquet tables, tablecloths, flower arrangements, waiters (in the open-air cordoned-off backstage area), and hundreds of lolling spectators (in the front area). It is a National Cancer Society fundraiser involving the unveiling of two new public artworks and a concert by The Strokes. Maris, the brains behind this event, provides Reena with an all-access pass, hangs the laminated card around her neck with her own excited hands. Both the park and the time are radiant and full. The trees' leaves overhead are turned jewel-like by the sun's rays and a massaging breeze. Even the squirrels are intoxicated, joyriding the branches of the trees. Joy joy enjoy yourself. Joy is the core of horror is joy. There is a whole scheme going on here. It is alive.

"Hello. How are you, Laser Girl?" Desire, light like spiders' webs.

Maris—in white dress and white flower for the hair, immaculate face—greets and chats with the various Cancer representatives, often posing in front of the banner for photographers and giving short statements to the roving TV crews. Reena is a picture too, a bit dazed by the too bright sun and a leafy, ballsy smell mixing with uptown perfumes and sweat. It all starts to happen. Cell growths? Ego growths. You bet!

"Thank you all for coming!"

Microphone feedback and the giddy, raspy voice of Maris draw the crowd's attention to a giant, guarded, veiled box on the Great Lawn. Cords are cut, champagne corks pop.

"Quand l'Institut d'..."

aaaaach . . .

A gust of wind rips the vinyl tarpaulin free and carries it across the park like a flying cartoon ghost. Laughter as it gets snagged in an elm in the distance.

"I ope zat you wheel fourgeev my purringleesh, butt I wood lyke two speek dearrectly wizzyoo. Zare cannes beano commune itay—an thees ees wat we arh ear four, no?—know commune itay bee tweanuz eef wee arh sep arated buy long weege. ok. Bon. Donc. ..."

A disheveled French dude is now addressing the crowd from atop an enormous, freshly assembled garage-like structure. The English Translator, stopped in his tracks, reverses, takes two steps back down: no way will he climb this thing.

"Zeese wurk ees ovcuss amposseeblegh wizzout urr partiseepassion: zee four gottun meedil glassis. Ovcuss, sum wheel ownly sea zees struckture az a skullpture. Zare wheel be fotograves een magazeens of zeese construckshun an deesgushun ov aow eet wuz maid an aow eet ree laytes two my pree vyurs work. Nun ov zeese wheel shuhoh aow wee av kree eighted aye tempura airy or tonomuss zoan, annaow een zeese zoan, wee arull phree phrum ze rolls sosaiyeetay as preeskribed fourruhz. Pfeyenally eye sinksat twogezur wee wheel demmonstraight aow eet eese posseeblegh tuesskayp suhtch conpheinz. Az yuno, eet wuzwonov yoohoo caim upwizzee solooshun: you entair ear anpark ur veehickle. Zen you parse sroo ze deevaidink aria eentwo ze meedil zoan wear you wheel poot ur kah keese eentwo a bowelle. Een zeese meedil zoan, ucann 'angoot' weese udder partiseepants, aneet ze fude eyewheel pre-pair (sum lyte snaques andeeps). Wen you won toogo, utayke anne udder set ovkeese. Weese zeese keese you parse eentwo ze phinal aria ... wear, you wheel get eentwo aye deefair aint veehickle anne dryve a weigh phrum ur ohled lyve."

Reena feels the feeling of all-out exposure and it isn't just her. It's everybody exposing everything. All frills, all ferocity. How is it possible? There are little fires of hate and little fires of excitement. It is a high intensity mingling. She is happily shaken. Ecstatic for a moment. Then instant doom is setting in, dark spirits come out to play. Happiness feeds paranoia and vice versa. Sorrow laughs joy weeps. She sees upright braziers and men with goatees. buzz. Buzzzzz. Things, very untidy, damaged and unresolved. She sees her whole life laid out in front of her … she knows that she will collapse under the weight of her own ambitions that have never been expressed. Now she will save herself, she instantly says the magic words "I Is Had Gone" and all ambitions have zoomed out of her, forming an ethereal cloud over the tent. Reena matter. Discarded again.

It is already two hours into the event and the barriers are melting down. The VIP area and the semi-VIP area seem to become one united land of chat and socializing. The buffet-zones have been entered. Vertigo and thirst. Blubbery lips, naked brains and lusty bodies keep on oscillating. A roadie passes Maris a splif. Maris's voice is by now coarse and loud and she won't stop talking about The Strokes.

… the first time I saw a Stroke was at Amanda de Cadenat's birthday party. It was actually one of those groovy Hollywood parties where both Ione Skye and Mathew Perry were making the scene. It was at Keanu's mother's house though of course Keanu was off shooting the Matrixes. I was staring at this guy who looked like he was totally imitating Jeff MacDonald from Redd Kross's look circa their Montsano period, but he was prettier, rosy cheeked. Cherry-lipped, in fact. His clothes were also totally clean and new looking, creating an overall 'fresh' look. His Converses were so new that I felt deeply offended. Who does this guy think he is posing as a Ramone? As I so exclaimed to my friend, he said, "That's The Strokes' guitar player." Of course it was, how blind could I be (this was before I'd met Reena). It was like someone hit me over the head and into bizarro world. And there was the drummer hanging out with Drew. They make really good boyfriend-as-accessories, I have to say. The cute edge that doesn't threaten, more pink than black. That's how the nite started, very pink. My friend introduced me to the guitar player (can't remember his name). We started talking about NY, of course, both being NEW YORKERS … turns out he'd never heard of DNA the famous No Wave band that was a huge part of the 'cool NY scene' of the late '70s and early '80s. He seemed very eager to learn, but my friend pulled me away mid-sentence and said, "Don't tell that asshole." Next he introduced me to Mathew Perry who said he loved my work. I thought that was the most insincere thing but I wasn't sure, or wanted to believe, so I told him I loved his work. But then thought that he must of thought I was totally full of shit to use a word like "work." Things were beginning to turn dark. I was beginning to feel too Hollywood and unclean. Time to go. The next time I met the jolly Strokes was at a Marc Jacobs show. They were very friendly and sweet. The one who looks a little like Billy Joel was swigging off a bottle of wine, didn't catch the label … true rock 'n roller, I guess. Bending reality has become the all-over occupation of the party. Everybody is playing. Nobody knows the game of tapping into the "noir universe." What happened to the glamorous, dark and truly charismatic shit. Does it exist? Did it ever?

Something about the pitch of her voice and the way her face is contorting is hurting Reena, as if when Maris spoke, it triggered inside her a torture instrument that crushed her organs. Reena says she'll be right back and, waiting in line at a bank of porta-potties, she meets, of all people, the Slovenian philosopher Slavoj Zizek.

Zizek is immediately charmed by the gleaming, beaming Reena and has ditched his own dude-swarm entourage of academic types. The music is very loud so it's hard to hear all the words, but Reena is all ears as he tells her about his new book, *The Ghost of Negation*. His sentences come like a continuous attack, deep rumbles of artillery shells, first from a distance, then progressively closer, but it is a benign fire. A search for truths. While he speaks there are fast successions of hand gestures, ticks, and his lips are wet from spit. Music starts blasting. Reena offers Zizek a powerbar. Balance, Detour, Yo-Bar, Zone in different colors. She could not help but pocket the whole range and put it in her purse. There was even a "will to powerbar" with the philosopher Nietzsche's head printed on the wrapping. She is truly excited to be able to offer this particular thing to Zizek. Massive fuel for the already massive machine. Zizek, in an all-gray flannel outfit—symbolizing some kind of phase in his life, serves as a most spectacular projection site and all possible spurts of thought need to be embraced. Reena seizes the moment and loves the abuse, quite naturally.

Behind a group of ladies dressed in pastel colors, who after liquid and/or pharmaceutical breakfasts are now huddling in the brisk park afternoon, the second of the two public artworks is being unveiled. It resembles a mixture between a bus shelter and a romantic folly, while of course never offering any interior space that is not immediately visible from the outside—no junkie shoot-up shed, rapid dark alley, bum bedroom this—and waiting for the one possible redemption of some Brooks Brothers wearing kids burning it to the ground.

I can feel it all slipping through my hands, Maris was thinking as she ran her fingers through the bowl of roasted peanuts on the rock 'n roll offering table backstage. The Strokes were on stage, stroking it up. The table was laden with herbal ham, olives, carrot sticks, little puff-pastry pizzas, jellybeans, pickled chili peppers, all arranged in a mandala-like spiral pattern. Roasted peanuts are a dieter's nightmare, but what about unroasted peanuts in the shell? Minutes ago, Maris decided to give everything up, eliminate everything toxic about herself: stop cigarettes, stop alcohol, stop fat and fried foods, stop male fantasy, stop psychoanalysis, stop the overextended and ambitious projects, and once again and always, to stop thinking about the outcome of situations. If I think about myself, this minute, I feel an enormous guilt about all the things that I am fucking up right now. My teeth are clenched, they should be relaxed. My boyfriend will arrive soon, and I wonder if he even is my boyfriend, does he want me that way, do I want him that way? I shouldn't care one way or the other when we're together. It just doesn't matter, and I should only matter in the way I am at any given moment. But I don't know who I am, what I am. I really want a cigarette.

Zizek was still Zizeking it up, saying that the drive is inherently ethical, not "blind animal thriving" but an ethical compulsion which repeatedly compels us to mark the memory of a lost cause. The drive is the compulsion to revisit, to encircle again and again those sites of lost causes, of shattered and perverted dreams and hopes, not out of some nostalgic longing but because the marking of lost causes signals the impossibility of a totalizing morality, the necessity of a method called "ethical bricolage" that he borrowed from compadre-philosopher Laclau.

When Julian Casablancas opens his lopsidedly curled lip to sing, his voice doggie-paddling through the airy slush of soft kiddie guitar pop, all I can hear was him whispering in my ear. The occasional guitar jabs are not enough to disturb the dreaminess but eventually the shivers down my spine surprise me so much that I blush and look around to see if anyone noticed. Where is Reena? Central Park is confusing, so many different guards. Julian's resemblance to Roger, my teen crush is becoming a disturbing image. They both have that english boy with slightly curled up girly hair on the ends look, complete with milky pale skin and lips more curled than mick jagger pouty. Roger was sixteen and I was fifteen. He had a twin sister and they lived on nob hill in San Francisco. We would take a little acid, just so we were all giggly and drive around in their parents' Bentley. The Strokes were like mini rockstars, that's what made them appear so cute on stage, not that they are small in size, only that because their music is small in scale, each song like an 8mm movie backdrop for Julian's vocal: "ooh, ooh yeh …" I can't really make out the lyrics but it doesn't matter because I know they're all love songs to me … and I've been waiting so long for Roger to just hold my hand, I can't stand it, I've never met a boy so shy, and gentle … the beginning and end of my desire for the passive, evasive, boy. He can't move toward you only out into the air … to open his mouth and sing. He grabs the pole and drops off the stage into the audience … where is he? It's so dark. Blue-black with just a spot of pink light searching in the crowd for Julian. I look down at my pink stockings. Their shiny iridescence makes my head swirl, and I suddenly feel sick to my stomach and puke on some guy's shoes standing next to me. I panic and push my way through the crowd. Inaccessible immensity, a hard-won state of mind. I'm loving every minute of this.

Zizek knows that Maris doesn't care about cancer, doubts if she even knows what it is, that it is the condition of one times one times one always equaling one. What Maris knows is bringing one thing into contact with another, one plus one. The Strokes and cancer. Zizek and Reena. The cameras and the trees and the kids and cancer and chaos. One thing into contact with another. Cancer. A lot of us have it, or will have it soon. Cancer, the condition of self being referred to self, is hard at work today, and Maris is making it work twice, three times. Bricolaging it.

Zizek brings his spitty lips close to Maris and begins to suggest radical changes in the structure of her company, Vive la Corpse. VLC should not pass up the opportunity to provide proof that it is our fantasies that support our sense of reality, that this is in turn a defense against the Real. The Real is the hidden/traumatic underfelt in strange and unexpected places: the Lacanian Sublime. He tells Maris she should figure out, with all her connections and her bricoleur's instinct, how to invoke this Sublime in ever more enigmatic ways. One elementary procedure could be moving forward from establishing shots of reality to a disturbing proximity that renders visible the disgusting substance of enjoyment, the crawling and glistening of indestructible life. And to combine this with new ways of invading daily existence. If the subject is a function of the difference between "subjective" pathologies and the libidinal economy of the "objective" ideological system, it must be precisely the gap between these two systems that founds the inherently split subjectivity. So, think about a company that grabs the leading edge in causing outbursts of the Real, with reality and its fantasmatic supplement acting side by side as though existing on the same surface. Reena Spaulings, you are this surface! You are the bricolage! Maris, Vive la Corpse is the perfect embodiment of difference. Work on the gap! Maris nods, a Yo-for-women powerbar clamped between her teeth like an old bone. She stares out into the crowd that has gathered around The Strokes and is terrified.

There is a person I imagine I want to be, someone different, different gestures, different reactions. I is had gone. Always thinking about death, my own, since I was nine years old. By now I should see it as a cheap fantasy: we die and then it's all over, good night, Irene. But what if death is a conversion into the most impossible, torturous beginning imaginable? You die, and are pressed into slavery to serve the will of some ruthless cosmic organism. Sure, maybe time and space doesn't exist anymore, but that's only to make you more efficient. All this means that human life on this planet is like some kind of vacation away from the grueling prison of the universe. That explains all the steady over-population over the ages. We got wise and tried to make life as long as possible, and now word's getting around about how great it is here. All those souls crammed around the entrance, waiting for a uterus to take them through to the other side—either a middle-class jewel of existence worrying about getting a decent job to pay for all the comforts; or two weeks before being massacred with a machete in a jungle, anything, a floor scrubber, a pirate, a policeman, any form will do to forget, for awhile at least, the fluid formless coordination of the before and afterlife. That's why most people are terrified of dying. That's my fear of dying. When I look up at the stars, I see pure malevolence hiding behind the sheet of the atmosphere. Those simultaneous engines. Science wants to ruin everything, pull down the sheets and try to get the image a little clearer. The spirit of progress is a restraining device programmed at the genetic level, to keep us clamoring for something new, "the unknown," while deep down we know that we have become attached to this life and will suffer miserably to lose what's around us. I resolve to be more conservative. This moment has to last forever, and if it can't I will do something to freeze myself, begin to cry and never stop, retreat into the last reaches of my self and sew up the borders, so that no one will ever hear from me again. I need to ground myself. What if I ground myself on Zizek over there? What am I doing with my hands right now? One is on my hip and the other is holding a newly-lit cigarette. How'd that happen? Didn't I just throw my pack away? Zizek is standing right next to me, and he's putting away a cigarette case. So it was him. We've been having a conversation. Good, at least I'm not losing my mind.

Reena gets up and goes and sits behind an amp. Maris follows her though and starts crying on her shoulder, confessing her anxieties about soon having missed her chance to have a child, crying until all her tears are spent. Reena, crazily energized by her Zizek fix and a newfound sense of command over all this nothingness, cheers her up with her idea for a new project: a live riot, a music, a Battle On Broadway, an untimely spectacle which she would like Maris to produce with underwear money. It will be called "Cinema of The Damned," and Reena will be its star. Maris prefers "Battle On Broadway." As The Strokes kick out their final jam, Jane feels another death drive coming on, and she will not go home tonight, not ever. Susan is deaf but can feel the song thudding repetitively against her eighteen year old flesh. Like a washing machine. Murielle is glad to be here and decides that New York can have her now, fuck Brussels, she's its. The Central Park event is ending. The crew of middle-aged white roadies in black jeans and band t-shirts start unplugging and winding the endless yards of electrical cords, packing up the equipment and amps and loading them into trucks. Reena's "bad idea" is floating there and refusing to go away, hooking into that part of Maris that makes her machine go, meshing with what she thinks of as her gears. She is emotionally spent and remains crumpled against Reena's shoulder, but in some part of her that never stops, she is working. Sensing the perfect moment, Reena convinces Maris to name her vice president of Vive la Corpse. The Strokes come backstage amidst a bustle of press, give a few interviews, drink a beer, and take off for their hotel. The Cancer people bid Maris and Reena goodbye with afterglow. Somehow Vive la Corpse had distributed some kind of monstrous but ungraspable desire all over the place, like walking sprinklers. And in the west the sun was setting.

Seth Price

Was ist Los?

Originally published as "Unique Source/All Natural Suicide Gang," in *New York Twice*, Bettina Funcke, ed., Paris: Air de Paris, 2005

Here is an operation. In 1988 the composer Steve Reich, whom at one point was called a minimalist, used the relatively new technology of the sampler to create a work based around the digitized human voice. The work grew out of phrases and sentences, the cadences of which suggested corresponding musical figures. Double strands laid out like objects upon their shadows. The voice writes the music. Listening through this music, specific language emerges: testimonials from Holocaust survivors, overburdened with meaning, unassailable. Well, a thing only really appears when it's turned into a weapon. Ovens, showers, lampshades, soap: an innocuous group of words, unless we're told that the context is Germany in the 1940s.

Where to locate the power in this operation? First, let us try to assemble some of its recognizable traits. It is an act of writing that does not hesitate to remove material from its native context, a move often seen as inappropriate or even criminal, at least in the realm of pop culture. According to this logic, an original is somehow violated through the creation of its double, a process seen as one more step in the lamentable cultural slide from representation to repetition.

In fact, sampling is not concerned with repetition. Its purpose is the creation of new, discrete events. Each reproduction is an original and a new beginning. Each, in fact, is the first in a potentially infinite sequence, which is to say an infinite sequence. This is where the gesture's violence is to be found, and why it is attended by cultural anxieties. These concerns are often understood to be copyright related, which means money motivated, but it's likely that they stem just as much from misgivings about the implications of instrumentalizing human expression. In any case, there's no longer such a thing as a copy.

Artists are universally recognized as experts in the field of human expression. Naturally they have been quick to recognize these issues. I wonder ... if sampling may be understood as a process of using stolen documents as raw material for form abuse, might this not be true of all advanced art? Luckily it isn't necessary to answer this question, as a thing doesn't have to be true, merely testable. With this task in mind we turn to the realm of music, a superior place to test artists' reactions to the intrusion of digital techniques, which were introduced to music quite early relative to other art forms.

The notion of "intellectual property" as regards most written material was codified in Europe in the sixteenth century, a response to the new text-copying technology of print. It was almost a hundred years before this notion really took hold in the world of music and a composer might actually own his composition. Previously, songs were understood to be common property, and, what's more, mutable, much in the way computer programs were initially understood as communal efforts to be shared, altered, and re-distributed. A one-hundred-year lag! Although in this respect music seems to have fallen behind the printed word, it soon leapt ahead. The practice of text copying has aged gracefully since the dawn of intellectual property, and its main exponent remains the printed page, but music has all along been subject to sudden shifts in the controlled reproduction and dissemination of commercial recorded material.

Let us reflect on these changes. To take an example from opera, Toscanini's tenure at La Scala wrought changes that would eventually turn the form into the consummate bourgeois entertainment. Prior to his arrival, the orchestra was seated on the same level as the audience, an audience with none of the docile characteristics of today's opera-goers, rather, a mob of hardy commoners, robust peasant folk, loyal to the toil of the soil, drinking, eating, and jesting in the manner of her C's, U's, and T's: "Let us meet at the opera and then decide whence we go … ," "Well-met, friend, pray share this flagon … ," "Scubberdegullion," "lass," etc.

This is the lumber of life.

It must be emphasized: Toscanini had the luck of good timing. Architecture is the model in Western metaphysics, and as such is a necessary corollary to ritual. At just this moment the bourgeoisie was working itself into a supreme ecstasy of privacy, decorum, and interiority. Built spaces were spaces of fantasy. The opera is such a fantasy, a ritualized repetition of aristocratic tradition. A depletion but also a preservation of forms lacking the vitality to proceed under their own power, delivered in the sorts of patrician packaging necessary to fire the bourgeois imagination. The emptying gestures of ritual are a force of preservation, just as death is the romanticizing principle in life. In this light, the phenomenon of a proper house for opera can be seen as a secret handshake between the middle classes and the aristocracy. For their part, aristocracies dutifully keep alive those endangered pleasures that repel the bourgeoisie. Now, as then? In our time there is no such thing as a bourgeoisie. Yet … Well, why not? One dreams all day long, just as during the night. It is possible that cultured people are merely the glittering scum that floats upon a deep river of production.

But what results from this? If architecture is the model in Western metaphysics, we are in some sense the inhabitors of older buildings, and ours is the business of living in a ruined house. It's useful to take a hard look at the word *ruin*, a word that splits. On the one hand, it could refer to the sorts of ancient structures cherished in the early nineteenth century: squalid, overgrown, graffiti-covered, surveyed at sunset for best effect. Yet it might also indicate those same ruins today: sandblasted free of graffiti, restored and conserved, made lucrative, seen only in the full daylight of "open hours." In the first example, ruin implies benign decay; in the second, active preservation, make-work, and industry.[1] Locating pleasure in benign decay is a perversion, for these structures are useless and wasteful, a spilling of seed, like gay sex, like gay sex.

All that which is not made useful and which serves no profitable function is seen as the unrecuperable waste of a society. This material may be understood as a force that crystallizes society's blockages, making visible a sort of cast of its bowels. The Boston Museum of Science features a display of "petrified lightning," which is merely a lumpy brown rod of sand fused at the instant of extreme heat. The exhibit stands for the operation by which a scientific process is mystified, replaced by a ruin under glass, making a fetish of waste.

My anecdotal mention of this exhibit itself belongs to a certain class of artistic vitrine, and one could treat cultural detritus the same way, wringing art from suburban architecture, or exurban wasteland.

It is here that our strands come together, for it is in music that one may now locate such fetishes and vitrines. In the era of the picturesquely crumbling abbey or castle, poetry was king of the arts, and it was this form that drew all the radical young dudes. A century later, on the other side of Modernism, in an age when any ancient scrap heap is carefully made over in the image of safety and security, music is the art toward which all the others aspire. It's here you'll find the young romantics. What accounts for this change? As with the adoption of ideas of intellectual property, the schematic shifts in music lag behind those of the written word.

This is the lake of our feeling.

It was not until the affront of the sampler that music really went to work anxiously mapping and itemizing the husks of metropolises constructed by earlier settlers. Seeking a new Classicism. With all the hedonism that follows a period of calamity.[2] The Classical style (if one may be so vain as to label something that exists beyond time) is often said to stretch from Haydn to Beethoven. It might be best understood as a single unbroken lineage in which Brahms writes with Beethoven looking over his shoulder, a carefully organized sequence of events, preserved on paper and embodied in the concert hall. The twentieth century, however, put an end to this careful sequence, substituting a wildly metastasizing growth based on the duplicable recorded signal. The arrival of the digital copy crystallizes this development neatly, almost allegorically, almost too neatly. One might think that music is in dissolution, heading away from form, increasingly resistant to the physical, and so also to structures of ritual,[3] but this may not, in fact, be the case.

Come what may, everything is reused. Artists rummage through the toolkits of past artists for approaches they may make use of. The task is to take these instruments and fashion new tools. You want a fine-art approach, you borrow the tool from commodity culture. Look for the use, not the meaning! And if it's done wrong, no problem, there is produced a nostalgia for the done-right way. For these reasons, the modern idea of a renovated ruin may be more relevant for art than the nineteenth century model of picturesque decay.

It still eludes me … what is so particular about the sampler? Take a close look at the economic and technological particulars of this tool. In 1979, the first commercial sampler was put on the market for around $25,000. The *Fairlight*. What a name! Ha, ha, ha. The steep price was typical of these early machines, which were consequently purchased by institutions, primarily well-funded university composition labs. In other words, this was a brief period when most of the people exploring sample-based music were classically trained academic composers, who recognized in the computer a spectacular means of testing their high-flying propositions.[4]

This moment is emblematic of music's Modernist style, which all along had a tendency, as with the abstruse proposals of Schoenberg or Webern, to make advanced theoretical training a prerequisite for participation. Now it was expected of students that they not only cultivate a familiarity with the usual histories and methodologies, but also rely entirely on the academy for production tools. After all, many middle-class homes featured a piano, but none a computer workstation. It was a natural endpoint to Modernist music's evolutionary chain, which flourished on a delicate diet of technology, money, and control. Hardly characteristic of Modernist music alone, it is true, but this moment so beautifully illustrates it.

But this moment was fleeting. The sampler's arrival upset the balance, and, as often happens with young technologies, the market seeped in, all the strictures slipped, old model of the pyramid, new model of the pancake. Ten years after the introduction of the Fairlight, any composer could buy a decent sampler for under one thousand dollars, adding a newly available personal computer to yield a versatile home studio. The same was true of any teenager producing dance music or rap music.[5] All this headlong change left a wake of wreckage and trauma, and, in academic computer music, a unique and peculiar musical period, a curiosity, the equivalent of a geographically isolated evolutionary zone where unique life forms go largely undiscovered. Actions of concealing belong to violence. A bruised music, which seems still to have no name, unsure whether it was the start or the end of something.

Around the same time sampling was introduced, the music industry developed MIDI, a kind of universal machine language that allows electronics to synchronize and exchange information. Packets of information, commands in fact, are relayed from one piece of gear to the next, allowing a synthesizer of one manufacture to get in line with a drum machine of another. These silent commands, such as *start note* and *end note*, are known as events. Arguably a language, and certainly a system of control, destined to be the new coin of the realm, a currency of loins and coins. Because it was intended for swift, industry-wide adoption, the concept had to be widely familiar, rather than intelligible only to technicians, engineers, and programmers. That meant attaching a friendly front-end to the code. The public happens to be most comfortable with the piano, and this became electronic music's user interface. This is why the events lurking behind most of the music you hear on the radio actually preserve the slight, barely perceptible movement of a fingertip somewhere striking a key. Strike the key and trigger an event, which is immediately sequenced in a series of other events. A chain of control achieved through a simple depression. When I am depressed, there is power at work somewhere.

Many are interested in the idiom of a form, few in the grammar. Personal computers, for example, were originally made so as to be programmable by their owners, but when consumers eventually rejected this aspect it was removed or hidden. Similarly, while the combination of sampled sounds, MIDI, and digital manipulation promised all sorts of possibilities, it turns out that most people don't want to build sounds that have never been heard. They want sounds corresponding to existing phenomena, invocations of reality at the touch of a finger, like paint straight from the tube: brass, woodwinds, car accidents, shrieks, breaking glass. The machine recalls events and dispatches them in a digital relay that is by design simply on or off, making obsolete the weak signal, the half-understood communication. A zero-sum spell.

So, you found the sampler's perfect expression early on, when you hit on the idea of employing sampled human voice as a re-pitchable synthesizer sound. An electronic keyboard simulates a piano, often noting even the force with which the keys are struck: it wants you to believe that it is a percussion instrument. The voice-sample technique, then, is the process of generating limitless copies of a unique and resonant human utterance, refashioned as a sprawling kit of silicon-calibrated fake drums. The voice becomes a structural element under total control, it is made useful, as opposed to evocative or expressive. That which reliably promises communication becomes pure instrumentality, a move based on the notion that instruments give us what we want—predictability, security, control—rather than the confirmation of an accurate representation of the real. It goes to show you that when your desires become reality, you don't need fantasy any longer, nor art.

The technique was immediately popular among academic composers and pop producers alike,[6] but soon disappeared from both realms, possibly because it seemed dated, but more likely because sampled and repitched voice is disturbing, a speech terrible and inhuman, an emulation gone bad. The sampled word is the zero degree of the word, as found in the dictionary, or in poetry. Here the communicative imperative, which depends on repetition and difference, was symbolically short-circuited, and, moreover, from within the cloak of language. It is not surprising that the technique fell into disfavor. Man fall from a tree, that tree be felled, man fall in a well, that well be filled.

Samplers continue to offer one entirely new experience, at least on the level of consumption: the recognition, while listening to an unknown piece of music, of the basis for a sample used in a familiar piece. As you look up with bewildered pleasure, the music charges on, diverging from the repetition you expected. You briefly glimpsed a private, inaccessible field between two disparate experiences, a mental correlate to the phantom step at the top of the stairs. Whatever pleasure you can sustain must rely on simultaneous presence and absence.[7]

Digital duplication was one of the twentieth century's few new schemas. Such developments draw the curtain on older powers, and, by the end of the 1980s, around the time Reich completed his sample-based work, the configuration *avant-garde music* was thoroughly depleted, a constellation made cold from forgetfulness. All forms of depletion are heralded by the degradation of language, and, just as the eclipse of Rome's power was contemporary with the decline of Latin, so the eclipse of avant-garde music was indicated by its wish to transform embodied language into an instrument. A desire to *be*, rather than to *seem*.

You could argue that sampling poisoned the well. On the other hand, it is true that in homeopathic medicine, and sometimes in magic, you put a drop of the bad thing, the thing you fight, into water or some other medium. Sampling may be invasive, negating repetition, disordering us, but then that's the wish of every man: to disorder, to mayhem. You must fight something in order to understand it! Voice sampling, possibly all sampling, gives us a text that is critical of reading.

Graffiti performs a similar operation. The gesture of graffiti must preserve that which it seeks to destroy. Were it to entirely efface its object, its particular critique would vanish. None, after all, is worse shod than the shoemaker's wife. The work of Marcel Broodthaers occasionally follows this logic, most clearly in his piece *Un Coup de dés jamais n'abolira le hasard*, with its pleasantly incestuous abuse of the Francophone avant-garde. The publication of Mallarmé's poem "Un Coup de dés jamais n'abolira le hasard," a work dis-tinguished by its typography and disposition of the words upon the page, marked the first time that a poem's conception and meaning was determined through the mechanical printing process. A lyric automation of the design function. In 1969, Broodthaers made a series of pieces that reproduced the exact page layout of Mallarmé's poem, and the layout alone, since he effaced each line of text with a solid black bar. This gesture, while it banished all communicative symbols, retained the striking look and feel of the work.[8] Mallarmé's piece was emptied-out, reduced to seductive packaging. This is a move typical of "appropriation," which may be considered simply an advanced form of packaging.

These depleted forms were engraved onto aluminum plates, as if prepped for mass production, and presented as fine art. Broodthaers claims and then augments Mallarmé's poem to produce a new, third body, a field between the works. The whole is without novelty, save the spacing of one's reading; the blanks, in effect, assume importance. The madness of the "a self-annihilating nothing" prescription. But this was only to be expected, since Broodthaers was an imitation artist. It may be that the supreme triumph of such advanced art is to cast doubt on its own validity, mixing a deep scandalous laughter with the religious spirit. There is a violence in this turn, the same violence that attends graffiti: "*Don't think, look!*"

In regular usage, the word graffiti describes an urban decay-threat, akin to mold, understood as pathology. It may be pathological, but not because it's vandalism, rather because it dreams of total saturation through an open-ended sequence of events, each a slight variation on the last. Such total coverage is a futile and perverse premise, an infinite possibility wedded to perpetual disappointment, a pursuit ripe with frustration. Like the poor man who sells his saucepan to buy something to put in it.

Then again, graffiti, like any human expression, is basically a search to find a style and context that makes further expression possible. Graffiti Culture (and why does it take so long for people to map a "culture" on to their violence?) represents the anarchic, expressive territory of those who have subverted painterly representation from the standpoint of cool alienation. A person inscribing a coded sign on the side of a bridge piling enacts a ritual repetition: Language is defaced by pictures. Writing that will never have a book. This isn't the business of living in a ruined house; it's the business of representing a ruined house, its interior trappings sketched out for all to see. The art object is seen as an object of contemplation, not to be parsed, but to be puzzled over. Its secrets may have to do with art, but with something else as well, which hovers beyond, with no name forthcoming.

In my view, it's refreshing to watch a form deplete itself: "Ah, now it becomes easier to see it as not a belief but a historical movement, which is to say a movement of thought. Easier now to trace the social shift and extrapolate out as far as desired: all design, all art, all packaging."[9] Take vacuum-forming, an industrial process that gives us the ubiquitous polystyrene packaging of batteries, toys, and toothbrushes, as well as of luxury items like boxed candies and cosmetics. Casual research into the use of this process in the plastic arts suggests that the chief instances, including Broodthaers' rectilinear plaques and Öyvind Fahlström's Esso/LSD reliefs, take the logic of the commercial sign as their model. This is congruent with a sustained twentieth-century artistic investigation of advertising and display, from Rudy Burckhardt or Walter Benjamin's interest in the sloughed-off detritus of commodity culture, to a more recent fascination with corporate monograms. What would it mean to employ such a process for the purpose of reproducing not the structures of language and capitalist syntax, but those of the human form? Making a package for conservative statuary and classical figuration, for art itself: a violent cough, as when the human voice is "repurposed" as an instrument.

What it means is, it shows how far we've come with our packaging. Full circle, the lowest shall be highest. In the evenings, you can stroll out to see how we are coming along with the construction of the temple.

Notes

1. The French have a saying: "the consumer has only three basic needs: to be safe, to be loved, to be beautiful." This is the desire of ruins in our time.

2. Historically, all new forms attack Classicism; it's a move characteristic not only of Romantic poetry, but also of the Neo-Expressionist painting of the 1980s, for which the darkest place was under the lamp.

3. The sudden shift from wired phones to mobile phones. The telephone is introduced as a wire-bound domestic appliance, a singular site, in fact often attached to the wall, and it serves multiple people, whether through the party line, or later the shared "phone in the hall," or, ultimately, the family phone. With the introduction of the mobile phone this model is upended, replaced by a roving non-site at the service of one.

4. It's the engineers who strike ground in digital creative arenas. This pattern is apparent not only in early computer music, but also in early computer graphics experiments, and in the earnest, fresh-faced CompSci graduates who are now enabling Hollywood's growing dependence on CGI. Something to do with Leonardo.

5. This raises the question of amateur production. As with all strategies of appropriation, sampling cannot be conceived of in terms of amateur or professional roles. This is part of its violence. Collecting and illegally redistributing material has no professional dimension; the person who compiles a mix tape for a friend is not an amateur. A licit practice that approximates this maneuver is that of a corporation that cheaply purchases rights to *déclassé* cultural material, like bygone dance music, from those now forced to part with it cheaply, thence to repackage these goods for re-consumption, either under the banner of nostalgia (the low-end approach), or for the archiving fetish of the would-be collector (the high end approach).

6. I once recalled someone standing by a keyboard, blurting out "I don't know what to say!" The phrase belonged to a female character on an early Cosby show, and was spoken into a new sampling keyboard demonstrated by Stevie Wonder, who appeared as himself. With some deft adjustments he multiplied her apparently random words across the span of the keyboard, repitched appropriately, basso profundo to mezzo-soprano, all subject to easy control through key depression. It was in fact Stevie Wonder, in 1981, who purchased the very first of the famous Emulator samplers, fresh off the assembly line. A quaint memory. What a time I chose to be born!

7. This experience is utterly different from that of recognizing one composer's melodic quotation of another's work, as different as is the scan from the photograph.

8. "Look and feel," a term popularized by the computer industry, is often used to describe the overall aesthetic of a particular operating system. Like the shade of seduction used to paint the information architecture. A well-known example is the Macintosh's successful graphic user interface, which was subsequently copied throughout the industry. The term gained notoriety through a series of lawsuits—Xerox against Apple, Apple against Microsoft and Hewlett-Packard—brought on the basis of whether or not it was legal to appropriate aesthetic qualities crystallized in code. Look and feel, in its current sense, is a notion that did not really exist prior to the personal computer, but one that now affects all consumer realms based on digital technology.

9. Compare emblematic New York graffiti tags of the 1970s, like Zephyr, Futura, or PhaseII, with those of the 1980s such as Sony, Seiko, and Casio, and then with those of the 1990s, by which time the best sense-making letter combinations were used up: Revs, Kuma, Sems, Naers. A graceful arc from poetry to consumer fetish to emptied form. Digital tags such as screen names and internet addresses will not follow this arc, which belongs to the past. Décor Holes.

Kirk Varnedoe

Why Abstract Art?

From *Pictures of Nothing: Abstract Art Since Pollock*
(Princeton, NJ: Princeton University Press, 2006)

The main title of this year's Mellon Lectures, "Pictures of Nothing," is from an essay by William Hazlitt about one of his contemporaries, the early nineteenth-century English painter J.M.W. Turner. Turner was celebrated (or notorious) for painting vaporous and indistinct conjurings of atmospheric effects, as you can see from one of his landscapes of the 1840s, *Snowstorm: Steamboat off a Harbour's Mouth*. In his essay, Hazlitt reports the remark of a dyspeptic viewer about one such work: "'Pictures of Nothing,' the viewer harrumphed, 'and very like.'"[1] This attitude, skeptical at best, dismissive at worst, seems as premonitory of modern reactions to abstract art as Turner is of abstraction itself. Because such skepticism is what I want to confront, and because issues of both nothingness and likeness have a looming presence in these lectures, the borrowing from Hazlitt seemed to me an appropriate provocation with which to begin.

Throughout these lectures I am going to talk about abstract art during the last fifty years or so. The big question I want to ask eventually is the one you are entitled to ask up front, and it is the title of today's talk: Why abstract art? But let me dodge that question for a moment and start with a second one: Why abstract art of the last fifty years? The quick answer is that fifty years takes us to the mid-1950s, a crucial juncture in twentieth-century culture.

* * *

I take this topic ultimately because it seems to me one of the most legitimate and poorly addressed questions in modern art. Put another way, I want to ask whether there is any grounding for abstraction, perhaps an underlying logic, or specifically a "logic of the situation," to borrow a term from E. H. Gombrich. Almost fifty years ago, Gombrich gave the epochal Mellon Lectures that became his book *Art and Illusion*, and I want to recapture some of the excitement that must have filled the National Gallery's lecture hall in 1956 when Gombrich spoke. He asked at that time one of the most resounding questions of all: Why does art have a history? Gombrich wanted to crack what he called the "riddle of style," that is, to find an explanation for the succession of odd stylizations by which different epochs and civilizations have represented the visible world.[2] Given that the elements of the natural world have always looked as they do, and given that human vision has always functioned as it does, Gombrich wanted to know why ancient Egyptians and medieval Italian monks and baroque ceiling painters depict the world so differently. He was intensely dissatisfied with explanations that rested on some quasi-mystical spirit of the age or zeitgeist. Instead he wanted an explanation of the history of art that had more scientific and philosophical rigor, that would take into account both the "hard-wiring" of human perception and the way knowledge has progressed cumulatively through successive ages and societies. Gombrich's proposal, which drew on the best minds of his time in areas such as perceptual psychology and the philosophy of science, was that within the confounding variety of the history of Western art one could trace a long, halting, but ultimately rational progress toward the development of a credible illusionism, that is, the feat of getting a viewer to conjure from painted marks on a flat surface a convincing illusion of such things as seamlessly receding space and three-dimensional volumes. Albrecht Dürer, in his 1525 woodcut of an artist trying to reason out the correct way to show a lute in perspective, reminds us how long and hard artists had to work to achieve this illusionism.

Gombrich delivered his Mellon Lectures in 1956, the year of Pollock's death, when, as we have seen, abstract art appeared to be spreading triumphant. At the same time, realist illusionism, propagated on every pulp page and street corner billboard by magazine illustrations, advertisements, and above all by photography, was taken for granted by the wider public. Gombrich wanted to reproblematize that commonplace: to show that, far from being a merely servile copying of nature—we see it, we draw it—illusionist representation was a willed, hard-fought achievement of human culture. It was the result of a cumulative dialogue between invented conceptual schemas and their corrections—a dialogue that was worthy of being regarded, like science, as a unique virtue of the Western tradition, stretching from what he called "the Greek miracle" in the vase painting and sculpture of the fifth century BC, through Dürer and the Italian Renaissance up to John Constable's naturalist landscape paintings, such as his beautiful 1816 picture of *Wivenhoe Park, Essex* from the National Gallery of Art collection.

But this noble progress foundered when it came up against the wall of the oncoming twentieth century. As much as Gombrich cherished the triumph of illusionism, he disliked and mistrusted its demise in abstract art. The antipathy was partly personal. Gombrich was, after all, a Renaissance scholar, and his tastes and sympathies were grounded in an earlier humanism. But his was also an intellectual and even ideological bias. Gombrich thought that abstraction was understandable as an extension of the history of decorative pattern-making, as in Alhambra tiles, rugs, basket weaves, tile work, and the like. But—if I can risk summing up and interpreting his many writings on the subject of abstract art—he saw the claim that modern abstract art might be something more than decoration as based either in mystifications about abstraction reflecting hidden metaphysical truths or in specious arguments that the tides of history somehow required such innovations.

It was precisely that lethal combination of belief in "higher ideals," stretching back to Plato, and pronouncements about the "requirements" of history, grounded in Hegel, that Gombrich's close friend, the philosopher Karl Popper, in his wartime book *The Open Society and Its Enemies*, had recently scourged as the false philosophical foundations of totalitarian thinking, propounded by both Fascism and Soviet Communism. Thus, to put it far more crudely than Professor Gombrich, the implicit message of *Art and Illusion* is two-fold. On one hand, Gombrich argues that the construction of illusionist naturalism is directly consonant with the neurological hard-wiring of human nature. On the other, he suggests the progressive way illusionism developed also makes it the appropriate "house style" of the best liberal traditions of free inquiry and criticism in the open society of the West. Conversely, Gombrich's subsequent put-downs of abstract art present its excesses as being, at best, whims of trendy fashion, and, at worst, tainted with the most dangerous policies of totalitarian thought.

I admire so much about *Art and Illusion*. Rather than critique the flaws that have become evident in Gombrich's arguments over time, I want to wonder with you whether there can ever be an argument for abstract art that is as good, as generous, as ambitious, and as challenging as Gombrich's argument for its opposite. Because as Sir Ernst rightly saw, all the many claims about timeless universal forms and historical destinies that have been used to explain modern abstraction are, however sincere or sophisticated, intellectually bankrupt. There are not any "hard" reasons why abstract art has to be. Nor any teleology that explains why it developed as it did. And it is useless to keep looking for those kinds of justifications.

This does not invalidate abstract art. The familiar arguments that abstraction is just a big hoax, a colossal version of the "emperor's new clothes," perpetrated on a duped public by cynical art mandarins, seem like tiresome whistling in the dark. Abstract art has been with us in one form or another for almost a century now, and has proved to be not only a long-standing crux of cultural debate, but a self-renewing, vital tradition of creativity. We know that it works, even if we're still not sure why that's so, or exactly what to make of that fact. To borrow the phrase of the apocryphal contemporary academic, "Okay, so it works in practice. But does it work in theory?" What is still needed, what seems well overdue, is to make the case for a logic of abstract art, as *Art and Illusion* made the case for illusionism, that would describe it (with respectful opposition to Gombrich's own dismissals) both as a legitimate reflection of the way we think individually and as a valid and valuable aspect of liberal society.

This is, of course, a tall order, not least because at the start of the twenty-first century we have very different ideas about how our minds work and how a just society functions. Looking at early minimalist works by artists such as Sol LeWitt and Dan Flavin necessitates revising and expanding Gombrich's idea of *making*, by which he meant the invention of forms and schemas, the mind's primal work in building knowledge. Especially in the last fifty years, a lot of abstract art has demonstrated that our intelligence innovates not by making things up out of whole cloth or by discovering new things about nature, but by operating with and upon the repertoire of the already known: by adapting, recycling, isolating, recontextualizing, repositioning, and recombining inherited, available conventions in order to propose new entities as the bearers of new thought. In the case of art, these conventions are dumb, man-made forms like cubes, stripes, and other architectural configurations. With illusionism, the argument could be made that art progressed by a series of corrections, made according to the unchanging standard of nature and perceptual mechanics. But there obviously is not any standard of measurement or external resemblance by which we would correct abstractions such as LeWitt's or Flavin's, or establish their relative success or failure. So we have to expand our sense of the drives wired into human cognition, recognizing that we are set up not just to make connections and find resemblances, but also to project meanings onto experience.

In *Art and Illusion* Gombrich discussed the classic drawing that looks like both a duck and a rabbit. We can see either the duck with its beak to the left, or the rabbit with its ears to the left, but we cannot see both at the same time, so we have to decide to see it as one animal or the other. Gombrich uses the drawing to illustrate the way that our visual perception involves what he calls "the viewer's share," that is, the active imposition of an interpretation on incoming experience. The point made by the duck-rabbit drawing can be broadened into a suppler and more inclusive notion of cognition as a process of finding meaning in the world.

Gombrich's model reminds us that works of art are vessels of human intention. The problem is that he judges artistic schemas exclusively by how well they transcribe reality. This is a useful yardstick for discussing representational art, but it is not much help in talking about artists whose goal is to have *no* reference. In abstract art, we face the problem of interpreting images that resemble any number of things, but look like nothing in particular.

Where Gombrich remains useful, here, is in reminding us that abstraction, even more than illusion, can never reside solely in the intention of the artist, but must also be in the eye of the beholder. Artist X may think he's making something that looks like nothing, but Viewer Y may think the work is just the color of Aunt Emmy's purse, or curves just like the bent blade of his favorite golf club, or invokes the key principles of 1911 Picasso. I could take the case of Judd's early minimal sculptures as somewhat comic examples. These early Judds are what he called "specific objects," that is, things that do not seem to be either painting or sculpture, that escape category, that are not familiar, that cannot be pinned down as to what they are.[3] Judd intended these works to be entirely idiosyncratic, outside the common bounds of descriptive language. But in fact he himself, and his viewers and critics, immediately started to categorize these objects, and continued to do so. In the literature on Judd, one of these weird works is known as the "Letter Box," while the other is commonly referred to as "The Bleachers." Other early Judds got nicknamed "The Harp" and "The Lifeboat."

Almost as fast as artists can open blank slates, others hasten to inscribe something on them, trivially at first, as in this case, but eventually with more serious freights of meaning. Hence the difficulty of enforcing the "abstractness" of abstraction. Pollock told an interviewer that when he poured his paintings, he was ever mindful to suppress unwanted imagery or any apparent figuration that his lines might inadvertently suggest. "I try to stay away from any recognizable image; if it creeps in, I try to do away with it."[4] Since then artists have worked harder and harder to keep the crutch of resemblance permanently kicked out from under their viewers. They understand that abstraction is most successful and effective when association and meaning appear to be out of r each. The absence of resemblance allows the work to embrace a great range of intuitions barely imaginable before the work was done, and only marginally present in the artist's conscious intention.

Take for example the huge painting—about four by six meters—done in 1970 by Twombly. Drawn with what looks like chalk but is actually an oil crayon on gray ground, it is one of his so-called blackboard series; this label is itself a kind of joke, like the descriptive titles people gave Judd's work. In fact, it is not a blackboard, and this forces us to deal with what it is. But what is it? It is a kind of furious scribbling, a seemingly mindless repetition of the same hand-drawn gesture. But the gesture is repeated so often and on such a scale that it begins to vault into a different set of references. We lose sight of the arm or the wrist, and begin instead to be aware of the scale of the whole body. And then, because the overlays and densities begin to create a sense of space or depth that is nowhere cued by perspective but is suggested by the blurring, cloudlike structure, we lose awareness of the scale of the body as well. My wife, who is an artist, said of this picture that it's so large and complex that it has its own weather. We sense that it has a kind of energy to it, a pulse like that of a cosmic nebula. And we keep reaching for analogies—weather, night sky, impulsiveness—for a vocabulary that in the end describes nothing other than this picture. We grapple with the combination of things the picture presents: with minute, intimate, and grand scale; with flatness and depth; with huge energy and vast, dissolving serenity. And we continually wind around something that never becomes any particular thing but itself, that has all of the complexity and energy that only it has, and that did not exist before.

Gombrich showed that, in representation, recognition and resemblance required interpretation. But abstractions such as Twombly's show that interpretation does not demand recognition or resemblance and may in fact profit from its absence. In cases like this, abstract art absorbs projection and generates meaning ahead of naming, establishing the form of things unknown, sui generis, in their peculiar complexities. This is one of abstraction's singular qualities, the form of enrichment and alteration of experience denied to the fixed mimesis of known things. It reminds me of the joke about the person who invented the cure for which there was no known disease.

At the same time, this expanded, open-ended process of matching forms with meanings, by means of project and cued invention, constantly turns abstractions into representations in a broadened sense, and defines the nature of abstract art of our time. In early modern art, abstraction was often promoted (or scorned) as a final destination, an ultimate endpoint of art, the culmination of a progressive divorce from appearances, or the terminal cancellation of everything that art required. But by now we have seen art declared "dead" too many times, and we're weary of going to fake funerals. (My colleague Robert Storr taught a course in abstract painting a few years ago that he called "Dead but Won't Lay Down.") In our model of history, there is not any progress at all, in the sense of straight-line, cumulative refinement toward a fixed goal. We have seen the end of the line become a departure station frequently enough to understand that even the seemingly purest abstraction that looks like a fat zero is in fact often an egg waiting to hatch. Not the period at the end of the story, but an ellipsis … (to be continued) within a looping and branching system that ties together a wide range of visual representation: loquacious, laconic, dumb, and all stops in between. Within that system, the abstract artist may colonize a new realm of feeling, as Twombly does, unique to his or her forms, and may also invent a new alphabet which a great many others—artists, designers, filmmakers, and so on—can use to represent the world in different ways.

For an example of how things get recycled, let's look at the use of mirrors in minimalism and postmodernism. In 1965, Robert Morris created a set of untitled mirrored cubes that were just that: cubes with mirrors fixed to the five visible sides. These may have had something to do with his desire to produce a totally neutral, industrial-looking form—something that seemingly is not made by the human hand, has no room for touch, is absolutely hard—and with his desire to force us to recognize the space around the object as part of the work of art.[5] Then, in 1968, when a new organicism appeared in minimal or postminimal art, Morris created a very different piece, using mirrors stuck into a pile of thread waste.

In the same year, Robert Smithson made his *Red Sandstone Corner Piece*. This is like an inside-out version of one of Morris's mirrored cubes, with a pile of broken sandstone inside it. Smithson may have got the idea of using mirrors from Morris, but his use of them was radically different. His combination of mirrors with natural materials had to do with a science fiction idea of crystallography, with the notion of the inertness of mineral matter as a paradigm for the entropic universe and for the way that life forms lose their energy; it had to do with the idea that glass is made by grinding up sand, and that the two are different states of the same thing. For Smithson there was a pseudo scientific rationale to using mirrors, but the mirrors themselves functioned as abstract elements in his work.

In the 1970s the young artist Jeff Koons comes along and puts an inflatable rabbit and flower on a mirror in the floor corner position—the same mirror arrangement that Smithson used, but with a completely different effect. We are no longer in the world of entropy and crystallography; we're in the world of boutique design. The mirror suggests glitz and glamour. This evolution reaches its final realization when Koons puts the mirror *on* the rabbit by recasting the rabbit in shiny stainless steel instead of plastic. This amazing object is often taken to be the ultimate symbol of Reagan-era glitz, a critique of the commodification of society. So the inclusion of the mirror begins as a neutral, formal element in Morris, becomes a sci-fi image in Smithson, and finally provides Koons with a symbol for the hard sheen and glamour of American consumer culture.

In this fashion, abstract art, while seeming insistently to reject and destroy representation, in fact steadily expands its possibilities. It adds new words and phrases to the language by colonizing the lead slugs and blank spaces in the type tray. Seeming nihilism becomes productive, or, to put it another way, one tradition's killer virus becomes another tradition's seed. Stressing abstract art's position within an evolving social system of knowledge directly belies the old notion that abstraction is what we call an Adamic language, a bedrock form of expression at a timeless point prior to the accretion of conventions. If anything, the development of abstraction in the last fifty years suggests something more Alexandrian than Adamic, that is, a tradition of invention and interpretation that has become exceptionally refined and intricate, encompassing a mind-boggling range of drips, stains, blobs, bricks, and blank canvases. The woven web of abstraction is now so dense that, for its adepts, it can snare and cradle vanishingly subtle, evanescent, and slender forms of life and meaning. The tradition of abstract art has recently shown time and again that, for those who learn it, it can make something out of apparent nothing. All in all, this is a good thing.

Like Gombrich's illusionism, abstract art is a construction that began in Western Europe but that has proved useful for a broader world.

Early modern society created—and we have inherited—that paradoxical thing: a tradition of radical innovation. Abstraction is a remarkable system of productive reductions and destructions that expands our potential for expression and communication.

Just the same, this is a risky business. Abstract art is a learned language, and not always easy to understand. I do not mean there is nothing to be had from an unprepared, naïve encounter with Flavin's *"monument" for V. Tatlin*, or with a blank, waxy monochrome canvas by Brice Marden. Nor do I mean to endorse the sense of cultish elitism that requires an MA in art history and a subscription to *Artforum* to understand what goes on in the Chelsea galleries. Dealing with recent abstraction is neither like falling off a log nor like solving differential equations. But the fact is that it does profit from some prior knowledge. Because contemporary abstract art operates within a long tradition, it helps to be aware of the parameters and rules of that tradition.

Understanding the tradition of abstract art sharpens our experience of what we are seeing. The idea that you need to learn about abstract art to enjoy it strikes some primal nerve, arousing our anxiety about authentic versus fake experience. It offends the know-nothings, who fall back on: "I don't know art, but I know what I like." But this cliché flies in the face of our common sense awareness, reinforced a thousand times in our life, that some of the most deep-seated pleasures of our natural selves—from sex and food on up to music—involve appetites that had to be educated. If these pleasures are rooted in crude instinct, we acquire hierarchies of discrimination, until second nature is nowhere separable from the first. Yet visual art—and abstract art most particularly—remains one of the last bastions of unashamed, unrepentant ignorance, where educated experience can still be equated with phony experience. In regard to abstract art, this syndrome becomes ever more acute as the tradition gets fatter and the works get leaner. What we see gets simpler, and what we can bring to it gets more complex. So we are constantly worried that we are being played for fools by works like Flavin's sculpture or Marden's painting. What makes the anxiety even worse is the fact that this is an art that, by its very nature, willfully and knowingly flirts with absurdity and emptiness, dancing on the knife edge of nonsense and beckoning us to come along.

Why put up with it? Because we want what only this risk has been able to give us. Of course, what we want from many of the forms of our culture is comfort and continuity, a sense of connection to enduring traditions, a respite from the relentless clocks that drive our individual lives. But, in modern society, we also live with a sharply ambivalent, painfully keen awareness that our lives are irremediably different from those of the past. We rise each day to a particular mix of sharpened pleasures and deepened anxieties that quickens our sense of separation from other days—a century ago, a decade ago, two years ago. This arouses in many of us a hunger for a culture that affirms this sensation, by giving us new forms that give shape to *our* feelings, *our* moment in history—as distinct from the feelings of our forebears, even of our youth. We torment (and flatter) ourselves with the belief that it has not all been said, that life as we live it is more complex than has until now been articulated. And in order to allow room for the new cultural forms we feel might be adequate to this vivifying hubris and doubt, we are willing to accept the destruction of past cherished norms, to endure large measures of disorientation in the present, and to sift through a great deal of dreck.

Abstract art is propelled by this hope and hunger. It reflects the urge to push toward the limit, to colonize the borderland around the opening onto nothingness, where the land has not been settled, where the new can emerge. That is part of what drives modernity: the urge to regenerate ourselves by bathing in the extreme, for better and for worse. What is remarkable is that abstract art, which was initially advanced by its advocates as a culture of crypto-religious, timeless certainties, associated closely with the new monolithic collectivism in society, should have been reinvented and flourished the last fifty years as a paradigmatic example of secular diversity, individual initiative, and private vision. It is a prime case of modern Western society's willingness to vest the fate of its communal culture in the play of independent subjectivities, and to accept the permanent uncertainties, pluralities, and never-ending, irresolvable debate that come with that territory.

Notes

1. William Hazlitt, *Complete Works. Centenary Edition*, ed. P.P. Howe (London: J.M. Dent and Songs, Ltd., 1930–35), 18:95.

We here allude particularly to Turner, the ablest landscape-painter now living, whose pictures are however too much abstractions of aerial perspective, and representations not properly of the objects of nature as of the medium through which they were seen. … They are pictures of the elements of air, earth, and water. The artist delights to go back to the first chaos of the world, or to that state of things when the waters were separated from the dry land, and light from darkness, but as yet no living thing nor tree bearing fruit was seen upon the face of the earth. All is without form and void. Someone said of his landscapes that they were like pictures of nothing, and very like.

It should be noted that this was written in 1916, when Turner exhibited *The Temple of Jupiter Panellenius*.

2. Ernst Gombrich, *Art and Illusion*, 2nd ed. (Princeton, NJ: Princeton University Press, 1961), 33.

3. Donald Judd, "Specific Objects," *Arts Yearbook* 8 (1965), 74–82; reprinted in *Donald Judd, Complete Writings, 1959–1975* (Halifax: Press of the Nova Scotia College of Art and Design; and New York: New York University Press, 1975), 181–189.

4. Pollock's remarks were captured in Dorothy Seiberling's notes for her profile of Pollock in the August 8, 1949, issue of *Life* magazine. Seiberling's unpublished notes are cited in Steven Naifeh and Gregory White Smith, *Jackson Pollock: An American Saga* (New York: Clarkson N. Potter, 1989), 591.

5. In "Notes on Sculpture, Part 2," originally published in *Artforum* (October 1966), and reprinted in Gregory Battcock, ed., *Minimal Art: A Critical Anthology* (New York: E.P. Dutton, 1968), 232, Morris writes that: "The better new work takes relationships out of the work and makes them a function of space, light, and the viewer's field of vision."

Tim Griffin

Editor's Letter

Artforum, vol. 42, no. 2, October 2003

It is subject to debate whether an art publication, or any other entity, can today offer a generative platform for the formation of a public sphere within which contemporary artistic production may be considered. But the terms of that debate—still resonant for practices engaging with politics and social representation, as well as with modes of appropriation in light of evolving mass media and attendant commercial forces—provided the substance for the following editorial statement in Artforum International. *This text appeared in* Artforum's *October 2003 issue, when the publication came under new editorial direction. It has been slightly modified for inclusion in this volume.*

Less than a week before "putting to bed" the second half of *Artforum*'s two-volume look back on the '80s, organized by my predecessor, Jack Bankowsky, I found myself seated across from sculptor Haim Steinbach at a Brooklyn kitchen table, a late winter light waning on the running tape recorder and half-finished plate of marzipan between us. Our interview had already lasted a couple of hours, and we had reached the kind of conversational pause that usually precedes a conclusion. But then Steinbach said something that caught me completely off-guard: "There seemed to be a reevaluation happening [in the '80s]. But the discourse did not really challenge participants to try to figure out what was going on—actually, there was no discourse."

Of course, Steinbach's version may not ring true to many of the period's active participants. Yet his implied desire (even hunger) for a venue to stimulate critical conversation among individuals with diverging artistic practices recalled the hunger I felt throughout the '90s and still feel today, when the languages of art seep ever more deeply into the tissue of mass culture. Information-based industries knowingly re-purpose the art-historical lessons of dematerialized objects. ("You see coffee," reads one recent Sprint ad featuring the image of a single steaming cup. "We see data.") Even something so intangible as emotion is today fully acknowledged in the business pages as a source of value, with products designed to transform living into lifestyle as part of the "experience economy." (Consider "blue" becoming the more leisurely "Bondi Blue," named after an Australian beach, in iMac coloration.) While one predominant theme of technology is ever more precise and pervasive control—which pertains to everything from subtle contouring on automobiles to genetic engineering and surveillance techniques—another is the mutability of perception. Extending the idea that depictions of space are determined by material (a trope of midcentury modernism), technology provides novel encounters with space and calibrates our experiences with traditional materials anew. In fact, the emergence of new media underscores the urgency of art-critical interest in medium specificity. (Even such a colloquial phenomenon as the rise of moblogs, for instance, might through its ephemeral yet—by virtue of their perpetual electronic relaying—fundamentally additive character shed a provocative light on our thinking about photography, especially in regard to this medium's changed relationship to the indexical.)

All these subjects give dramatic cause for discussion. Artistic discourse, as an interrogatory realm for emotions and ideas, provides the perfect analytical lens through which to consider developments in contemporary culture; and, in turn, looking back through culture compellingly illuminates questions long important to artists, art historians, and critics. This discourse must engage culture strategically in order to make art matter, to underline the gravity of contemporary problems such as the mass media's relationship with art, criticism's relationship with artistic practice, connoisseurship versus cultural studies, collectives versus institutions, emergent globalism versus identity politics and ethnicity, and simulation versus psychology.

Obviously, there will be failures in any attempted exchange—fragmentation, incompatibility, even intransigent opposition. One need only turn to scholar Jonathan Gilmore's recent discussion of *Art History After Modernism* (2003), the latest volume by the German art historian and theorist Hans Belting, to gain a baseline sense of the challenges for critical dialogue today: "Art history ... must be defined so disjunctively that it often isn't clear whether there is anything on which feminists, poststructuralists, social historians of art, queer theorists, iconographers, connoisseurs, and so on might agree such that their disagreements could offer a productive exchange."

There are nevertheless models to engage. Considering, for example, feminist theory's influence on recent and contemporary art practices, curator Catherine de Zegher has cited the growing prominence of artists who are posing "questions of audience and distribution ... making art imbued with thoughtful reciprocity between artist and viewer." (In this vein, de Zegher's further mention of "partial subjects co-emerging and co-affecting" is apt when considering how disparate entities may resonate with each other today and yet remain resolutely themselves.) The tactical interplay she notes sounds among many other voices in contemporary art. In this particular issue of *Artforum*, Collier Schorr's discussion of photography and desire—as well as her reading of Richard Prince's *Spiritual America*, 1983, through the prism of media critiques of the '70s and '80s (specifically, she describes how the conveying and experience of male desire may be mediated by feminist and postfeminist theory)—resonates with Prince's fictional screenplay treatment "In My Movie." [Writing for the magazine, Prince here made himself a character operating on the same narrative plane as Kate Moss, whom he had recently photographed in a nurse uniform for the fashion publication W; the artist's text appeared alongside images of his then-new Nurse paintings.—*Ed.*] The dynamic of exchange reverberates within the still-developing oeuvre of cover artist Roe Ethridge, who reasserts the discrete values of typologies within photography only to revel in their unmooring: their placement in a system activated by a millennial marriage of German typological and Pictures-generation photography. Seen in the greater context of artistic production today, his artistic move articulates a recurring theme of abstraction among artists—of revisiting now-established categories, from photographic genres to feminism (and perhaps even "art"), only to see their value evacuated or transposed, at the risk of leaving the original form an empty shell. For me, what critic Kate Bush has called "postappropriation" in his practice is indicative of the shifting of terms inflected by new technology, when one era, shaped by mechanical reproduction, gives way to another, shaped by replication, with all its attendant metaphors.

The pervasiveness of fragmentation and abstraction in today's art and discourse perhaps signals that resolution is not an appropriate goal for this historical moment. I am reminded of a passage from Jean Genet, in which the author describes the practice of Japanese vase makers who, on encountering a flaw in the object before them, allow their work to both emanate and evolve from that imperfection. *Artforum* will explore and uncover (and inevitably produce) any number of such liminal flaws, both in art and its culture, and will migrate to them as the places from which new dialogue is most likely to unfold—and where pleasure promises to be the payoff. In fact, pleasure might arise most clearly from happy coincidences and correspondences: Genet's vase makers find an interesting correspondent in the characters of Prince's "In My Movie," who play a round of poker called "accidentally on purpose," a phrase that, in turn, describes Ethridge's cover image of a bird in flight. The bird seems randomly caught in motion—and yet the simple image is only arrived at through an elaborate technique. Indeed, the bird itself is more than it seems, having been taught to perform for various films and rumored to have been trained by the same handler who worked on Alfred Hitchcock's *The Birds*. This knowledge, there to be found just beneath the surface, creates a rich, unexpected tension that should always find its way into these pages—from this issue, my first as editor, forward—and into the broader engagements of art.

Ralph Rugoff

Circling the Center

From *Overlook: Exploring the Internal Fringes of America with the Center for Land Use Interpretation* (New York: Metropolis Books, 2006)

The Center for Land Use Interpretation is one of the most intelligently provocative organizations that I have ever had the good fortune to encounter. What exactly it is up to is another matter, but before I wade into the muddy waters of speculation regarding the Center's possible functions—which are not at all obvious—a few facts are in order. The Center is a nonprofit educational organization that examines how we use, envision, and think about different kinds of landscapes in the United States. A few individuals from different backgrounds who nonetheless had come to think and work in similar ways founded the Center in 1994 in Oakland, California. Operating out of a rickety office along that city's industrial waterfront, they began presenting exhibits that examined areas where the man-made, the cultural, and the natural seemed to merge. They also conducted tours focusing on little-observed features of the surrounding urban area, and installed interpretive plaques commemorating unusual types of land use (such as one marking a site in New Mexico where in 1957 a hydrogen bomb hit the ground after having been accidentally dropped from an airplane).

Audiences for these initial programs were small, but that was of little consequence. What mattered was that the Center was inventing, piece by piece, a new type of institution: a grassroots clearinghouse that presented documentation of the curious, astonishing, and sometimes alarming transformations of the contemporary American landscape. Looking at material that was off the radar of both the mass media and mainstream academia, the Center's programs addressed not only the way that land is used, but also how it is perceived. To a certain extent, even, it could be said that its real subject is how we look at, and conceptualize, the world around us (but more on that later).

I first picked up on the Center in 1996 after it had relocated to Los Angeles, opening a small office next to another unique organization, the Museum of Jurassic Technology. The Center's exhibits in its new home c ontinued to look at aspects of how the country's lands are used and perceived, examining an eclectic array of sites ranging from field-test facilities for high-impact tech-nologies to sites of "geo-transformative" activity undertaken by government agencies. Among other memorable exhibits from those days were a display of aerial photographs of open-pit mines, shot as a hobby by a retired mining engineer, that were disconcertingly beautiful, and a screening program featuring films of nuclear testing programs of the world's declared nuclear powers (which was a study of different cultural approaches to propaganda as much as it was about perspectives on land use).

Over the years, the Center's exhibits and publications have been remarkably astute, noteworthy not only for illuminating our understanding of mundane as well as extraordinary landscapes, but also for their evenhanded and lucid exposition. Even when describing odd, disturbing, or even potentially humorous phenomena, the tenor of these presentations is never dramatic or self-conscious. Texts tend to be straightforward and factually oriented, while the Center's photographs typically resemble the seemingly authorless images compiled in government and industrial archives (though, for the most part, these photographs are produced by the Center's extended family of volunteers). In their tone, at least, these programs conjure the work of a benevolent social science agency or think tank, or perhaps a forward-looking research division of the US Army Corps of Engineers. (The Center's name likewise suggests some such bureaucratic organization.) And as it has grown over the past decade, this organization has in many very real ways come to resemble a public research institute, developing an impressive array of databases, libraries, and archives as well as far-flung "research training stations" and myriad outreach programs.

Yet unlike its institutional counterparts, the Center has remained curiously unmoored from any recognizable policy platform. Its programs —as far as I can discern—reveal no overt or even implicit political or social agenda. Indeed, whether documenting nuclear proving grounds or the architecture of show caves (subterranean caverns that have been decorated and turned into tourist attractions), its exhibitions and publications are always disarmingly—at times, almost unnervingly—free of any editorial viewpoint. They are equally detached from the positions of environmental politics as from those of the military or commercial industry.

But if this organization is not trying to sell us an ideological bag of goods, what purpose(s) could possibly be motivating its public exploration of how land is used and apportioned in the United States? It is not only the more cynical among us who may regard the Center's ostensible neutrality, its flagrant nonpartisanship, as slightly suspicious as well as provocative. Its nonjudgmental attitude goes against the grain of our expectations, especially when it is applied to contentious subjects like nuclear weapons testing or stripmining, which we are accustomed to considering within an explicitly political or moral framework.

This conspicuous absence of editorial slant is paralleled by the expansive—almost indiscriminate—selection of criteria used by the Center in choosing subjects for its exhibitions and publications. Besides reportage on such topics as shipping channels, defense installations, and aspects of urban infrastructure, the Center's purview embraces less straightforward phenomena: underwater towns created by dam-produced floods; fictionalized spaces ranging from movie set locations to civilian emergency training sites where lifesize props simulate toxic fuel spills and collapsing buildings; and the alternative universe of the Nellis Range, a five-thousand-square-mile area of military-controlled terrain in Nevada, which since 1940 has been a virtual nation unto itself, a kind of time capsule cut off from the rest of American society. Significantly, the Center treats all these diverse subjects in an identical manner, assigning no more weight to an exhibit on anti-terrorist barricades than to one looking at period travel postcards. Within the broadly defined field of "land use interpretation," they are all comparably noteworthy.

In this way the Center's programs deliberately bypass the familiar categories and classifications that we rely on in making sense of the world.

A very curious effect results from this benignly subversive approach: we may end up looking at one place or activity through a lens we normally reserve for evaluating another. By treating a nuclear test site in the same manner as an outdoor sculpture, for instance, the Center's exhibits gently prompt us to reconsider the sculpture as possible waste while appreciating the aesthetic value of the radioactive hole (think of it as a type of vast earthwork). In engineering this subtle shift, the Center introduces us to a landscape of uncertainty where our ready-made convictions and judgments lose their traction. But it undermines our assumptions in a very generous manner, encouraging us to look at things from more than one perspective and alerting us to other ways of understanding that can renew our interest in the larger landscape.

From another point of view, of course, it can be argued that the Center's apparent lack of editorial bias is itself a kind of editorial stance—though one directed not against any particular issue so much as the fallibility of our knowledge in general. Indeed, a tonic trace of skepticism runs just beneath the surface of many of the Center's activities, including its archival projects that involve ordering mountains of information so they can be productively mined. Yet even while it divides this material into categories and subcategories, indexing it with keywords and cross-references, the Center seems to subtly acknowledge that its own ordering system is inevitably flawed—that to arbitrarily classify things and place them in conceptual cubbyholes involves cutting them off from the continuum of existence.

In contrast to our culture of experts—the pundits, academics, and government analysts who regularly appear in the media to tell us what to think—the Center is a haven of amateur agnostics. Its members are specialists who specialize in nonspecialization. Their approach is not so much multidisciplinary as nondisciplinary: it traces out an underlying logic that connects disparate fields and perspectives, linking them to the common ground of land use and its interpretation. And on one level, at least, it speaks to a desire to transcend the increasingly differentiated, specialized, and disconnected worlds of science, commerce, culture, and politics.

To a certain extent, I think of the Center as a type of informational test site or lab where different models of presenting data are tried out and developed. In the process, its far-ranging programs have also charted an alternative map of the United States. Filling in blank spots in our collective perceptual field, they call attention to neglected, overlooked, and often highly telling aspects of the American landscape. And once exposed to this information, our everyday picture of the world around us—and our sense of our role in it—can never be the same again. Yet the specifics of how our perspective may change is something that each visitor works out on his or her own. The Center is not interested in lobbying us for a particular point of view or trying to mold our opinions. It simply suggests that things might be different than we had previously thought.

In other words, the Center never pretends to have all the answers. Instead, its programs suggest that answers often come in the form of questions, and as the result of finding the common ground beneath the middle of an apparent conflict. That conflict may be one of values. Many of the Center's projects emphasize the contradictory qualities of a given subject: a suburban landscape that is at once banal and melodramatic, an industrial harbor that is simultaneously unsightly and sublime. If the Center has a function—and I am not at all sure it does, at least not in any conventional sense—it might have something to do with recognizing and celebrating this kind of paradoxical perspective, and with disseminating the idea that truth exists only in conditions of contradiction.

Yet I suspect that the Center, however indirectly, also functions as an agent of intelligent change, possibly even revolutionary change. Its politics are oblique, of course, and it may be that they are most conspicuous in terms of the Center's decentralized organizational model. A largely volunteer outfit with contributors from across the country, independently researching and investigating and producing new materials about land use and its interpretation, the Center has continued to develop in unpredictable directions (I long ago lost track of how many desert research outposts, interpretative stations, and regional offices it has opened around the country). Distributing the fruits of this open-source research in myriad forms (including its excellent Web site and printed newsletter, *The Lay of the Land*), the Center eschews any central voice of authority. It presents no master narrative that demands an exclusive path of action. Its politics, if they can be described in such terms, are indirect and elusive. They evade conventional forms by refusing to embrace recognizable "positions"—positions that easily become reified postures that can be targeted and dismissed. Embracing a post-protest ethic that moves beyond simple binary oppositions, the Center sets out to reframe the nature of debate itself. Its work confronts contradiction and gray areas, prompting us to question the points of balance in our existing notions about land use and to grapple with the daunting complexities and scenarios of contemporary landscapes. It presents opportunities for opening up new avenues of knowledge rather than reinforcing ready-made conclusions. Needless to say, the question of land use is an area of increasing concern, and I imagine that the future impact of this organization's work will grow exponentially in the years ahead. Of course, what we do with the awareness it provokes is up to each of us in the end, but on its own the Center is already evolving tools that can transform the way we think—not only about politics, but about the very ground beneath us all.

Matt Wolf

New Live Queer Art

LTTR 3, 2004

It's June 2003 at the Fez Café in New York City and drag king Murray Hill is hosting the annual Miss Lower East Side Beauty Pageant. A panel of downtown personalities is judging the competitive event by collectively rating the contestants' fashion, poise, and talent routines. Artist and *LTTR* coeditor Emily Roysdon takes the stage to compete not as an individual model, but as *LTTR* incorporated. Dressed in a grandma-chic floral jumper and too-big high heels, she rambles with slurred speech and begins her routine for the talent competition. Immediately, the crowd is silent—save for a few murmured "what the fuck"s—as they watch Roysdon reenact artist Carolee Schneeman's legendary performance *Interior Scroll* (1975). Liberally tracing Schneeman's footsteps, Roysdon unrolls a paper scroll from her vagina and she recites its contents: her self-authored text, "democracy, invisibility, and the dramatic arts," which first appeared in *LTTR*.

In the original performance, Schneeman unrolled the scroll like an umbilical cord and she proceeded to read criticism about her artwork's "personal clutter" and its "persistence of feeling." As feminist critic Lucy Lippard described, Schneeman read "the inside story from a woman's body."[1] The audacious, liberated strategy of embodiment poignantly dramatized the experience of dismissal and dilemmas about formal mastery and failure. Although *Interior Scroll* became the icon of 1970s feminist art, queer critics later questioned if any one artwork or "inside story" can sufficiently explain our bodies.

Roysdon's performance offered a different generational point of view by redoing Schneeman's historically canonized art in a club context. This seems indicative of many new queer art projects by predominantly young artists who possess a sharp generational self-reflexivity. These performers and producers traverse subcultural, academic, and high-art references with remarkable ease and a keen sense of their historical precursors.

The following ephemeral, temporary, or performance art projects developed alongside recent cultural moments or social phenomena. Queer culture always creatively defines itself, lately against the grain of media frenzy and mainstream political debates. As a result, new live artists make queer social spaces and conceptual scenarios in which we can pause for a moment and begin to make sense of all this material.

* * *

Grrrl love = Grrrl power, or so the saying went among young punk feminists in the early nineties. By November 1992, Riot Grrrl had hit the mainstream. The movement was prominently featured in a *Newsweek* article about "a sassy new breed of feminists for the MTV age."[2] By that point, many of the Riot Grrrl founders and leaders grumbled angrily about the media's misrepresentation of the movement, and the forgotten politics that originally inspired a national network of girl-punk organizations. Loosely or perhaps ambivalently modeled after seventies consciousness-raising feminist groups, Riot Grrrls, often in high school or in their early twenties, traded zines, made music, and talked about sexism, abuse, racism, and punk rock. The Riot Grrrl movement began informally in Washington D.C. and Olympia, specifically with the bands Bikini Kill and Bratmobile. Girl fans and friends followed by starting their own bands and making xeroxed zines with personally charged and politically evocative rants, which grrrls traded through a grassroots peer network.

Many Riot Grrrls felt that the mainstream media coverage over-hyped an "angry girl" cliché, falsely elevating rock star Courtney Love as their patron saint. Riot Grrrls adopted a bold fashion with baby boll dresses and cat-eye glasses, and many would write slurs like "slut," "bitch," or "rape" with black markers on their arms and bodies. These subcultural gestures and styles, much like the pointed emphasis on being "grrrls" rather than women, aggressively repossessed sexist labels and exorcized patriarchy. As a result, the imitable fashion attracted a second generation of even younger Riot Grrrls, who read about the revolution in *Seventeen*, *Sassy*, *Glamour*, and *Rolling Stone* magazines. Perhaps partially divorced from the politically sighted, revolutionary claims of the early Riot Grrrls, younger participants nonetheless cultivated a far-reaching feminist peer community with a powerful network to distribute women's music, writing, and art.

So when the Spice Girls claimed "Girl Power" as the global pop mantra for pre-teens in the late nineties, many believed that the Riot Grrrl movement had sufficiently lost its steam. Indeed the unique style and language of Riot Grrrls had informed many vacuous pop correlatives like Lisa Loeb's Gen-X anthems, or Baby Spice's powder-blue velour jump suits. Certainly an attempt to cursorily narrate a Riot Grrrl history inheres in the reductive traps of the *Newsweek* and glossy-magazine articles. But the Riot Grrrl music and aesthetics, not to mention contemporaneous queercore bands from the nineties, left a lasting impression.

In 1998, Kathleen Hanna, who was reluctantly dubbed the spokes-person for Riot Grrrls, formed the band Le Tigre with queer video artist Sadie Benning and zine producer Johanna Fateman. The band brilliantly blended a feminist punk sensibility with electro-pop keyboards and samples. Le Tigre would show slides during songs like "Hot Topic," which pays homage to feminist and queer artists, activists, musicians, and intellectuals. Their aesthetic was decisively lo-fi, with a signature pastel color palette in accompanying art. JD Samson of Dykes Can Dance joined Le Tigre, and the band collaboratively produced and commissioned a series of videos to accompany live performances of songs from their album *Feminist Sweepstakes*.

As digital video equipment and editing software became increasingly accessible to consumers in the nineties, a new generation of artists and musicians started producing video art that sampled the television and pop culture saturating our daily lives. At the same time, the gallery art world finally accepted video art as a viable commercial entity, and video installations, sometimes with the production values and scale of feature films, began filling galleries. Many gallery artists engaged in performance-art strategies, which were slickly represented in large-scale photographs and looping DVDs. Although pop stars had incorporated multimedia into arena concerts for years, independent and punk rock bands, particularly in the queer underground, began integrating video into their acts to re-imagine the rock show as a visual performance.

The Ssion (pronounced "shun") from Kansas City, Missouri, performs a punk rock, high-school-style musical theater spearheaded by artist and musician Cody Critcheloe, with backup singers Taylor Painter-Wolfe a nd Shannon Michaels. Critcheloe's intricate animated videos, with hand-drawn collages and lyrics, screen behind the band like motivational karaoke. They were dressed as a chicken, cow, and lion with giant exposed genitalia, in sync with the videos, while using their cardboard instruments, props, and scenery for added effect. In early performances, the Ssion took on gender politics with literally cartoonish irreverence. For "I Got AIDS Off a Toilet Seat," Cody drew a caricature of himself with dancing women's legs, which rhythmically tic-toc to the beat of the song. When animated Cody enters the "Lil' Gay Bar," blood squirts from his eyes, ears, and crotch, followed by a set of disembodied cocks, which proceed to squirt more blood over the bar, its toilets, leather daddies, punk twinks, and Cody. In the song and video "Anorexia Rules, Ok!" the Ssion performs with an animated chorus of suffragettes. The cartoon feminists raise their picket signs and sing the mantra, "we want it all ... we want what's just begun," followed by the lyrics, "Keep your fingers crossed, and keep your legs spread ... Anorexia Rules, Ok!" The song and visual performance broach the sensitive subject of eating disorders—a vital topic among Riot Grrrls —by expressing with acidic enthusiasm a sense of personal and political anxiety or failure. In other performance videos Cody incorporates cartoon caricatures of Kathleen Hanna and Courtney Love to indulge a budding Gen-X nostalgia with tongue-in-cheek, albeit affectionate, post-Riot Grrrl parody. The Ssion trade the revolutionary scope and lyrics from the Riot Grrrl heyday for dark humor, crass queer star-fucking, and summer-stock theatrics.

In the band Tracy and the Plastics, artist Wynne Greenwood literally talks to herself. Part living-room band practice, part one-woman video play, Greenwood embodies the character Tracy and sings electro-punk riddles in front of a small video projection, along with her avatar bandmates Nikki and Cola (aka the Plastics). The virtual band of three is really just Greenwood, who appears on stage as Tracy and simultaneously in the low-tech videos as both Nikki and Cola. During inter-song skits, Tracy's argumentative alter egos talk back to her, forcing Greenwood to look at her pre-recorded image, while shifting between personas on screen with crooked platinum wigs and slight wardrobe transformations. Tracy negotiates a fragmented lesbian personality that draws from conflicting cultural and social spaces and voices. Greenwood recounts "Nikki [asking] Cola why she puts socks down her pants—to look like a dick or a third dimension? Cola turns to me, Tracy, and asks my advice. 'I don't put socks down my pants,' I say. Cola says she does it to look more real. There's a history, a reality created by the interaction between the self and the image of the self."[3] These conversations recall seventies performance artist Joan Jonas's preoccupation with media technology and female psychology, particularly in the video *Vertical Roll* (1972). Jonas makes a compact physical space by purposefully generating a television technical malfunction, in which her costumed figure persistently gets wiped on and off the screen. In other works, Jonas relates the theatrical space of her live performances to the virtual space of electronic media. Much like Greenwood, Jonas performs an enigmatic mythology with costumes and gestures in a televisual environment.

During Greenwood's video concerts, she always plans beats during which she addresses the audience and requests their participation. In her essay "CAN YOU PAUSE THAT FOR A SECOND ... and let yourself groove" Greenwood writes, "When I'm on stage as Tracy, I often doubt my relationship to my audience so when I pause my video during a performance I say, 'What's up?' I say, 'What do you want to say to me? What are we doing here? Together.'"[4] Greenwood reprograms relations between the audience, performer, and her screen in a continuous flow of feedback and interference. The deliberate technical difficulties (exaggerated stutters and awkward silences) in a Tracy and the Plastics concert retard the temporality of the "live" show to simulate what Greenwood considers to be the political space of a video pause. In that discreet moment of control when Greenwood halts the video image and music, she finds an entry-point for participation in media, despite the pervasive realities of surveillance, vacuous static, and commercial noise. Wynne addresses the audience as a queer-feminist community and she asks them to rearrange our world until it's "how we want it."

Greenwood writes, "I'm spitting out these word bones. Stuttering out these quickly glued-together phrases and half-thoughts."[4] In poetically cryptic lyrics, Tracy relays sometimes private but often convincing messages: "We'll have to knit or stitch a claw... we'll have to drop the guns to draw."[5] When Tracy talks to herself on stage, she negotiates the creative conflicts with the collaborating Plastics (herself), and she also dramatizes the inevitable psychic fractures for a multifaceted lesbian identity, which exists in an exclusionary popular culture. Hence Greenwood is constantly reconstructing her message or "the band" with a unique video language. She samples the dominant culture and makes its missing images, suturing extreme close-up details from suburban carpet and upholstery with appropriated television shots from women's golf tournaments. Sometimes she's in imaginary spaces and landscapes, rendered in blunt monochromatic colors or with digital abstraction. But at any given moment, Tracy might hit the pause button to interrupt the alluring score and steady stream of visual imagery. She'll ask you to stop and to let yourself groove.

* * *

Drag performance artist Vaginal Cream Davis recently adopted as her newest stage name, Ada Smith, the black Vaudevillian nightclub owner whose 1920s-era Parisian club, Bricktop, hosted some of the best entertainment for intoxicated expatriates and cabaret enthusiasts. Cabaret performance became wildly popular in Europe following World War I, particularly in Germany, where the Weimar government dissolved most forms of censorship.[6] Berlin clubs in the 1930s boasted satirical routines, transvestitism, and general debauchery with a sociopolitical edge. While American cabaret lacked the intellectual ambition of its European predecessors, mob-style speakeasies in the heyday of prohibition hosted glamorous and clandestine entertainment with alcohol. Cabarets were a unique space for otherwise rare inter-class, -race, and -gender socializing. In the post-Stonewall 1970s, the nascent gay culture sought its own types of entertainment. Cabaret became a vital form of performance in bathhouses, where gay men had public and anonymous sex. Bette Midler famously began her career performing for towel-wearing mixed gay and straight crowds at the gay Ansonia Baths on Broadway in New York City.

Now Davis's regular Friday-night Bricktop event at the Parlour Club in the Russian Quarter of West Hollywood, California, draws a genuinely mixed crowd of postpunk fags, heterosexual flappers, LA lesbians, and the occasional celebrity. Recreating an amalgamation of Weimar Berlin, Paris café culture, and downtown New York bohemia, Bricktop presents Davis's multimedia monologue-scats, plus eclectic guest performances that often pay tribute to esoteric personalities from the Jazz Age. Targeting "literate clubgoers sick of the corporate careerist vulturism and youth-culture myopia that plagues the tired and stagnant LA club scene,"[7] Bricktop does salvage cabaret with a fair dose of parodic kitsch. Davis's weekly event is steeped in admiration for the historic "lost generation" and for the vital intelligentsia fringe, which these expatriates cultivated.

For decades now, Vaginal Cream Davis's prolific suitcase of performance personalities, concept bands, tell-all diaries, and guest-star appearances have mixed up the LA punk scene. The six-foot-six veteran paved the way for a younger generation of performance artists, like Wynne Greenwood, who utilize the sounds, styles, and venues of punk culture for something radically different. Davis published an infamous zine called *Fertile LaToya Jackson* in the 1990s, which queersploitation filmmaker Bruce LaBruce called "an underground rag that featured SoCal punk scene gossip, photos of hot Huntington Beach surfers and wistful musings by Miss Davis herself, gregarious gossipeuse and poetess extraordinaire."[8] The name Vaginal Cream Davis was inspired by radical black activist and media personality-*cum*-professor Angela Davis. By sampling (and in turn parodying) various subcultural and mainstream personalities, aesthetics, and clichés, Davis cultivates an entertaining militancy, which assaults the conventional tropes of camp sentimentality.

Davis's interest in Black Power inspired the 1980s *a capella* performance group Vaginal and the Afro Sisters. Davis and her backup ensemble of white girls in Afro wigs did the show "We're Taking Over," which portrayed the "Sexuales Liberation Front," whose mission was to kidnap the heads of white corporate America and to "put big black dildos up their lily white buttholes and hold them for ransom."[9] Davis also drew inspiration from her Chicana heritage with the band ¡Cholita! (billed as the female Menudo), which performed Latin pop music on a cassette album that obtained a modest cult following. Other theatrical personalities have included the Chicana gang member Graciela Grejalba, a white supremacist named Clarence, street preacher Rev. St. Salicia Tate, and diva character Voodoo Williams, fashioned as the doña of dance.[10]

José Muñoz's book *Disidentifications* discusses Davis's performance as an alternative to the nineties "multiplex" drag in films like *To Wong Foo, Thanks for Everything! Julie Newmar*, *Priscilla Queen of the Desert*, and *The Bird Cage*, or Ru Paul's tenure as a talk show host on VH1. Muñoz writes, "Commercial drag presents a sanitized and desexualized queer subject for mass consumption. Such drag represents a certain strand of integrationist liberal pluralism. The sanitized queen is meant to be enjoyed as an entertainer who will hopefully lead to social understanding and tolerance."[10] Muñoz distinguishes Davis's countercultural style of gender play as "terrorist drag" for its unrelenting cultural critique and "ground-level guerrilla representational [strategy that portrays] some of the nation's most salient popular fantasies." As white supremacist Clarence in the performance "The White to be Angry," Davis inverted racist blackface Sambo or minstrel caricatures into an aggressively fetishistic ultra-white, ultra-right-wing heterosexual drag. Davis as Clarence injects the seeds of racial politics into the dominantly and ambivalently white punk subculture. Instead of using the conventional first-person rhetoric of identity, Davis mocks and performs its extremist versions in a subversively combative form of cabaret drag.

* * *

In 1999, police and firefighters started arriving unannounced at New York City nightclubs to inspect for illicit drug use, but, more importantly, for unlicensed dancing. Causing alarmingly literal pre-Stonewall déjà vu, DJs and club owners switched the music off and the crowds froze during police raids.[11] When New York City Mayor Giuliani resurrected the 1926 "cabaret law," unlicensed bars were subject to massive fines and even padlocks if their patrons were caught illegally dancing. Framed as a safety issue by the city government, clubs were required to make expensive upgrades to sprinkler and fire-alarm systems and to face a mammoth city bureaucracy in order to obtain a cabaret license. The queer performance venue the Slipper Room, which hosts DJs and burlesque performances, including drag king Murray Hill, was a prime example of an underground club targeted by these new standards. In the spring of 2001, the Slipper Room received its first ticket for illegal dancing, which resulted in a $150 fine. All was resolved for one year, until the club was randomly inspected on a Thursday evening, quickly padlocked for cabaret violation, and issued a lethal $30,000 ticket. The Slipper Room hired famous civil liberties attorney Norman Siegel, a pro-dance ally, who successfully got the charges dropped by the Department of Consumer Affairs.[11]

Obviously the cabaret law debates are not merely petty disputes about noise, safety, commercial zoning, or quality of life: the laws raise more worrisome flags about diminishing First Amendment rights to expression and the freedom to dance. In 1926, the cabaret laws were created in part to prevent multiracial socializing in Harlem jazz clubs. The recent revival of the law and its arbitrary implementation continued this discriminatory legacy.[6] As a logical response, artists revived public-dance theater as a form of interventionist protest. François Boué's Super-8 film *Life, Liberty, Etc. …* documents a spontaneous rave protest that occurred in Tompkins Square Park during the summer of 1999 in response to the cabaret laws. Shortly after, artists Tara Mateik, Emily Roysdon, and JD Samson formed the group Dykes Can Dance, whose manifesto promised, "… To endorse creative costuming / To combat lesbian domesticity and, even worse, bed-death / To congregate / [and] To break the law."[12]

Other new interventionist dance groups, including Free Dance Lessons in Toronto and the Chicago booty-dance protest group Pink Bloque took boom boxes to the streets. Alienated by sixties approaches to radical politics, Pink Bloque set out to make protests more visually striking and fun by appropriating the sounds, iconography, and corporate lingo from popular culture.

The Radical Cheerleaders made similar protest innovations with lefty cheers performed as punk homecoming queens. The loose-knit group began in Florida in the early nineties and spread by word-of-mouth to other activist communities around the world. Some Radical Cheerleader groups design pristine uniforms, while others cheer wholeheartedly in androgynous rags. Pink Bloque avoided the traditional slogans of activism altogether, and instead studied videos by superstar choreographer Darrin Henson, famous for "training" Britney Spears and N'Sync. The dancers made their debut at Chicago's May Day protest in 2002, an annual event for workers' rights demonstrations. Clad in pink hoodies with the attached slogan "2 cute 2B Arrested," Pink Bloque performed a boy-band-inspired routine to Donna Summer's "She Works Hard for the Money." By practicing "tactical flirting" with police officers, the dancers evaded heckling and continued grinding alongside their banner: "U.S. women earn 27–36% less than white men for the same work." Other protest dance routines have included Janet Jackson's "Nasty Boys" at the Transatlantic Business Dialogue and Mary J. Blige's "Family Affair" at Chicago's International Day Against the War.

In a more overtly hedonistic vein, the Dazzle Dancers began performing in New York nightclubs, bars, and theaters in 1993 with the simple intention of spreading a message of love and sexual freedom with purposefully amateur and baroque body slamming. They prefer to be nude while performing spastic moves, covered only in glitter and employing a low-budget-Bollywood sensibility. Toronto artist Will Munro similarly encourages people to take it all off, or, more specifically, to reveal his elaborately stitched underwear art. Munro organized a performance in a Toronto strip club in which a variety of masculine body types—from hulking bears to trannies and everything in between—wore Munro's personalized Y-front briefs in an attempt to corrupt the hygienic fetish of Calvin Klein. Far from CK whiteness, Munro uses thrift store fabrics granny-like afghan quilts and heavy-metal t-shirts as base materials to construct his underwear. Instead of the standard stripping rules, Munro collaborated with the unconventional queer models by choosing briefs that best fit the strippers' music tastes and personalities.

New York artist Lynne Chan also meticulously studied stripper protocol for her pole-dancing demonstrations at the Skowhegan visual arts residency program. Chan's performance work involves athletic mastery and comically daring showmanship. Often performing as the mutable personality J.J. Chinois, Chan cultivates a fictional fan base for Chinois's ultra-suave performances, which recently included a demolition derby competition. While working at Skowhegan, Chan visited a local strip club and found a willing mentor to teach her the complicated routines from stripper-themed films like *Showgirls*. Chan then hosted a pole-dancing seminar for fellow residents. Using the stylized charisma and homosexual extremity of Richard Simmons, these sessions had the methodical underpinnings of a group power-yoga session. The pole-dancing demonstrations present the stripping as an athletic skill that thoroughly unravels social boundaries. Chan built a temporary stage with a prominent performance pole at Skowhegan that served as a social focal point in a converted barn. During one social event, the pole catalyzed a unique dance party in which some of the most inhibited personalities called attention to their bodies by demonstrating an acquired mastery of pole-dancing techniques.

Instead of liberally exposing herself, London-based artist Oreet Ashery hides her body in intensely repressed and socially patrolled settings. Ashery regularly defies religious law when she performs as her Hasidic Jewish male alter ego, Marcus Fischer. In May 2003, Ashery went to the north of Israel for an annual religious event that celebrates the death of Rabbi Shimon Bar-Yochai, author of the "Zohar," a Kabbalistic text. Jewish tradition doesn't call for mourning during the hours before Bar-Yochai's death, but rather for intense dancing. Ashery describes the forty-eight-hour event as a religious rave with plenty of homoerotic groping. Because the sacred celebration is explicitly limited to men, Ashery surreptitiously participated in Hasidic Jewish drag—an intrusion that could have easily lead to violent repercussions. This performance intervention occurred around the same time that two suicide bombers dressed as Orthodox Jews enacted separate bombing attacks in Israel. Like Vaginal Cream Davis, Ashery engages in "terrorist drag," posing a serious security threat in politically and religiously dangerous spaces. In order to safely participate in the public dance, Ashery must "pass" as Marcus Fischer and disguise any visible indicators of her female anatomy.

* * *

In recent years, queer culture was transformed by the increasing visibility of transgender identity, shifting gender pronouns, gender-neutral names, and —perhaps most radically—with surgery. In the past few years, this new gender frontier has expanded, thanks to FTM (female-to-male) trannies, who dissolve or translate lesbian or butch codes and sensibilities into a non-normative transman, trannyfag, or androgynous identities. Transexualism was considered a disease in the past, and sex reassignment surgery (SRS) treated the supposed gender ailment.[13] The goal of "passing" typified most sex-reassignment surgery, and resonated in the familiar transsexual sentiment: "I'm a man living in a woman's body," and vice versa.

Certainly these feelings represent many transgender people's experiences. Nonetheless, the values of "gender queerness," predominantly adopted by a younger generation, involve new gender presentations that deliberately dissolve the categories of "male" or "female" altogether.
Top surgery recently became the most visible manifestation of transgender expressions. FTM trannies are now regularly opting for bilateral mastectomies (usually with no intention to receive a phalloplasty operation to construct a penis). Some trans people choose to take hormones that facilitate ongoing transformations, while others pursue no forms of body alteration at all.
The heterogeneity of gender variance makes every gender-queer body and expression different. So by mismatching and re-signifying coded feminine and masculine styles, bodies, and behaviors, gender queers engage in a project often termed "gender fucking."

Particularly for gender queers, these new modes of expression were partly informed by theoretical discussions about gender and sexuality that emerged in many liberal arts colleges and activist communities during the rise of queer studies in the nineties. Cultural theorists like Judith Butler had immeasurable impact on young feminist and queer students, who developed political and personal agendas to dissolve the theoretically termed "gender binary system." Gender queerness is a radical lifestyle—a political and body praxis. This subversive strategy of integrating critical theory and living politics also arose during the eighties and nineties when AIDS activists mixed cultural theory with political activism. Douglas Crimp's *AIDS Demographics* (1990) and the 1987 edition of the journal *October* that Crimp edited, titled "AIDS: Cultural Analysis, Cultural Activism," mix the expertise and perspectives of both activists and theorists.

Gender-queer identity both theoretically and socially transformed the lesbian community. There was increasing pressure to differentiate between butch lesbians and FTM trannies, which often provoked an unspoken schism. When trans people began widely shifting pronouns in both personal and professional settings, many queer people (not to mention the broader world) ignored or refused to acknowledge these legible indications of transgender identity. As a result, many transgender people feel pointed sensitivity and anger about mistaken or misused gender pronouns, thus splintering the queer community into the "trans-phobic" and the "trans-friendly."

In certain ways, trans experiences were expressed in many of the first-person identity-politics models adopted from discussions of race, class, gender, sexuality, etc. Additionally, many artists simply focused on body alternation as an art project in itself. Artist Tara Mateik credited his surgeon, Dr. Brownstein, in his video installation *Video Kourous* (2002). The video quite simply shows Tara's healing flat chest, adorned by his gold nameplate necklace "Tara." Tara's torso floats in and out of frame, much like Maya Deren's filmed dance sequences in her 1945 experimental film *Study in Choreography for the Camera*. Mateik uses the art-historical reference to Archaic Greek *kouroi* statues, which depict the nude bodies of boy-like soldiers. The projected image of Mateik's trans "top" locates the carved bust in a history of sculptural forms.

Mateik has also pursued quasi-biological research to find instances of gender variance in the animal kingdom. In an effort to make the often-earnest topic of transgender identity comedic, Mateik has developed a performance project about sea horses, the only fish that experiences male pregnancy. The sea horse's reproductive process begins with daily pre-dawn dances in which fish couples intertwine their tails for up to eight hours. In Mateik's project, he embodies the essentially transgender sea horse in a fish costume and choreographs a mating dance routine with his partner, who is also in sea-horse drag. Mateik has also proposed yet-to-be-realized projects that involve these performances underwater in aquariums among other marine wildlife.

Animals have long been a thematic focus for artists exploring gender nonconformity or variance. Recently artist Lynne Chan coined the term "manimal" to explain a new gender frontier. In 1976, feminist sculptor and video artist Lynda Benglis made the video narrative *The Amazing Bow Wow*. Filmed in a carnival sideshow, Benglis plays a dominatrix-style roadie who obtains and wrangles an unparalleled freak show attraction named Bow Wow—a hermaphroditic talking dog. Benglis depicted Bow Wow in a life-size dog suit with giant exposed intersex genitalia. The supremely bizarre video critiques the politics of display and the fascistic distinction between man and his "other."

Certainly artist Matthew Barney produces the most mainstream transgender-coded artwork, arguably from an overtly heterosexual point of view.

The *New York Times* proclaimed him to be "the most important artist of his generation,"[14] and his work was the subject of a recent mid-career retrospective at the Guggenheim Museum in New York. A master of hype and mythological grandiosity, Barney is best known for his prolific *Cremaster* cycle, a series of five films that incorporate allegorical performances, extravagant sculptural props, and "lavish" scenery with a sophisticated filmic language. The films generally feature Barney playing cryptically loaded roles, such as a satyr, Harry Houdini, or a ram. Interestingly, the title of the film series refers to the muscle that raises and lowers the male reproductive system according to temperature, external stimulation, or fear. During *Cremaster 3* (2002), Barney shows close-up shots of his amended genitalia with radically reformed orifices, which constitute his own imaginative species. For Barney, the crux of mythological mystery and power exists in the muscular functions of the disappearing testicles. His work usually explores hybrids of animal and human forms. In an earlier video performance, *Envelopa: Drawing Restraint 7* (1993), Barney performs as a hairless cloven-hoofed man-animal with concealed and erased genitalia.

In *Virginia Puff-Paint*, donut-hole orifices, elephantiasis snouts, ribbed-foam phallic swords, and debutante-style lace and tassels comprise the hand-stitched costumes of collaborating artists Jeremy Laing and Will Munro. The Toronto performers dress as baroquely adorned queer beasts, and they unzip, pack, and unravel their multi-layered entrails and orifices that are stitched onto pink spandex body suits. The sexual theater in *Virginia Puff-Paint* demonstrates extreme gender fucking with prolonged cycles of bestial penetration. At Zsa Zsa Gallery in Toronto, Laing and Munro installed *The Pavilion of Virginia Puff-Paint*, an elaborately constructed textile palace of fuckable furniture, including orifice-laden and phallic pillows, a pearl-trimmed commode, and a butt-plug stool. The installation also showcased a large coat-of-arms banner, from which the penetrable pillows could be hung with buttons and loops of trim. Viewers could reach inside of the *Pavilion* or peak through lace-lined glory holes for hands-on participation and voyeurism. The creatures proceed to have "sex" for an exhausting four hours by removing, untangling, and sharing their assortment of phallic cones and tactile holes. From a padded stomach cavity adjoined by a zipper seam, one beast removed a long tube of intestinal objects. These innards are made with foam shards stuffed inside of a sausage-like chain of stockings. The *Puff-Paint* partner proceeded to stick this intestinal object into its donut-shaped sequin holes, which line the chest, crotch, and bottom regions.

This curious form of mutant play uses the lacerated and malleable body to express corporeal relations that exceed human gender or sexuality. There is a horrific sense of unknown sensation during a Virginia Puff-Paint performance. Nonetheless, the artists use fussy adornments like tassel, lace, sequins, and sticky glitter that have an almost childlike (or even grandma-friendly) material sensibility. The artists' emphasis on handcrafts and ephemeral performance creates a wildly tangible sensuality. Virginia Puff-Paint's kind of imagination dissolves legible roles, positions, or bodies drawn from pornographic fantasy. Instead, the creatures combine their insides in a ritualistic form of unification.

* * *

When freshly elected San Francisco mayor Gavin Newsom began illegally issuing marriage licenses to gay couples in February 2004, hundreds of people began lining up in front of City Hall. With puffy white dresses and tuxedos, the wedding lines became international news and a striking visual representation of the political issue, which became a hot topic for competing presidential candidates. Perhaps as a result of the media coverage and the recent wave of gay television programs, queers became valuable pawns in American social-issue politics.

In 1997, Ellen DeGeneres appeared on the cover of *Time* with the cheery caption, "Yep, I'm gay." The article prefaced Ellen's coming-out episode, furthermore the first ever "outing" of a main character on a primetime sitcom. The emergence of gay television undoubtedly changed queer culture forever. The Museum of Television and Radio in New York City recently hosted the series "Not That There's Anything Wrong with That," which outlined the extensive history of gay representation on television.[15] The first known story about homosexuals appeared in a 1964 episode of *Espionage*. In 1977, Billy Crystal's character Jodie Dallas on *Soap* was the first successfully integrated gay character in a television series. Other milestones included the 1983 episode of *St. Elsewhere* in which a popular councilman was told he had AIDS in television's first representation of the epidemic. Not to forget Ryan Phillippe's 1992 appearance as the first gay teen on television in an episode of *One Life to Live*, in which Phillippe helps a priest display the AIDS quilt.

Along with gay visibility on television came slippery new standards for inclusive and "good representation." In 2001, the Los Angeles-based queer-feminist performance group Toxic Titties responded to furniture store IKEA's television commercials, which explicitly targeted domestic gay couples. The artists jumped into model bedrooms at IKEA Burbank and posed as a polyamorous gay family for faux-advertisement photographs. The revisionist pictures attempt to jilt prude images of gays, whose homogenous television depiction suggests widespread homosexual suburban malaise. Likewise artists in Chicago are planning Pilot Chicago, a four-day collaborative event in October 2004 for queer and feminist artists to spontaneously build sets, converting a giant loft space into a fully functioning do-it-yourself gay television studio. While artists now are repossessing and critiquing gay television, in the early days of media exposure the differences between positive and explicitly hostile depictions of queer people were more easily distinguished. The Gay and Lesbian Alliance Against Defamation (GLAAD) was formed in 1985 to promote and ensure fair, accurate, and inclusive representation of gay people and related news events in the media. One of GLAAD's earliest victories was persuading the *New York Times* to begin using the word "gay" instead of "homosexual" in 1987. GLAAD also ensured that Bob Hope produced a public service announcement condemning anti-gay violence after he used the word "fag" on a 1988 episode of the *Tonight Show*.

In contrast to GLAAD's tactics, AIDS activists from ACT-UP staged a more guerilla-style media intervention on January 22, 1991, on the evening before the widespread "Day of Desperation." Complementing other dramatic takeovers, including a gigantic action at Grand Central Station, activists invaded *CBS News with Dan Rather*, and for a brief second stormed in front of the newscaster and flashed (live on camera) the protest sign: "Fight AIDS, not Arabs; AIDS is news!"[16] Although present for only a few frames before crew and authorities yanked the civilian imposters, ACT-UP activists made AIDS and queer protest visible on mainstream television.

In the following years, GLAAD successfully utilized more mainstream styles of activism and PR that strategically changed aspects of popular culture. The organization was instrumental in shaping sympathetic press coverage of Matthew Shepard's murder. GLAAD became a watchdog for the gay community, and publicly criticized Elton John and Eminem's duet at the Grammy Awards. The organization's decisions about "bad" and "good" representation could not always encompass the full scope of queer political perspectives. In this respect, GLAAD's full-throttle advocacy of gay marriage alienated many queer critics of matrimony.

Whether or not marriage is a blessing or a threat to gay culture is a drained debate. The potential phenomena of gay divorce or the widespread transfer of gay ghettos from urban enclaves to suburban sprawl is perhaps more interesting. Alternative or "radical" queer people have generally been vehemently opposed to gay marriage. Viewing the institution as defunct and patriarchal, many feel that the normalizing force of gay marriage threatens the autonomy and ideals of queer culture. Toronto-based band the Hidden Cameras, a gay folk-*cum*-church-rock group, made the convincing song "Ban Marriage," which says, "And as I looked him in the eye I heard my best friend cry / That we aren't fool to fall in love but let coupledom die." The Toxic Titties also responded to gay marriage in their 2002 performance *Toxic Union*. The artists enacted the signing of their business contract in the form of a wedding ceremony at an art gallery. Reframing the marriage event as a legalistic celebration of bureaucratic arrangements, the artists formed an alternative structure for obtaining partial equity.

As the possibility of gay marriage becomes increasingly realistic and gay identity wins even more mainstream fans, many cling nostalgically to previous modes of queerness in search of a countercultural or underground authenticity. Numerous art projects mentioned here have deliberately injected perversion, obscenity, or sexuality into public performances, likely in reaction to the mostly sterile presence of gayness in popular culture. Perhaps the new generation of queers shifts from "liberated" to "post-liberated" points of view. So it's difficult to say, for example, if *Queer Eye for the Straight Guy* is neo-minstrelism for gay product placement or something actually much more subversive. The show's hosts regularly touch straight men's bodies, interfering in their most private spaces to hopefully spice things up. While the program affirms latently homophobic audiences with entertaining gay clichés, it does persistently emphasize that gay men, and their repressed or clueless straight male contemporaries, have sexuality and that they should express it. Whether or not you call this post-liberated representation good or bad, it undoubtedly has changed our society.

* * *

Queer culture will continue to form itself, even if the major networks and presidential candidates are on the job too. Modern American queer history is so nascent that we acutely focus on its temporality: our pre-histories, recent pasts, current events, and fast-changing cultural futures. We recognize every historical shift because we still can, so the rapid transfer of political and aesthetic values from one generation to the next is very visible and filled with pangs of nostalgia and optimism. These young live artists and many of their mentors set up situations, scenes, and scenarios that make us pause to consider the variety of social and political forces affecting our bodies and our lives. And right now, if one thing is for sure, gay people have got a lot going on.

Notes

1. Lucy R. Lippard, *The Pink Glass Swan* (New York: The New Press, 1995), 104.

2. Farai Chideya, Melissa Rossi, and Dogen Hannah, "Revolution Grrrl Style," *Newsweek*, November 23, 1992, 84–86. http://cerebro.cs.xu.edu/~tankgirl/twelvelittlegrrrls/articles/newsweek.html.

3. Wynne Greenwood, "Give me video, give me air," http://www.tracyandtheplastics.com/writing/videoair.htm.

4. Wynne Ryan, "CAN YOU PAUSE THAT FOR A SECOND … and let yourself groove" in *LTTR 2: listentranslatetranslate-record*, 2003.

5. Tracy and the Plastics, *Knit a Claw, Culture for Pigeon*. Troubleman Records, 2004.

6. "Cabaret 101 – Part I," http://www.musicals101.com/cabaret.htm.

7. "Vaginal Davis News and Updates," http://www.vaginaldavis.com/new.shtml.

8. Guy Trebay, "Ready to Fade Into Obscurity. Wait, He's Already There," *New York Times*, May 23, 2004.

9. Vaginal Cream Davis in José Muñoz's *Disidentifications* (Minneapolis: University of Minnesota Press, 1999), 98.

10. Ibid., 99–108.

11. Tricia Romano, "The Safety Dance." *Village Voice*, December 27, 2002. http://www.villagevoice.com/issues/0248/romano.php.

12. Tara Mateik, Emily Roysdon, and JD Samson, "Dykes Can Dance Manifesto," 2000.

13. Dean Spade discusses power and medical institutions related to transexualism in the essay "Mutilating Gender," 2000. http://www.makezine.org/mutilate.html.

14. Michael Kimmelman, "The Importance of Matthew Barney," *New York Times*, October 19, 1999.

15. "Not That There's Anything Wrong with That," Museum of Television and Radio http://www.mtr.org/exhibit/gaylesbian/index.htm.

16. "Day of Desperation Synopsis," http://www.actupny.org/diva/synDesperation.html.

Artists

Murray Hill, http://www.mrmurrayhill.com
Carolee Schneeman, http://www.caroleeschneemann.com
Le Tigre, http://www.letigreworld.com
Ssion, http://www.ssion.com
Tracy and the Plastics, http://www.toopure.com/tracyandtheplastics/
Vaginal Cream Davis, http://www.vaginaldavis.com
Joan Jonas, http://www.queensmuseum.org/exhibitions/jonas.htm
Pink Bloque, http://www.pinkbloque.org
Radical Cheerleaders, http://radcheers.tripod.com/RC
Dazzle Dancers, http://www.dazzledancers.com
Will Munro, http://www.willmunro.ca
Lynne Chan, http://www.jjchinonis.com
Oreet Ashery, http://www.foxyproduction.com/artist/view/18
Tara Mateik, http://www.taramateik.com
Lynda Benglis, http://www.eai.org
Matthew Barney, http://www.matthewbarney.com
Virginia Puff Paint, http://www.trrill.com/archives/virginia_puffpa/
Toxic Titties, http://www.freewaves.org/festival_2002/artists/toxictitties.htm
Pilot Chicago, http://www.pilotchicago.org
Hidden Cameras, http://www.musicismyboyfriend.com

Hamza Walker

Renigged

Freestyle, New York: Studio Museum in Harlem, 2001

I became black around 1987, when I suddenly had a choice in the matter. I mean, I could've become African-American. Until that point, I never realized how much I liked being simply black. I was surprised to learn that my grandfather shared similar sentiments, in fact even more vehemently than I. That year, during college spring break, I came home to find him angry about our new hyphenated designation. I had no idea Henry Brown was so down with "black." Here was a man from the era of "highballs" and Pall Malls, an easygoing, retired gent of seventy years, nary a pomaded hair out of place, visibly upset. Having been Colored, Negro, and Black, he felt entitled to protest because the rather broad line between self-determination and just being plain fickle had been crossed. Against the backdrop of a crack-cocaine epidemic, and alarming figures on the Moynihan barometer of black "well-being," "uplift of the race" through a shell-game/name-change more than ruffled the crease in this man's jeans. Initially, he suspected that the desire to be called African-American, like the transition from Negro to Black, represented yet another generational schism and that I, as a younger man than he, might be in on it, much the way my mother and father were previously adamant about being called black. I assured him that I too shared his concern about denial through pride.

In high school, I could not fail to perceive hyphenated American identities as the basis for exclusion and irresponsible behavior rather than as a genuine expression of pride. All the ballyhoo whites made about being part this, that, or the other ever really amounted to was an excuse to get drunk and offend someone—namely me—with half-baked ideas about race relations inherited from God knows where, their parents or some Norman Lear concoction. The term African-American did not conjure its corollary, Euro-American, as readily as the more specific categories Irish-, Italian-, Greek-, or German-American, strands of that monolithic narrative known as the immigrant success story. I was intuitively wary of combining a hyphenated identity with the desire for a black cultural patrimony because it blurred the incommensurability of the immigrant success story and black American history. What paved the way for this semantic merger was a reading of black history precisely as a narrative, one with a beginning, middle and successful conclusion, i.e., the civil rights movement. This reading masked the profound ambivalence of the movement's legacy and implied a sense of closure, making the term African-American unconsciously complicit in announcing the death knell of an era. As if the television show *Happy Days* (appearing in the middle of the 1970s) was not offensive enough, by the mid-1980s it seemed that on every front, whether political, social, or economic, the 1960s were being declared dead, making way for a wave of nostalgia that persists to this very moment. History was fast becoming an endless Motown special launched by the *Big Chill*, a film whose title was more ironic than anyone could've guessed. The new hyphenated designation failed to capture my own existential free fall which went well beyond any sense of tokenism. To state it more accurately, it was not that I became black, nor wanted to be black in an essentialist way, as much as I preferred at that time remaining in the black.

In 1989, an article appeared in *Newsweek* proclaiming an end to the era of integration. Given the overall socio-political climate after eight years of Ronald Reagan as president, a reneging on the "ordeal of integration" should hardly have come as a surprise. It would certainly sound impressive to my grandchildren to say my life began with the "end of an era." Yet it felt more as if a football referee, in his all-too-symbolic black-and-white striped jersey, had thrown a yellow flag and blown his whistle, declaring that my adolescence and early adult life were simply a "false start." So we had gone from post-segregation to post-integration. What happened to integration proper? I had negotiated an inferiority complex reinforced by demeaning experiences great and small, not the least of which were the daily slings and arrows of being called "Uncle Tom," "white boy" and "oreo" by my black classmates, in particular Roosevelt Drummond, aka Beau. And for what? Hardly something as intellectually romantic as DuBoisian double consciousness. A double dose of alienation was more like it. How was it that, through my parents' effort, I managed to drag my ass from the northwest side of Baltimore to a school downtown? Yet few if any of the white peers I had toward the end of college exhibited, on an interpersonal level, so little grace when it came to race.

I arrived at the doorstep of diversity very angry. I experienced multiculturalism as the sound of a door closing rather than opening. In fact, it felt as if debates about affirmative action were slamming the door shut behind me. All I really had to do to get an answer to the question that bothered me was to ask white friends how many black people they knew, really knew. Yet by and large I held my peace. Integration, thus far, had been a one-way street. I was willing to accept that fact. But I couldn't accept movies, television shows, literature (no matter how great), not to mention the ubiquitous commodifiable representations of blackness—ass-whoopin' rapper #1; the soulful, no-nonsense talk show host; the athlete; the sociologist; you name it—as a substitute for an exchange with someone other than the doorman. I was down with cultural studies as far as diversity was concerned—the sharing of values, stories, etc.—not to mention cultural studies as a form of social critique. But diversity as a lived reality was another matter altogether. As I entered the work force, I quickly learned any institution could be diverse: all they had to do was count the "greater support staff." Black and white weren't talking to one another. We were talking at one another through representations—good, bad, and just plain ugly. My life circa 1990, as subject to the lens of history, was undergoing a reverse-zoom shot. The lens zoomed forward while the camera moved backward. The scope expanded to reveal the subject in greater context but the overall camera movement was backward nonetheless. As for the 1970s ideal of racial utopia, which I had been fed as a lower-middle-class-to-poor black child, the only thing missing was a unicorn.

Just as representations of blackness mediated black-white relations, they also mediated black-black relations and ultimately the relationship I had to myself. Each and every image of someone black was speaking to me, at me, and for me. A "we" was assumed, imposing itself on whatever meager sense of self I could muster. "I" could start the morning off as Michael Jordan or Michael Jackson (or Michael Jordan Jesse Jackson) and end the day a crime statistic. Likewise, whenever whites in any discussion concerning race addressed me as "you," was it in the singular or plural? Were "they" talking to "me"? Or, if it was plural, as in "you people," which narrative were "we" being weighed against? Was it comedy or tragedy? Was it the Huxtables or the homeless? A sense of self, as it was constituted in language, was irrevocably shattered. I found discussions about race incredibly difficult to maintain because I had no idea for whom I was speaking, if anyone. The only voice I had was negational, one I certainly could not imagine useful for constructively answering questions about an artist's relationship to his or her audience. Racially, it appeared as though I had flatlined. But, in essence, I had repressed a great deal of anger which provided something of a pulse. And that is when I found myself "renigged," a term that I use strictly in a personal sense as I ask myself questions about change and historical agency—questions that each generation will have to come to terms with, at some point. Given that history would appear to repeat itself in the most uncanny fashion, as the 1992 LA riots would attest, perhaps the voices which spoke the first time around are adequate for speaking the second time around. But what happens when history does not repeat itself? Surely new voices will emerge, ones that will grapple with questions of historical change, perhaps implicitly as opposed to explicitly, fashioning a style capable of capturing a free-fall. Can I get a witness?

Paul Chan

Sublime Humility

Originally presented at "Approaching Humility: An illustrated lecture series,"
September 10, 2003, New York

Let us reject the blindness of isolationism, just as we refuse the crown of empire. Let us not dominate others with our power—or betray them with our indifference. And let us have an American foreign policy that reflects American character. The modesty of true strength. The humility of real greatness.
President George W. Bush, campaign speech

Never let 'em know where you live
Never let 'em get familiar wit your doe or your kids
Always stay quiet, humble
But don't be scared to take it to the knife or the gun in the rumble
Ruff Ryder recording artist Jadakiss, "We be like this"

William Hawkins. Born 1895 in rural Kentucky. Moves to Ohio in 1910 to escape the reconstruction that never came. Mops floors, drives a truck, runs a small brothel, and paints. Starts to sell his work around 1930. Paints. Suffers from a stroke in 1989, which leaves him partially paralyzed. Still paints. Dies several months later. 79 years old.

I do not mourn the passing of William Hawkins until the year 2000, when folk-art scholar Lee Kogan shows me a slide of his work. The painting is entitled *The Last Supper #9*, and it is. Bright reds and yellows that swirl in an obscure pattern frame the traditional grouping of the apostles and the triangular focus on Jesus that is the hallmark of last-supper paintings. It is faithful to the traditional pictorial demands of this famous scene, albeit with the vibrant colors and aggressive line quality befitting a painter who was also a janitor, a truck driver, and a pimp. But wait. What's that in front of Jesus? Is that fried chicken? It is. And more. Collard greens. Mashed Potatoes. Rib tips. Judas stares at a peach cobbler.

I don't remember what Da Vinci and the others served Jesus in *their* last supper paintings. But it doesn't matter. I'm transfixed. And now, something changes. What psychoanalytic philosopher Jacques Lacan calls an anamorphic shift takes place, and a minor, supplementary detail becomes the anchor point around which the whole obsessively revolves. The last supper is transformed. And it becomes beautiful to me, perhaps for the first time. Not because I love peach cobbler, but because I feel and see the weight of what is depicted, and, at the same time, the lightness of the intervention that distorts the matrix of the formal and historical tradition of the painting, and *still* at the very same time continue to feel that weight. It is actually heavier. Hawkins did not want to make light of the last supper, nor make it somehow more contemporary. He wanted to honor and obey the law of the last supper. Above all, he wanted to love it, in an excessive way, which is to say in a personal way. And surely you know one loves the other by feeding the other a good meal. Even if you know the other will betray you. Perhaps it is precisely *because* the other will betray you that one has to make the extra effort to make great gravy before the betrayal. Certainly before the redemption.

* * *

Let's start with the obvious: There is no humility without humiliation. In the old and new testaments, humility is an essential characteristic of true piety, of men and women who are right with God. "God humbles men in order to bring them to himself" (Deuteronomy, Chapter 8, Verse 2). And "when men humble themselves before him then they are accepted" (Kings, Chapter 12, Verse 29). The state of grace that frees one from pride and arrogance, the quality of mind that fixates on unworthiness and imperfections for a greater good does not result from the practice of faith or the accumulation of knowledge. It comes from the act of submission. Humility is learned at the end of a whip.

It is important to note here that the state of humility that comes from the grace of humiliation is not a cycle one studiously avoids. This cycle is, in fact, very pleasurable. It also serves a long tradition. There is, of course, that legendary institute for the research and practice of debasement and Eros known as the Catholic Church. No less grand is philosopher Georges Bataille's work, which is a blend of theology, Marxism, and bathroom graffiti. Bataille writes, "Since it is true that one of man's attributes is the derivation of pleasures from the suffering of others, and that erotic pleasure is not only the negation of an agony that takes place at the same instant, but also a lubricious participation in that agony, it is time to choose between the conduct of cowards afraid of their own excesses, and the conduct of those who judge that any given man need not cower like a hunted animal, but instead can see all the moralistic buffoons as so many dogs." And of course we must mention philosopher Jean Paulhan's introduction to the classic story about the erotics of humility and humiliation, Pauline Réage's novel *The Story of O*. Paulhan begins by describing a slave rebellion in Barbados in 1838, in which the slaves, just weeks after they fought and freed themselves, returned to their former master and demanded to be taken back in. Paulhan's essay is entitled "Happiness in Slavery." Pleasurable yes. And hence popular.

Evocations from President Bush and Jadakiss aside, the production of a state of lowliness of the mind and the perpetual reminder of our fundamental imperfections for the service and consolidation of power is a venerable tradition in America. Can we not make the sincere case that the reason why the United States has the lowest voter-turnout rate of any democratic nation on Earth is that the people of the United States have been thoroughly humbled? Isn't the idea of true humility what motivates pop sensation Britney Spears, in a recent and bizarre interview with CNN teenage conservative Tucker Carlson, to answer, in response to Carlson's question about her opinion on Bush and Iraq, "Honestly, I think we should just trust our president in every decision that he makes and we should just support that." Not only is humility *not* missing in the general discourse, it virtually blankets the whole of our social milieu with its terminal smog of faith and goodwill. Humility, as the pleasure from the passivity that duty demands, calls us from every US department of whatever and every cable news channel as insistently as the Islamic call to prayer in the mornings and afternoons that echo throughout cities in Jordan, Syria, and what was once Iraq.

* * *

On the one hand, the cycle of humility and humiliation, a movement that serves to consolidate power and bind us to a contract not unlike a slave to a master. On the other hand, a complete disavowal of this unsavory cycle, risking political and cultural alienation. Is there a third way?

I thought I saw a glimpse of it in Hawkins's painting. No church, Catholic or Protestant, would hang Hawkins's painting in their house of worship and risk questions like, "What is the meaning behind the enormous plate of rib tips next to Jesus?" But Hawkins did not paint the last supper for a laugh. The reverence in the painting betrays an intention beyond parody or critique. Hawkins's painting, rather, resonates with a kind of excessive love that results from a profound embrace of the duty toward the depiction of Christ and the ideas motivating that depiction. It is as if Hawkins imagined he was the only painter with enough experience, knowledge, and love to adequately represent this pivotal scene in Christianity. He cuts out the middle man, as they say, and paints the core of the last supper with what he had and what he knew, in a loving excess above and beyond the law, which is to say, the church, to answer the calling of another master, *another* law. His painting is his answer to this call. And it is dutiful, excessive, sublime, and humble.

The master. The call. The duty. More than the problematics of psychology, education, or their relations to art history, these are for me a truer measure for the "outsiderness" of outsider art. The sordid history of outsider art is a long apologia for misfits and crazies, which is not unlike the sordid history of insider art. But there is a kernel of difference between the two worlds of work. For outsider art, the duty is to the law, not to the new (or more precisely the longing of the new) which is the calling of contemporary art. In other words, the transgressive nature of outsider art is not the pursuit of novel forms and expressions that yield and articulate new pleasures and possibilities. It is, rather, the total embrace of the established forms and traditions that elevate those forms from mere things to "objecthood" or art. The embrace, however, is so tight that it threatens to collapse the forms themselves in a suffocating excess, and in the process, transform the very traditions that elevated those forms in the first place. The weight of the embrace. The honoring of the form. The excessiveness with which they answer the call of a law beyond themselves. Aren't these the hallmarks of the great outsider artists like Henry Darger, Lee Godie, and Howard Finster? And do they not point the way toward a kind of humility that ruptures the Christian cycle of humility and humiliation? A kind of sublime servitude to the law above and beyond the established earthly embodiments of that law, and finally, against the powers that speak for the law, because the true servants of the law know that the law does not speak. It is silent. And it must remain so, humbly, if it is to keep its promise of a more just future to come.

Perhaps this is the crucial difference between true and sublime humility: One serves the present, the other serves the future. Are there other servants of the future besides painters from Kentucky and homeless portraitists wandering the streets of Chicago? Yes, I think. They are in our midst, like traitors waiting for the right moment to betray the law that speaks only of power and the appalling freedom of the blind. At this very instant, while 130,000 soldiers are serving the will of literally five lonely men in power, seven Americans are in Baghdad serving the goodwill of the American people and the ideals that founded our humble republic. Members of the Chicago-based group Voices in the Wilderness have been serving both the Iraqis and Americans since 1996, openly breaking the unjust US-backed UN sanctions against Iraq, bringing medicines and toys into that country and reminding the rest of us quietly, gently, that life, liberty, and the pursuit of happiness are ideals worth fighting for beyond the fifty states. Members of Voices are now working in the middle of a war zone once known as Baghdad to bring an end to the occupation. Unreasonable? Yes. Crazy? Yes, yes. All guts. No glory. Not even a decent paycheck. Still, they practice their outsider politics and serve us, with us, perhaps even against us.

They are not the only ones. Before Voices in the Wilderness, there were the Quakers and the Mennonites, the liberation theologians, Dorothy Day and the Catholic workers. And way before them the Antinomians, the Levellers, the Ranters, the Diggers, the Ishmaelites, and maybe we can also ask our founding fathers to join this quintessentially American list of humble radicals who bring trouble, honor justice, and serve the law against power.

Perhaps this is why I was so moved when I saw the Black Bloc at the March 2003 anti-war protests in Washington, DC. The Black Bloc is a loose anarchist collective that is universally dismissed as a fringe star in the constellation of contemporary activism. They are young. They dress in all black. They tattoo anarchy symbols all over their ratty backpacks and hoodies. They are blamed for everything from broken windows to injured cops. They're wild and they endanger the legitimacy of the movement, many say.

But they're also the ones who wrap strips of cloth dipped in vinegar around live tear gas canisters thrown at protesters by cops so nobody gets stung by the fumes. I have seen them form phalanxes to crash through barricades so demonstrators could escape the billy clubs and rubber bullets. They serve the movement while remaining excessive to it, and in doing so transform the very nature of that movement.

And you know what they did back in March? They wore these funny hats. I didn't recognize the hats at first, but then someone clued me in: they were the black tricorns worn by George Washington and his rebel crew during the American Revolution. And like Hawkins's painting, the gesture did not feel like parody or critique. It felt, rather, like a kind of honoring. A radical embrace. A mere 220 years later, the Black Bloc dons the same symbol of rebellion that founded our country, fifteen or twenty of them, patriots all, facing down a nervous battalion of riot cops by themselves, trying to expand the perimeter of the protest on the street; for us, with us, against us, beyond us.

Giorgio Agamben

No to Bio-Political Tattooing

Le Monde, January 10, 2004

The newspapers leave no doubt: from now on whoever wants to go to the United States with a visa will be put on file and will have to leave their fingerprints when they enter the country. Personally, I have no intention of submitting myself to such procedures and that's why I didn't wait to cancel the course I was supposed to teach at New York University in March.

I would like to explain the reasons for this refusal here, that is, why, in spite of the sympathy that has connected me to my American colleagues and their students for many years, I consider that this decision is at once necessary and without appeal and would hope that it will be shared by other European intellectuals and teachers.

It's not only the immediate superficial reaction to a procedure that has long been imposed on criminals and political defendants. If it were only that, we would certainly be morally able to share, in solidarity, the humiliating conditions to which so many human beings are subjected.

The essential does not lie there. The problem exceeds the limits of personal sensitivity and simply concerns the juridical-political status (it would be simpler, perhaps, to say bio-political) of citizens of the so-called democratic states where we live.

There has been an attempt the last few years to convince us to accept as the humane and normal dimensions of our existence, practices of control that had always been properly considered inhumane and exceptional.

Thus, no one is unaware that the control exercised by the state through the usage of electronic devices, such as credit cards or cell phones, has reached previously unimaginable levels.

All the same, it wouldn't be possible to cross certain thresholds in the control and manipulation of bodies without entering a new bio-political era, without going one step further in what Michel Foucault called the progressive animalization of man, which is established through the most sophisticated techniques.

Electronic filing of finger and retina prints, subcutaneous tattooing, as well as other practices of the same type, are elements that contribute towards defining this threshold. The security reasons that are invoked to justify these measures should not impress us: they have nothing to do with it. History teaches us how practices first reserved for foreigners find themselves applied later to the rest of the citizenry.

What is at stake here is nothing less than the new "normal" bio-political relationship between citizens and the state. This relation no longer has anything to do with free and active participation in the public sphere, but concerns the enrollment and the filing away of the most private and incommunicable aspect of subjectivity: I mean the body's biological life.

These technological devices that register and identify naked life correspond to the media devices that control and manipulate public speech:

between these two extremes of a body without words and words without a body, the space we once upon a time called politics is ever more scaled-down and tiny.

Thus, by applying these techniques and these devices invented for the dangerous classes to a citizen, or rather to a human being as such, states, which should constitute the precise space of political life, have made a person the ideal suspect, to the point that it's humanity itself that has become the dangerous class.

Some years ago, I had written that the West's political paradigm was no longer the city-state but the concentration camp, and that we had passed from Athens to Auschwitz. It was obviously a philosophical thesis and not historic recital, because one could not confuse phenomena that are proper, on the contrary, to distinguish.

I would have liked to suggest that tattooing at Auschwitz undoubtedly seemed the most normal and economic way to regulate the enrollment and registr-ation of deported persons into concentration camps. The bio-political tattooing the United States imposes now to enter its territory could well be the precursor to what we will be asked to accept later as the normal identity registration of a good citizen in the state's gears and mechanisms. That's why we must oppose it.

Translated by Martin Rueff and Leslie Thatcher.

Critical Art Ensemble

When Thought Becomes Crime[1]

March 17, 2004

How did it come to this?

Only a perverse authoritarian logic can explain how Critical Art Ensemble (CAE) can at one moment be creating the project *Free Range Grain* for the "Risk" exhibition at Schirn Kunsthalle in Frankfurt, reconfiguring it for "The Interventionists" exhibition at Mass MoCA in a second moment, and then suddenly have a CAE member in FBI detention. The US Justice Department has accused us of such shocking crimes as bioterrorism, health and safety violations, mail fraud, wire fraud, and even murder. Now, as we retool *Free Range Grain* for the "Risk" exhibition at the Glasgow Center for Contemporary Art, the surreal farce of our legal nightmare continues unabated.

Of course, we always knew that cultural-interventionist work could have serious consequences. And over the years, predictably, CAE has been denounced (and threatened) by all varieties of authority: cops, corporate lawyers, politicians, all types of racists, and church groups—even the Archbishop of Salzburg. But to be the target of an international investigation that involves the FBI, the Joint Terrorism Task Force, the ATF, the Department of Homeland Defense, the Department of Health and Safety, numerous local police agencies, and even Norwegian and German federal investigators goes far beyond the pale. As of this writing, CAE member Steven Kurtz and one of our long-time collaborators, University of Pittsburgh geneticist Robert Ferrell, are fighting the insanely real threat of being sent to federal prison.

So how did we create such a vortex of Kafkaesque legalistic repression? In the *Free Range Grain* project, for instance, CAE simply used molecular biology techniques to test for genetically modified food in the global food trade. We want(ed) this interventionist performance to demonstrate how the "smooth space" of global trade enables the very "contaminations" the authorities say it guards against. Now we, along with our colleagues on the CAE defense team, have been trying to understand why the authorities have taken such a reactionary position in regard to our art practice. We have come up with many reasons; we can address only a few in this brief article.

The first reason, we believe, involves the discourse in which we framed our project. By viewing the scientific process through the lens of political economy, we disrupted the legitimized version of science as a self-contained, value-free specialization. The powers that be would have science speak for, within, and about itself. This insularity is akin to Clement Greenberg's idea of letting art history explain the production of art, or Emile Durkheim's use of "social facts" to explain the social. But any discourse exists within larger historical and political contexts. It seemed self-evident for us to place competing discourses in conversation, and show the socioeconomic ideologies at work in food production.

From the perspective of authority, however, we were being subversive, deviant. For those who wish to preserve the illusion of the autonomy of science, citizens can discuss scientific structure, method, materials, etc., as long as they do not refer to the political or economic interests that impinge on scientific research. A biology club can talk all about cells, but if it goes beyond the institutionalized boundaries of the life sciences, look out for the Feds. The second challenge we posed came from our amateur approach to life-science knowledge systems, experimental processes, acquisition of materials, etc. An amateur can be critical of an institution without fear of recrimination or loss of status or investment. An art professor, for example, will probably not tell students that art school is a pyramid scheme into which they will pour a lot of capital, feed the higher-ups, and probably get very little if anything in return. That criticism is more likely to emerge from outside the power structure (or from disgruntled ex-students). In science, where the financial stakes are much higher, any criticism of resources may well result in funding cuts—a situation one can ill afford in such a capital-intensive discipline. So it takes an outsider to science—a creative tinkerer—to rattle the cage of the discipline's most dearly held assumptions and practices.

With special regard to the institutional financing of science, the amateur reveals the profit-driven privatization of a discipline that is purportedly —mythologically—open to all. By undertaking research as if science were truly a forum in which all may participate according to their abilities and resources, CAE angers those who manipulate scientific activity through capital investment. The financial stakes are so high that the authorities can imagine only one motivation for critical, amateur research, particularly if it is conducted at home outside of systems of surveillance/discipline. If that research intends to expose, disrupt, or subvert the meta-narratives that put scientific investigation in the service of profit, the amateur investigator must want to produce terrorist acts.

In the paranoid political climate of the US, American authorities leap all too easily from ideological criticism to terrorism. What's more, the CAE's legal battle reveals that the government has made *thinking* into a crime: a citizen can be arrested without having committed any act of terror or without having done anything illegal at all. Former US Attorney General John Ashcroft has unofficially reformed law-enforcement policy and practice according to the Bush administration's idea of "preemptive war." He has argued that if indicators—any type of dissent in relation to "national interest" or the interests of the investing classes—suggest that a person or group *could* do something illegal, then they should be arrested, detained, deported, or otherwise persecuted with the full resources of all repressive state agencies. Apparently, the US Justice Department is now trying to make CAE into an example of what can happen to citizens whose only "crime" is having thoughts of dissent enacted within the sphere of legality and with the alleged protection of constitutional rights.

For experimental art, political art, tactical media, and independent media in the US (and to some degree in other nations), the implications of Steven Kurtz's arrest are profound. The repressive forces of the state are directly targeting producers of cultural interventionist work. In past decades, policy-makers have often leaned on political artwork through financial penalties such as rescinding artist's grants, folding federal arts programs, and economically squeezing out the spaces that exhibit subversive work.[2] Now, these attacks on *civil* grounds have undergone a horrific paradigm shift, and individual artists are being charged with criminal activity. The persecution works slowly and insidiously, through silencing artists, looting their work and their research, and constraining their movement. We are no longer seeing cultural conflict in action, but a proto-fascist attack upon free expression itself.

Notes

1. The set of theses presented in this document were collectively developed through a series of lectures given by the CAE Defense Team. Contributors include Doug Ashford, Gregg Bordowitz, CAE, Natalie Jeremijenko, Claire Pentecost, and Lucia Sommer. Special thanks to Karen Schiff.

2. The New York Council for the Humanities recently rescinded a grant awarded to the City University of New York for its series on *academic freedom* because Steven Kurtz was one of the invited speakers!

Gregory Sholette

Disciplining the Avant-Garde

The United States versus The Critical Art Ensemble

CIRCA: Contemporary Visual Culture in Ireland, Summer 2005

> *It's vitally important that whenever we think about insurgency to remember that the essence of any insurgency and its most decisive battle space is the psychological. In the 1960s, insurgency was referred to as armed theater, which I think is a really poignant way of thinking about it.*
> Steven Metz, US Army War College Strategic Studies Institute[1]

> *There's somethin' happenin' here,*
> *What it is ain't exactly clear.*
> Buffalo Springfield

Birth of the Homeland Security State Apparatus

It has been three and one half years since President George W. Bush proclaimed, "you're either with us or against us."[2] Since that time the neo-liberal "revolution" has undergone a re-Balkanization in the United States. Gone is the ideology of fluidity and openness that presided over the post-cold war years and in its place comes a new nationalist spirit complete with rising trade tariffs and a variety of seemingly expedient security measures that have evolved into a new way of life.[3] From no-fly lists to ubiquitous public surveillance, from severe visa and immigration restrictions to the fingerprinting of tourists, "bunker America" is replacing the fantasy of globalization. Even unilateral military action is justified as a preemptive defense of the homeland. Meanwhile, the rest of the world is offered Pax Americana, a sanctimonious sop revealing perhaps what was at stake all along, nothing less than global supremacy. Less well known at home, however, thanks to guilt-free "happy" news and embedded reporting, is the targeted suspension of habeas corpus and mass cataloging of thousands of Islamic, Middle Eastern, and North African people inside the country. Thousands of individuals have been detained without trial, others deported, and some have been sent abroad into "extra-juridicial" zones within Pakistan and Syria where human rights do not stand in the way of extreme interrogation methods.[4]

It comes as no surprise that those who publicly question aspects of the new homeland security state apparatus also find themselves victims of government investigation and intimidation. While certainly not on par with disappearances and torture, scores of artists, journalists, and academics, including several high school students, have been questioned recently about alleged anti-American activities by a variety of federal and local law enforcement officials. In at least one case, the one that concerns this essay, the US government is aggressively seeking to portray a group of contemporary artists known for their politically provocative yet legal and constitutionally protected art as a full-blown terrorist threat to national security.

Since September 11, 2001, the FBI and the Secret Service have interrogated gallery curators in Chicago and Dallas for displaying images they deemed suspicious; accused a Nevada man of "borderline terrorism" because he had a bumper sticker that read "KING GEORGE—Off With His Head"; and detained and questioned a Colorado high school principal for permitting students to sing the Bob Dylan tune "Masters of War" during a public performance. Adbusters, the culture-jamming group, were questioned by government agents over a flag-like billboard they installed in Times Square. Secret Service agents even prevented two teachers from attending a Bush rally because they wore t-shirts printed with the words "Protect our civil liberties." The atmosphere of enhanced public security has apparently also emboldened some local law enforcement to disregard this very advice. Police in Albany arrested a man for wearing a peace sign on his t-shirt; a young man was arrested outside an armed forces career center in Boston for dressing up as a US torture victim in Iraq; six men were arrested in Pennsylvania for creating an Abu Ghraib-style human pyramid as the President's motorcade drove past; and in August 2004, during the Republication National Convention, the New York Police Department went so far as to take thousands of people into custody, holding them long past the legal twenty-four-hour limit in appalling conditions at a concrete and steel pier on the Hudson River.

Probing calls from federal agents to university administrators have added to a chilling climate of suspicion within academia already apprehensive over congressional debates about alleged anti-American curricula and over student groups like the ultra-conservative Campus Watch, who openly stake out "liberal" instructors in order to document their so-called Left bias. Professors at universities in New Mexico, Houston, Urbana-Champaign, South Florida, upstate New York, and even Columbia University in New York City have discovered that raising questions about US policy, Israel, 9/11, and homeland security inside the classroom can bring on disciplinary action and even dismissal. Regrettably, several university museum directors—at Arizona State University, the City Museum of Washington, and Ohio University—have gone so far as to actively self-censor their own exhibitions by removing socially critical work or by adding art that reflects a "conservative" point of view. Meanwhile, the firing of several prize-winning journalists effectively demonstrates that challenging Bush administration policy even from within mainstream media can have considerable consequences.[5]

The most alarming of these cases so far is certainly the US Attorney General William Hochel's unrelenting investigation of artist Steven Kurtz and his former colleague, Robert Ferrell. Kurtz is a professor of art at the University of Buffalo in New York. He is also a co-founder of the Critical Art Ensemble (CAE), an artists' collective that dates from 1986 which has become known for its multi-media projects splicing Brechtian pedagogy onto the comedic diligence of Mr. Wizard.[6] Donning white lab coats and assuming the personae of amateur scientists, they arm themselves with high school lab equipment as well as common household supplies and groceries in order to demystify, or, more to the point, democratize the increasingly privatized worlds of science, technology, and information networks. These often playful routines contrast with the serious intent and analytical approach of the group's numerous books and manifestos. In *Electronic Civil Disturbance*, CAE celebrates anti-corporate, "slacker" Ludditism and in *Digital Resistance* they provide plans for making graffiti-writing robots and reprogramming Nintendo games so that children will gain "the means to bring about a situation in which a process of broad spectrum invention, discovery, and criticality can occur." Whether in a museum, an international conference, on the street, or in print, the CAE's work unvaryingly aims to inform, entertain, and demonstrate the value of public knowledge.

For the past several years the group has focused attention on what they see as the misuse of biotechnology by private corporations operating outside the realm of democratic, public debate. CAE's tactical response is what they term "Fuzzy Biological Sabotage" (or FBS), a type of sophisticated prank that uses harmless biological agents, including plants, insects, reptiles, and even microorganisms to operate in the gray, in-between spaces as yet unregulated by institutional regimes.[7] In 2002 the group demonstrated one form of FBS in the project *Contestational Biology*, which was developed in conjunction with artists Beatriz de Costa and Claire Pentecost and installed at the Corcoran Art Gallery in Washington, DC. *Contestational Biology* consisted of an "amateur" scientific experiment that "reverse-engineered" samples of the Monsanto Corporation's Round-Up Ready corn, canola, and soy products, three of the many genetically modified organisms rapidly being integrated into modern agriculture industry. The ultimate goal of the installation, however, was to raise public awareness about the sweeping privatization of the human food supply by directly contesting Monsanto's right to create and patent customized life forms for corporate profit.

All of CAE's writings and projects converge around a single objective: a sustained effort to de-familiarize forms of civil disobedience in order to re-invent new ways of responding critically to contemporary social and political reality. They insist therefore that "outdated methods of resistance must be refined and new methods of disruption invented that attack power (non)centers on the electronic level."[8]

Strongly influenced by the theories of Michel Foucault and Gilles Deleuze, CAE perceives political power as operating more or less anonymously within, or across, a deterritorialized, postindustrial environment. In light of this, most past forms of activist confrontation are largely useless. Out of necessity therefore, political resistance must adapt by appropriating the same evanescent digital networks as corporate and state power, while endlessly recalibrating their critical interventions in the form of "tactical media."

According to David Garcia and Geert Lovink, "tactical media" occurs whenever cheap, "do-it-yourself" (DIY) media, made possible by the revolution in consumer electronics and expanded forms of distribution (from public-access cable to the Internet) are exploited by groups and individuals who feel aggrieved by or excluded from the wider culture.[9]

CAE's signature approach to tactical media is a decidedly self-reflexive one insofar as the group frequently applies do-it-yourself maneuvers to science and technology in order to reveal the underlying ideological administration of knowledge itself. At the same time, the group links tactical media to a distinctly anti-modern form of "cellular" collectivism and political autonomy.[10]

For now, I want to underscore the significance to CAE of this avowed amateurism while suggesting it may also be playing a central role in the group's recent predicament with federal authorities. CAE has stated that

> *amateurs have the ability to see through dominant paradigms, are freer to recombine elements of paradigms thought long dead, and can apply everyday life experience to their deliberations. Most important, however, amateurs are not invested in institutional systems of knowledge production and policy construction, and hence do not have irresistible forces guiding the outcome of their process ...*[11]

For a $33 billion homeland state security apparatus dedicated to patrolling the periphery and reinstating wartime discipline, such calls made by self-acknowledged dissidents for the founding of new, amateur forms of "fuzzy" resistance may seem merely curious. Or they may appear outright devious. As military theorist Steven Metz argues, the essence of insurgency is not seizing territory, but rather sending messages to a wider audience through a type of politicized theater.[12]

Art is not terrorism

On the morning of May 21, 2004, Steven Kurtz awoke to find his wife Hope lying unresponsive beside him. Kurtz immediately called paramedics. On arrival, the medical response team took notice of assorted laboratory equipment in the home, including petri dishes, microscopes, and test tubes. Nervously, local police alerted the FBI. The Joint Terrorism Task Force soon descended on the Kurtz home and, in a scene reminiscent of the 1971 techno-thriller *The Andromeda Strain*, agents wearing white hazmat (hazardous materials) suits cordoned off the house, confiscated the body of Kurtz's wife, and gathered a variety of materials for scientific analysis. They also impounded the artist's passport, lesson plans, books, automobile, computers, and cat.

By the next day New York's Commissioner of Public Health officially reported that nothing hazardous was discovered in the home and no danger to the public existed. Hope had died of a heart attack. Nonetheless, the house was under quarantine for six days, during which Kurtz was placed under surveillance for twenty-two hours. FBI agents did not arrest him, but they put him up in a hotel, together with collaborator and family friend Claire Pentecost, who had recently arrived from Chicago. The agency even purchased Kurtz dinner with the hopes of uncovering more information. At one point Pentecost was taken aside and asked if Kurtz had ever advocated the overthrow of the United States government.[13]

At the time of his wife's tragic death Kurtz and CAE were finishing work on a project entitled *Free Range Grain* involving a do-it-yourself DNA-extraction laboratory for testing for the presence of genetically altered genes, or trans-genes, in store-bought groceries. The project was to have been installed in an upcoming exhibition entitled "The Interventionists: Art in the Social Sphere" at the Massachusetts Museum of Contemporary Art.[14] It was the presence of these laboratory materials, together with three types of harmless bacteria procured for the group's next project about the history of US bio-warfare programs, that led to the investigation, because prior to the unexpected death of his wife there is no evidence Kurtz or CAE were of interest to the FBI.[15]

Eventually, Hope's body was returned for burial, but the FBI retained the artist's passport, books, and computer. Still, up to this point, the incident appeared to be a case of jittery officials who, in the aftermath of the still-unsolved anthrax mail murders of 2001, reacted to the discovery of a premature death and the presence of unexpected lab equipment with an indiscriminate response. That was the assumption at least until several CAE members and collaborators were handed subpoenas by federal agents at the MassMoCA opening that directed them to appear before a federal grand jury last June. Nine people were served subpoenas by then, and while neither the FBI nor the attorney general would make public the details of their probe, it was evident from the wording in the documents that Kurtz was being investigated under US Code Title 18, Part I, Chapter 10, Sec. 175: Prohibitions with Respect to Biological Weapons. The scope of this statute was greatly expanded by the USA Patriot Act of 2001. So much so that some speculate even the harmless research bacteria of the type Kurtz obtained for CAE art projects might now be labeled as a hazardous "biological agent."

Commenting on the potential charges, Donald A. Henderson, dean emeritus of the Johns Hopkins University School of Hygiene and Public Health, pointed out that

> *based on what I have read and understand, Professor Kurtz has been working with totally innocuous organisms ... none of the organisms noted to be present in this case are covered, nor should they be, by the post-9/11 provisions.*[16]

To the surprise of no one who knew Kurtz or the work of CAE, after it met on June 15 the grand jury rejected all charges of bioterrorism. Once again, the unpleasant incident appeared about to conclude, with Kurtz anticipating a public apology like that extended to Brandon Mayfield, the Islamic convert from Oregon who was escorted in handcuffs from his place of work and accused of involvement in the Madrid train bombings.[17] Optimism was short-lived, however. On June 22, CAE's publisher, Autonomedia, was subpoenaed, indicating the investigation was not yet over.[18] Before long, Kurtz and Ferrell found themselves facing up to twenty years in prison on downsized charges of mail fraud for the alleged mishandling of bacterial samples purchased from a scientific supply house.[19] As of this writing the investigation grinds on still, and renewed charges involving bioterrorism may be lodged soon, following a second grand jury hearing on April 19, 2005.[20]

The public sullying of a white and otherwise privileged academic's reputation is not unique these days. Dr. Thomas Butler, a world-renowned specialist who researches bubonic plague, has also received similar treatment by federal officials. In January of 2003, Butler noticed thirty vials of the bacteria missing from his lab. Assuming the samples were misplaced, but erring on the side of caution, he reported their absence to the FBI. As someone with a history of security clearance, he trusted the government and signed away his rights to legal defense. He was then arrested. "I was tricked and deceived," said Butler on CBS's *60 Minutes*. "I was naïve to have trusted them and the assurances they gave me." Butler was charged with sixty-nine criminal counts, including everything from bioterror to tax evasion, and even though the sixty-two-year-old scientist was, like Kurtz, acquitted of all terror-related charges, he was instead indicted for financial misconduct and has lost his job, his doctor's license, is broke, and still faces several years in prison.[21] The National Academy of Sciences and the Institute of Medicine sent a letter to the United States attorney general warning against "the impact that Butler's case may have on other scientists who may be discouraged from embarking upon or continuing crucial bioterrorism-related scientific research."[22]

Meanwhile, state intervention aimed at regulating scientific research has been increasingly visible of late. The Bush administration demanded the right to approve all American scientists selected for the World Health Organization; the US Department of Health and Human Services blocked scientists from traveling to the International AIDS Conference in Bangkok; and in March of this year, the US National Institutes of Health (NIH) received a letter charging it with creating "a crisis for microbiological research." The letter was signed by more than half of the scientists whom the NIH helps employ.[23] The charge of promoting "junk science" and manipulating data is now increasingly being leveled at the White House by members of the science community, including twenty Nobel laureates.[24] David Schubert, head of the Cellular Neurobiology Laboratory at the Salk Institute for Biological Studies in La Jolla, went so far as to say there has been

> *an unprecedented assault by the executive branch of our government upon the ability of U.S. scientists to freely share their data and insights about our world with the public. Much of the justification for this repression of scientific communication falls under the Orwellian concept of "sound science," which is clearly understood by the scientific community to mean the misrepresentation of scientific data to reflect the administration's political and social agendas.*[25]
>
> *All the while this dampening effect is taking place with regard to certain types of scientific research, and as restrictive prohibitions are enacted on information sharing, the U.S. government's spending on biological-weapons research has reached unprecedented levels.*[26]

Unlike many people who have been investigated or have outright disappeared since 9/11, the members of CAE are reasonably well-known figures within the international art world. Moral and material support have arrived from dozens of countries, and a recent auction of artwork by artists such as Hans Haacke, Andrea Fraser, Martha Rosler, Carl Andre, and Joseph Kosuth, among others, was staged at a major Chelsea art gallery in New York. Yet, while the Kurtz / CAE case has received a relatively high degree of attention in the mainstream press and within the art world, criticism of the federal government for its handling of this case has not been nearly as intense or widespread as the outcry during the so-called "culture wars" of the 1990s.[27] Gradually, however, these disturbing stories are beginning to align and in the process provoke an inevitable question: Is the United States re-entering a period of political and cultural repression like that experienced during the Palmer Raids of the 1910s or the McCarthy era of the 1950s? Without denying the possibility of a return to such overt political tyranny, I think it necessary to make this all-too-convenient hypothesis more problematic.[28]

For one thing, the abuse of civic and human rights has been an enduring feature of US military and law enforcement throughout our history, from Wounded Knee and the conquest of California to the annexation of the Philippines on up to the present. What has not happened to white, middle-class Americans since the early 1980s is the systematic retraction of constitutionally guaranteed civil liberties. At that time the FBI investigated and infiltrated US-based supporters of political refugees from El Salvador. For another thing, the very threat of such a return to the bad old days is useful in itself as a type of disinformation. Panic drove many in the 1950s to abandon hope of a constitutionally based legal defense. Self-censorship and political resignation soon followed. Even the Communist Party USA, the primary target of the government's assault, concluded it was better to go underground than publicly face what was wrongly theorized to be the rise of full-blown American fascism.[29] An ideological battlefield was quickly transformed into a game of shooting fish in a barrel.

Therefore, perhaps a better way to phrase our hypothesis is to ask why it is that the post-9/11 ideological landscape and the CAE investigation appear at once so familiar and simultaneously so very strange?

Managing Dissent

State intervention into the production and distribution of culture is as enduring as the history of nations is long. Think of Plato's injunction against poets and painters in his ideal republic, or Stalin's decree enforcing socialist realism in the mid-1930s, as well, of course, as the House Un-American Activities Committee's witch-hunting of Hollywood radicals in the 1950s. Modern bourgeois societies have evolved two seemingly contradictory modes of state control. One of these is the isolation and overt suppression of select individuals, groups, or ideological positions allegedly carried out in defense of the freedom or morality of an alleged majority interest.[30] This type of explicit control reappears cyclically in the United States, especially whenever government or big business is threatened by collective dissent emerging "from below." Its most recent full-scale manifestation took place immediately after World War II when militant labor unions, communists, and other Left radicals, grown strong during the anti-fascist Popular Front years, were systematically eradicated through a combination of legal and extra-constitutional measures. Before it was over, thousands of men and women were investigated, lost their jobs and/or were blacklisted in the name of freedom and democracy.[31] Many of these people worked in the culture industries and academia. While such overt repression is extremely effective in the short run, the same establishment that unleashed it will eventually denounce tyranny as antithetical to the free society it claims to protect. So even as the hammer of law enforcement was descending on individual radicals and nonconformists, a subtler means for managing dissent was coming to fruition. After all, the cold war was, aside from some hot moments in Greece, Korea, and Cuba, primarily a battle over which system could deliver a superior way of life to its citizens. Government leaders may have sought to overcome the missile gap, but just as significant were gaps in refrigerator, stove, and automobile production. Not surprisingly there was also a culture gap. As Eva Cockroft, Serge Gilbaut, and others have demonstrated, the US State Department actively supported the display and export of American art abroad. This included avant-garde painting and sculpture, which became a global advertisement for capitalism's apparently infinite tolerance of artistic expression and individual freedom.[32]

It comes as no surprise therefore that capitalist marketing barely broke stride as the counterculture blasted onto the cold war stage during the late 1960s. Corporate America, not the state, led the way this time, converting from the production of goods to the selling of lifestyles. Patched and faded jeans, Che Guevara accessories, and the homely VW Beetle were soon the ultimate symbols of hip, or what Thomas Frank describes as a countercultural capitalist orthodoxy.[33] And while resistance to the authority of state power remains tenacious, its changing forms are no less a product of the historical moment than is nationalism, imperialism, and so forth. Such opposition has run the gamut from bourgeois revolutionaries in the coffee houses of the seventeenth century to the Paris Commune of 1871 to the turn-of-the-century anarcho-syndicalism of the International Workers of the World (IWW). After the Second World War, the New Left turned against centralized Old Left politics as the civil rights and other minority-based liberation movements re-centered anti-nationalist sentiment around individual freedoms and/or cultural identity. Curiously, even the punks' overt negation of the 1960s was carried out in the name of anti-state cultural anarchism just as today, informal collectives such as Reclaim the Streets, Carnival Against Capital, and Indymedia reflect the green-anarchist and indigenous peoples movements that are militantly opposed to globalization and centralized authority. Under the circumstances stealing the state has been transformed into stealing corporate power in order that it may be redirected towards alternative, people-centered purposes. As the activist art group Yomango insists, "Dare to desire: YOMANGO is your style: risky, innovative. It is the articulate proliferation of creative gestures."[34]

Nevertheless it is crucial to note that powerful anti-state sentiments are also shared by right-wing libertarians and assorted religious fundamentalists, as well as by a group of high influential "centrist" policy makers who, not so long ago, prophesied a future in which the global marketplace would gradually subjugate national territories. Neoliberalism—from Reagan and Thatcher to Bill Clinton—is typically described as a response to the capital crisis of the late 1970s, and in his influential study *The Condition of Postmodernity* David Harvey argues that the floating exchange rates and financial networks of the 1980s permitted corporations to out-maneuver national interests in what he labels a regime of "flexible" capital accumulation.[35] Even if by some accounts Neoliberalism was only a method for stabilizing US national markets over and against all others,[36] a perspective that recent moves towards protectionism may bear out, one thing most analysts agree upon is that the last thirty years have seen a reduction of state influence in economic matters, the globalization of production, an emerging class of mobile, creative laborers, and a rise, especially evident in the immediate post-cold war era, of a technological entrepreneurialism that prompted one noted commentator to triumphantly proclaim the arrival of "a certain uniformity of economic and political institutions across different religions and cultures," and ultimately to theorize the end of history itself.[37]

This flexible accumulation finds its behavioral corollary in what theorist Brian Holmes describes as the "flexible personality":

> *an internalized and culturalized pattern of "soft" coercion, which nonetheless can be directly correlated to the hard data of labor conditions, bureaucratic and police practices, border regimes and military interventions.*[38]

According to Holmes, the new conditions erase the division between consumption and production, and worker alienation seems to vanish as "individuals aspire to mix their labor with their leisure." Even businesses begin to see themselves as a "sphere of creative activity, of self-realization" in which the new "net" worker becomes "the manager of his or her own self-gratifying activity."[39] That is, at least as long as happy-work leads to a product worthy of profitable exchange.

The end of the flexible personality?

It is at this moment, in the glow of these softly regulated modes of precarious, creative labor, that seemingly radical styles of business management emerge, directly modeling themselves after experimental, avant-garde, and even critical forms of culture. Frank's countercultural capitalist orthodoxy is one such example, with its rapid-fire absorption of all that is new and different, is then re-packaged and sold back to us as an ersatz "otherness." Consider now the highly successful CEO Al West, who runs a risk-management firm near Philadelphia in which employees serve on fluid, multi-disciplinary teams and re-arrange portable office furniture to suit the evolving needs of projects.

The few walls that exist inside the company's postmodern headquarters display contemporary artwork, some of it strange and disturbing to workers. West explains that his objective is to help people "get out of the box." "We want them to think creatively, so why not highlight these pieces? That's what art is all about—doing it in a different way." Meanwhile, West's management theory sounds as if it came from the pages of *Artforum* or even the anarchist zine *Clamor* rather than from the *Wall Street Journal*:

> *It used to be that information would flow up to one spot, and then the decision we make would flow back down. That's no longer a good model. In today's environment, you turn the organization upside down.*[40]

Drawing an even tighter circle around contemporary art practices and business theory, Matthew Jesse Jackson asks, in a recent piece for the *New Left Review* suggestively entitled "Managing the Avant-Garde":

> *Is it too far a stretch to suggest there exists a structural and historical correlation between such vanguard management ideology, with its flexible, at times experimental approach to worker productivity and happiness, and the forms (not content) of tactical media?*[42]

Significantly, it is this anarcho-capitalist dream of unimpeded financial networks and frictionless exchange that has recently hit a roadblock, or should I say "road-Bush"? Free-market subterfuge has been replaced by pious demolition and occupation. For compared to past conservative regimes in the US that have favored isolationism over militarism, the Bush Doctrine is something of a chimera.[43] With the appetite of unrepressed, free-market capitalism, its heart is filled with the moral righteousness of missionary Christianity. (Nor can one help but notice that its body is designed for old-fashioned imperialist conquest.) Therefore, when comparisons are made between past and present instances of state-sponsored oppression, contradictions of this magnitude must be factored in. Indeed, the modern state's apparently bifurcated response to political dissent—carefully targeted outright repression on the one hand, and repressive tolerance manifest by commodity culture on the other—is not, strictly speaking, an ideological reaction. For despite a superficial equivalence between conservative and liberal regimes respectively, the twin tactics of state social control more accurately correspond to the changing needs and pressures arising from the need to manage unstable markets for maximum capital accumulation. In other words, if flexibility, openness and tolerance were the watchwords of art, science, and industry, especially immediately following the end of the cold war, then the new maxims of the homeland security state apparatus are restraint, insularity, and suspicion.[44]

Conclusion

In this sense the seemingly post-rational political agenda of the Bush Doctrine might be a refreezing of selected portions of the de-territorialized network that Hardt and Negri posited in their influential study, *Empire*. Likewise, the investigation and intimidation of journalists, scientists, academics, and artists may be more than just a public scapegoating of relatively powerless individuals and groups. It might instead be aimed at loudly signaling an end to the interdisciplinary, transnational entrepreneurialism that dominated the pre-9/11 technological, economic, and cultural environment.[45]

That is not to say that capitalism will never again chant the mantra of 1990s management guru Tom Peters, "Never hire anyone without an aberration in their background."[46] Nor will it, at the mere invocation of anti-authoritarian ideas, react as it has in the CAE case, at least not based on the facts thus far. Instead, what sets this moment apart is the re-sanctification of the state as transcendent fetish and a concomitant re-disciplining of ambiguous, unmanageable forms. This includes CAE. When CAE transformed various insurgent theories—be these avant-gardist or radical-corporate—into accessible, DIY procedures, and then directed a diffuse yet unquestionably resistant force towards select private and governmental targets, it publicly demonstrated its ability to operate within the same nebulous terrain of power that the state now deems its privileged concession to own, lend out, or direct. Is it any wonder authorities compare CAE to terrorists? Kurtz and his colleagues sinned yet a second time when they published manuals explicating how to make use of this counter-knowledge, including its tactics and circuitry, and did so not with the ambiguous idioms of art-speak, but rather with the determined hyper-clarity of the techno-geek.

This is where something far more grotesque than a simple return to the past begins to be teased out of an otherwise incomprehensible instance of state censorship. It is a warning aimed as much at the avant-garde, entrepreneurial spirit of the dot-commers as it is against a group of interdisciplinary artists who refuse to stay in their assigned role as isolated cultural workers. Yet if the buzz word of "bunker America" is "get back in your box!" there must be no equivocation regarding support for those being targeted by the new, homeland security state apparatus. To speak up against its creeping authoritarianism, to do so loudly wherever we are, whenever we have the opportunity, in large or small ways, means never acting alone, but instead acting collectively. To not act, as Bertolt Brecht precisely summarizes, is to accept the ignominious verdict of history:

> *They won't say: the times were dark. Rather: why were their poets silent?*[47]

Notes

1. Steven Metz, "Relearning Counterinsurgency: History Lessons for Iraq, Afghanistan, and the Global War on Terror," The American Enterprise Institute, January 10, 2005; transcript at www.aei.org/events/filter.,eventID.982/transcript.asp.

2. George W. Bush in a joint news conference with French President Jacques Chirac, November 6, 2001.

3. Some who read this sentence will naturally question my use of the term "openness" and point to the harsh political attacks on artists such as Karen Finley, Robert Mapplethorpe, and Andreas Serrano among others in the 1990s over their allegedly subversive images and performances. But the so-called "culture wars" were really neoconservative ideology in vitro, whereas for neoliberals it was primarily about transforming the National Endowment for the Arts (NEA) into an institution actively promoting the privatization (commercialization) of culture.

4. The number of people involved is difficult to estimate but an excellent website that includes a database of some who have disappeared is www.disappearedinamerica.org.

5. Details on many of these cases and over a hundred others are compiled by Matthew Rothschild in his "McCarthyism Watch Updates," published by *Progressive* magazine and available online at www.progressive.org. See also: Temporary Services' special website on the Resurgence of the culture wars at www.temporaryservices.org/culture_wars.html.

6. *Mr. Wizard* was a popular US television show in the 1950s and 1960s in which an actor, Donald Herbert, demonstrated laboratory experiments for young people.

7. See: http://www.critical-art.net/biotech/conbio/index.html and *The Molecular Invasion*, published by Autonomedia Books in 2002.

8. *Electronic Disturbance*, p. 9.

9. David Garcia and Geert Lovink, *The ABC's of Tactical Media*, 1997; available at subsol.c3.hu/subsol_2/contributors2/Garcia-lovinktext.html.

10. Blake Stimson and I elaborate on this concept of post-war collective forms in our essay "Periodizing Collectivism," *Third Text* vol. 18 no. 6, pp. 573–585, and again in our forthcoming anthology *Collectivism after Modernism* for the University of Minnesota Press.

11. Critical Art Ensemble, *Digital Resistance: Explorations in Tactical Media*, Autonomedia Books, 2001, p. 9.

12. See endnote 1.

13. Related by Claire Pentecost in a presentation at The Cooper Union on October 25, 2004.

14. "The Interventionists: Art in the Social Sphere," Massachusetts Museum of Contemporary Art, March 20 – May 30, 2005.

15. No evidence of prior interest, with one, possibly coincidental, caveat: a lecturer at the University of Illinois at Urbana-Champaign who baselessly stated, "The Critical Art Ensemble paints a picture of cyber-resistance that looks a lot like the descriptions of bin Laden's alleged network." Whether Heidi Brush's paper, "Electronic Jihad," was noticed by federal agents is anybody's guess. It was, however, reported on by Kevin Featherly in *Newsbytes*, October 16, 2001, and it was circulated on the Internet, among other places at lists.virus.org/isn-0110/msg00110.html.

16. Quoted in "Anti-biotech Artist Indicted for Possessing 'Harmless' Bacteria," Brendan Coyne, *The New Standard*, July 6, 2004; available at newstandardnews.net/content/?action=show_item&itemid=646. Furthermore, the bacteria purchased by Kurtz and Ferrell is often used in high school and middle school classrooms.

17. An illegible fingerprint faxed to the US from Spain was later blamed for Mayfield's much-publicized humiliation and the FBI sheepishly admitted blunder.

18. The attorney general apparently dropped this aspect of the investigation after being pressured by the American Civil Liberties Union.

19. If Kurtz and Ferrell are guilty of what they're accused of doing, this would be no more than a contract dispute over $256 of harmless bacteria. Nevertheless, neither American Cultures, who supplied the cultures, nor the University of Pittsburgh, through which the transaction occurred, have brought forth any charges.

20. On March 17, 2005, almost a year after the initial subpoenas were issued, Steve Barnes, another co-founder of CAE, was issued a new subpoena listing, upon it the US Code Title 18 Prohibitions with Respect to Biological Weapons. Barnes testified on April 18 and reports that new charges of bioterror may be

pending in the case. See: "Artists Experience Déjà Vu in 'Bioterror' Case that Won't Go Away," by Brendan Coyne for the *New Standard*, April 25, 2005; also at newstandardtimes.net/content/?items=1733.

21. See John Dudley Miller, "Butler's last stand: plague researcher may receive a long prison term in fraud case," *The Scientist* vol. 18 issue 4, March 1, 2004; www.thescientist.com/yr2004/mar/prof2_040301.html.

22. The letter is available as a downloadable PDF file at www.fas.org/sgp/news/2003/08/nas081503.pdf.

23. Rick Weiss, "Scientists Object to NIH's Bioterror Focus," *Washington Post*, March 1, 2005, p. A13.

24. James Glanz, "Scientists Accuse White House of Distorting Facts," *New York Times*, February 18, 2004; www.nytimes.com/2004/02/18/science/18CND-RESE.html.

25. David Schubert's commentary was published in the conservative newspaper *San Diego Union-Tribune*, July 9, 2004, p. B7; available at www.organicconsumers.org/corp/bushscience071604.cfm.

26. According to Debora MacKenzie, grants "for work on non-biodefense disease germs fell 27%, while grants for studying model bacteria such as Escherichia coli fell by a whopping 41%," "Top U.S. biologists oppose biodefense boom," *The New Scientist*, March 2005; www.newscientist.com/channel/health/dn7074.

27. Martha Rosler pointed out to me that the CAE case is unlike that of Mapplethorpe, Serrano, *et al* insofar as it has not directly implicated cultural institutions or arts administrators. Is it also possible that "subversive" sexual imagery, when decried as amoral by the State, rallies those who defend individual liberty, whereas "subversive" activism, when decried as terrorism, has an opposite, censorial effect?

28. Australian artist and writer Anna Munster is one of the few to challenge assumptions about neo-McCarthyism. However, she hypothesizes a far more ominous, matrix-like "bio-logic" at work, and that CAE was snared by its self-regulating nodal network thanks to the chance occasion of Hope's heart attack. Although Munster's novel argument suffers from a lack of historical or economic analysis, she nonetheless offers several insights, including her statement that the charges facing Kurtz and Ferrell arise from their having violated "expectations pertaining to the conduct of intellectual and cultural work." "Why is bioart not terrorism? Some critical nodes in the networks of informatic life," published in the e-journal *Culture Machine*, no. 7, 2005; culturemachine.tees.ac.uk/frm_f1.htm. For a more grounded and thoroughly researched analysis of CAE see Claire Pentecost, "Reflections on the Case by the U.S. Justice Department against Steven Kurtz and Robert Ferrell," at: www.caedefensefund.org/reflections.html.

29. According to the *Encyclopedia of the American Left*, some ten thousand people may have lost their jobs during the McCarthy Era of the late 1940s and early 1950s. (Eds. Buhle, Buhle, and Georgakas, Garland Publishing, New York and London, 1990, p. 459).

30. Remarkably, it was to protect the minority interest that constitutional freedoms were initially devised.

31. See endnote 28.

32. Eva Cockroft, "Abstract Expressionism: Weapon of the Cold War," *Artforum*, June 1974, pp. 39–41. Serge Gilbault, *How New York Stole the Idea of Modern Art*, University of Chicago Press, Chicago, 1983.

33. Thomas Frank, "Why Johnny can't dissent," in *Commodify Your Dissent: Salvos from* The Baffler, eds. Thomas Frank and Matt Weiland, W.W. Norton & Company, New York and London, 1997, p. 34.

34. See Yomango.net as well as the Yes Men, who are perhaps the finest practitioners of pilfering corporate power today, at www.theyesmen.org.

35. David Harvey, *The Condition of Postmodernity: An Enquiry into the Origins of Cultural Change*, Cambridge, MA, Blackwell Publishers, first published in 1990.

36. "It was the threat of protectionism that the U.S. used to attack those [other] countries unwilling to go global thereby transforming the impulse for nationalism itself as a means of opening up markets," in "Finance and American empire," Leo Panitch and Sam Gindin, *The Socialist Register*, 2005, pp. 24 & 26.

37. Francis Fukuyama, "The Illusion of Exceptionalism," *Journal of Democracy*, 1997, 8.3, pp. 146–149; academic2.american.edu/~dfagel/Markets&democracyfukuyama.html.

38. Brian Holmes, "The Flexible Personality for a New Cultural Critique," in *Hieroglyphs of the Future*, Arkzin publishers, Zagreb, Croatia, 2001, p. 139.

39. Ibid., p. 122.

40. Quoted by John Dunn in "Designing a Business Revolution," *Georgia Tech Magazine*, vol. 76 no. 2, Fall 1999; gtalumni.org/Publications/magazine/fall99/west.html.

41. Matthew Jesse Jackson, "Managing the Avant-Garde," *New Left Review* 32, March–April 2005, p. 114.

42. Taking this one large step further, the networked operatives of the financial world who covertly seek to exploit or bankrupt other corporations and even nations are veritable

encyclopedias of tactical methodology. Indeed, one might even compare them to Al Qaeda agents if not for the premium they place on self-preservation. A good example is John Perkins, who "declares his guilt" in *Confessions of an Economic Hit Man*, Berrett-Koehler Publishers, San Francisco, 2004.

43. President Clinton's former undersecretary of commerce for international trade, Jeffrey E. Garten, has warned that the new nationalism will lead to "escalating tensions between the U.S. and Europe over export subsidies, steel, agriculture, genetically modified food, and privacy regulations." In "The politics of fortune: a new agenda for business leaders," on the website of American Economic Alert at www.americaneconomicalert.org/view_art.asp?Prod_ID=662.

44. Ironically, it is the liberal press that appears to be calling for a return to the cultural politics of the cold war years. In a *New York Times* op-ed piece from August 9, 2004, the "liberal" paper implored the State Department to find new public and private partners to help it shape a coherent cultural policy and construct a broader and more open system to select and finance artists for international exhibitions. Those artists are one of the best ways of letting the world know that cultural freedom and excellence matter in this country.

45. Undoubtedly, creativity and innovation will remain central to the weapons, security, and surveillance industries, especially.

46. Tom Peters, quoted by Stefan Stern in "A Guru Aims High on Prozac," www.work911.com/cgi-bin/links/jump.cgi?ID=4166.

47. "In Dark Times," 1936–1938, in *Bertolt Brecht Poems, 1913–1956*, eds. J. Willett and R. Manheim with E. Fried, Methen Books, New York, Toronto, London, Sydney, 1976, p. 274.

Alan Gilbert

Startling and Effective: Writing Art and Politics after 9/11

Pores 2, 2002; reprinted in *Another Future*, Middletown, CT: Wesleyan University Press, 2006

This past summer, as I was sitting in one of Anthology Film Archives' movie theaters waiting for the documentary film *Gaza Strip* (Longley, 2002) to begin, I overheard snippets of conversation coming from a group of six or seven women and men from different backgrounds and in their mid-twenties sitting in the row directly in front of me. One of them was providing some context for the film they were about to watch (it was produced by an American filmmaker who planned to spend a couple weeks in the Gaza Strip making a documentary about the current intifada, but ended up staying three months and filming everyday life under its harsh conditions); another person was talking about films she'd recently seen at Anthology (run by Jonas Mekas, Anthology Film Archives remains one of the few places in New York City, and the United States as a whole, that shows avant-garde and experimental films on a daily basis; even the films of old-school experimental filmmakers such as Stan Brakhage are screened monthly); another member of the group was talking about her new job. Then suddenly, or so it seemed to me because I hadn't heard any of the particular conversation leading up to it, someone in the group said: "It'll be twenty years before anyone makes an avant-garde film again." Intrigued as I was to hear any responses to such a claim, or further clarifications from the person who uttered it, I couldn't catch much else, and the movie started soon after.

Gaza Strip is a mostly conventional documentary that nevertheless eschews a number of conventional documentary techniques: no solemn voice-over, a certain amount of non-linear narrative and editing, and a sprinkling of digital effects that are meant to enhance moments of emergency and danger. Its organizing conceit is to follow around a Palestinian boy named Mohammed Hejazi as he throws rocks at Israeli tanks, sells newspapers, visits his young friends after they've been shot by Israeli soldiers, and joins funerals. But plenty of other aspects of life for Palestinians in the Gaza Strip are also represented: bulldozed houses, snipers firing on schoolyards, rockets fired into houses, and poisonous gas attacks; in other words, the film has everything except, as J. Hoberman pointed out in his *Village Voice* review, footage of the horrific carnage inflicted on Israelis by Palestinian suicide bombers (2002). But *Gaza Strip* isn't blatantly biased, nor is it overly didactic. Simply filming the Israeli army terrorizing Palestinians in the Gaza Strip is damning enough, especially when a soldier in one of its tanks rolls what looks like a metal toy toward a group of Palestinian children playing, only to have one of the kids discover after he picks it up that it's actually a small bomb which then blows most of his abdomen away.

The one-hundredth issue of the journal *October* is a special anniversary volume somewhat ironically dedicated to the topic of obsolescence. A number of artists responded to a questionnaire dealing with the concept, and two roundtables addressed it in relation to contemporary art criticism and "American avant-garde film," respectively. Both roundtables returned again and again to the idea of institutionality—in relation to visual art and the discourses surrounding it. In the roundtable on art criticism, institutionality was seen as a potential danger to art and art criticism, while, at the same time, all of the participants generally agreed on the difficulties of working, or even conceiving themselves, outside the art-world system. Andrea Fraser, whose renowned brand of institutional critique receives ongoing institutional support, was perhaps the most representative roundtable member in this regard. In contrast, the roundtable on "American avant-garde film" mostly embraced institutionality as the only way in which this film practice could continue to reach an audience beyond a very select few, the majority of whom are fellow avant-garde filmmakers.

The lone exception, experimental filmmaker Ken Jacobs, espoused a do-it-yourself 1960s—later punk, later Internet—fuck-the-system outsider stance in which artmaking isn't dependent upon institutional support for its vitality. He also fell back on what might be seen as a relatively separate strand of vanguardist innovation:

> *[Ken] Jacobs: ... But then you have things that uphold the idea of the avant-garde, which is to forage and get out there into new territory, to think completely freshly, come up with whole other ways of putting things together, unexpected things to go for. New things have been made all through these years. New things are being made now.*
> *[Paul] Arthur: I'm sure that's true, but I find this aspect of the cultural ideology somewhat suspect, even obsolescent. This idea of constant innovation, of stretching the envelope of what's possible in cinema ... I find that a problematic notion at this point.*
> *[Annette] Michelson: Why?*
> *Arthur: Because I don't see that much stretching these days, but I do see a very strongly institutionalized movement, and for me, that's the essential definition.* (2002: 117)

Here, film critic Paul Arthur is referring less to institutionality as a network of support encompassing the production, distribution, and screening of experimental film, and more to a codified, and even ossified, vanguardist aesthetics. If the notion of vanguardism is conceptually derived from the militaristic scouting forays made by the lead part of an advancing army, then maybe after a century of the worst warfare in human history and plenty of avant-garde experiments (many of them ending up in some dubious political affiliations), it's time for the avant-garde to drop back a little, not in order to march shoulder-to-shoulder with this army (as ethicist Emmanuel Levinas once described Martin Heidegger's booted march toward Being [1987: 40–41, 93–94]), but to meet it face-to-face. Semantically, at least, the avant-garde would no longer be an avant-garde; but, then, maybe the army would no longer be an army.

After the feelings of shock, sadness, and anger I experienced in the hours following the attacks on the World Trade Center, and when more information began to filter in about exactly what happened, my two initial thoughts were: 1) this will seriously damage the Palestinian cause, since sentiment in mainstream US media and society had finally begun to shift toward a less one-sided understanding of Israeli-Palestinian relations; and 2) this is partly the responsibility of the US auto industry—in collaboration with the major oil companies—for refusing to develop serious alternatives to the gas combustion engine. These may appear odd first thoughts; but one can imagine what it was like to be in New York City on the evening of September 11, 2001, watching the smoke rising from southern Manhattan's enormous scar billow against a spectacular sunset, rendered, it may sound grotesque to say (although people in Los Angeles experience this all the time), even more spectacular by the pollutants in the atmosphere. Everyone in New York City that day and in the following days was breathing in the cremated remains of thousands of people, though absolutely no one could say it—then, or even now. Instantly, what seemed like millions of flyers of missing persons with photographs and contact information for relatives and friends covered every available surface. Spontaneous public spaces were established in parks and open areas around the city; and while some writers exaggerated the level of civic discourse and debate in these temporary public spheres, they nevertheless were places where people congregated and dialogued freely and with a certain degree of self-allowed autonomy.

This made the authorities nervous, but the level of grief was so intense that even then-mayor Rudolph Giuliani—who was pleased to be able to finally run the city like the police state he always dreamed of, and who did a good job of it, if efficiently running a police state is something one can be complimented on or take pride in—couldn't tear down the flyers or break up the gatherings. But within a couple weeks he did, and suddenly the flyers were gone, as if overnight, and people no longer congregated in public spaces. The attacks also meant the Bush administration finally had an objective other than to loot everything in sight; and just as it's easy to forget how low Giuliani had sunk in the general opinion of New Yorkers before 9/11 (the second fatal shooting of an unarmed African-American man by his police corps was one of the final straws), to the point of excusing himself from his Senate race against Hillary Clinton, so, too, it is difficult to remember exactly what the Bush administration was up to before its attentions were turned toward Afghanistan and Iraq. Unlike the Reagan administration, which at least formulated a pernicious ideology of trickle-down economics to justify its greed, Bush, Jr., and his recycled Reagan/Bush-père cronies were/are only after one thing: wealth, and the most massive redistribution of it in the US since the latter half of the nineteenth century.

Exploiting contradictions is one strategy art, writing, and the larger cultural sphere might explore in the wake of 9/11. Focusing in on contradiction, exposing it without necessarily adding explicit commentary and/or a heavy-handed narrative structure, is a dialogic process, one that can be politicized without in turn being made demagogic. But an attention to contradiction is as much a strategy of reading as it is a mode of cultural production. In a so-called "Information Age" of media monopolies, with their consolidations and restrictions of available information, it's increasingly essential to read this information against the grain. It's also crucial to cultivate alternative sources of information, which are in wild proliferation, whether in print or on the Internet. Both attitudes toward information are summarized in Marshall McLuhan's declaration: "When information is brushed against information … the results are startling and effective" (1967: 76, 78). There's no reason why art can't be "startling" and "effective," even though the two categories have frequently been kept separate: the former associated with formal innovation and extravagance, the latter with dry political utility and pedagogy.

It's important that an approach to cultural production and reading that brushes information against information has a wide range of applications. For instance, I wouldn't be the first to point to the contradictions at the heart of David LaChapelle's photography and its very voguish attempt to blur the distinctions between fashion and art (2002, 1999, 1996). On the surface, LaChapelle's work is among the most effusive celebrations of celebrity culture currently produced today. It makes gushing television shows such as *Entertainment Tonight* and *Access Hollywood*, which also push celebrity culture and its products, downright dull in comparison. But perhaps LaChapelle's work is more complex than this. Perhaps Jeff Koons isn't Warhol's most immediate Pop offspring—LaChapelle is. (After all, he got his start photographing for Warhol's *Interview* magazine.) Like Warhol, the image factory and its resultant celebrity goods—and vice versa—is LaChapelle's world. Similar to Warhol's work as discussed by Hal Foster in *The Return of the Real*, specifically his '60s silkscreens of car crashes, criminals, and even celebrities (1996: 130–136), there's a sense of violence and death in LaChapelle's depictions of the commonplace-as-incongruous and the incongruous-as-commonplace in mass culture. Celebrities may strive to transcend mortality in both Warhol and LaChapelle (and in this their art subscribes to one of the most conventional of aesthetic notions), but death and the intrinsic, never-resolved contradiction it brings always sniffing at the edges of the frame.

At one level, Warhol and LaChapelle's projects couldn't make much more clear—without, that is, becoming purely "effective"—the primary relationship between consumption and death. To this I would add the relationship in capitalist societies between consumption, death, and war. But this connection is also a contradiction: to consume is to try to elude death, and to consume is also supposed to negate war, as Thomas Friedman famously remarked when he said that two countries with a McDonald's in them would never go to war (rather quickly disproved when the US bombed Serbia, to which Friedman responded that this exception actually proved his rule [1999]). In their most complex work, Warhol and LaChapelle bypass irony (the easiest of critical gestures) for contradiction. The very excessiveness of LaChapelle's depiction of celebrity and riches practically begs the viewer to read back critically into the constructed image and to understand that too much is literally too much. Of course, this begging is also a sign of the work's complicity, and one should be careful not to exaggerate the critical aspect of LaChapelle's images.

The contradictions I'm pointing to in LaChapelle's photography may serve as a reading of resistance, but the key is to link up this reading with larger social, political, and cultural formations and movements. And for that, a globalized view is necessary, an awareness that's becoming more widespread, if the unexpected strong-selling success of Michael Hardt and Antonio Negri's *Empire* is any indication (2000)—though *Empire* might do a better job of reminding its readers that without robustly functioning nation-states, transnational capitalism would collapse within months, if not weeks. If any contemporary photographer could be considered the polar opposite of David LaChapelle it might be Allan Sekula. Sekula's epic *Fish Story* was shown in its entirety at this year's Documenta. In his installation of the work and book of the same title (1995), Sekula documents global shipping routes and ports of transnational trade. If, on first glance, LaChapelle's work is "startling," Sekula's work might be considered "effective." Yet there's a rigorous attention to formal concerns in Sekula's photographs. Sekula may work in a somewhat traditional documentary mode, but unlike documentary that tries to capture an entire span of intellectual and emotional response within a single frame or film or video, a Sekula photograph is incomprehensible without the context he creates for it with accompanying images and text, which in turn comment directly on larger socio-economic conditions. The failure of traditional documentary is that it trusts the immediate impact of its images, and remains satisfied with these direct representations. This distinction between different documentary methods is cited by critic and curator Matthew Higgs: "Writing elsewhere on documentary photography, British artist Liam Gillick has described the kind of work that seeks meaning in the apparent profundity of its subject matter in lieu of offering a 'constructed critique' as a 'stunned mirror'" (Higgs 2002: 167). Sekula's quick movement in *Fish Story* between the macro and the micro, his constant historicizing as well as his attention to the smallest details, are the result of a complex formal and critical process. What at first glance makes Sekula's work appear the product of a classical documentary lineage turns out to be his refusal to accept consumption as the fundamental social and economic reality. Even in a world full of simulacra, most commodities still have to be produced and transported before they can be consumed. In a manner that's the complete opposite of LaChapelle, Sekula's work seeks to strip the commodity of its fetishistic dimension. This forces a reading of resistance to be read back, in turn, into a capitalist economy and social organization that uses an ideology of consumption—of goods and images—to camouflage inherent structural contradictions.

Unfortunately, not much has changed, in art or otherwise, after 9/11. At the same time, a quote such as, "It'll be twenty years before anyone makes an avant-garde film again," however off-hand, however unsubstantiated, however unjustified, perhaps could only have been made after 9/11. But has anything changed? A space has opened up within political discourse and artistic practice in the US, a space partially and metaphorically vacated by the Twin Towers, in which contradictions have the potential to become more evident. Yet if one of the main challenges of various forms of cultural production is to expose contradictions in dominant ideologies, then they must also learn to expose contradictions within themselves. Without serious self-critique, art slowly loses its capacity for anything more than shallow institutional critique. For the avant-garde in particular (or what's left of it), self-critique may allow it to step back—though not so far as to become a rearguard—and engage with the progressive cultural populism it needs in order to rejuvenate itself and again function as a radical project.

Works cited

Arthur, Paul, Brian Frye, Chrissie Iles, Ken Jacobs, Annette Michelson, and Malcolm Turvey. "Round Table: Obsolescence and American Avant-Garde Film," *October* 100 (Spring 2002).

Foster, Hal. *The Return of the Real: The Avant-Garde at the End of the Century.* Cambridge, MA: The MIT Press, 1996.

Friedman, Thomas L. "The Golden Arches Theory of Conflict Prevention," *The Lexus and the Olive Tree: Understanding Globalization.* New York: Anchor Books, 1999.

Hardt, Michael and Antonio Negri. *Empire.* Cambridge, MA: Harvard University Press, 2000.

Higgs, Matthew. "Same Old Same Old," *Artforum* vol. 41, no. 1, September 2002.

Hoberman, J. "Crime Scenes," *Village Voice* vol. 47, no. 31, July 31–August 6, 2002.

LaChapelle, David. *Photographs.* Vienna: Museums Betriebsgesellschaft mbH, 2002.

– *Hotel LaChapelle.* Boston, New York and London: Bulfinch Press, 1999.

– *LaChapelle Land.* New York: Simon & Schuster, 1996.

Levinas, Emmanuel. *Time and the Other* (trans. Richard A. Cohen). Pittsburgh: Duquesne University Press, 1996.

Longley, James. *Gaza Strip*, 2002. Directed and produced by James Longley.

McLuhan, Marshall and Quentin Fiore. *The Medium Is the Massage: An Inventory of Effects.* Corte Madera, CA: Ginkgo Press, 1967.

Sekula, Allan. *Fish Story.* Düsseldorf: Richter Verlag, 1995.

Robert Morris

From a Chomskian Couch: The Imperialistic Unconscious

Critical Inquiry 29, Summer 2003, pp. 678–694

Dr. Chomsky sits impassively behind the black leather couch. I lie down. Minutes pass in silence. I look up at the sign on the wall that reads It's part of moral progress to be able to face things that once looked as if they weren't problems.[1] *I imagine a faint smile crossing the lips of the doctor. He uncrosses his legs and recrosses them. And to help me along, says…*

Dr. C: There need be no objects in the world that correspond to what we talk about, even in the simplest cases, nor does anyone believe there are.[2]

A lexical item provides us with a certain range of perspectives for viewing what we take to be things in the world, or what we conceive in other ways … The terms themselves do not refer…[3]

Me: Okay, Doc, I'll just say what comes into my mind as I recline here on your couch. What could the perspectives be to the phrase *A century of unimaginable violence*? Or should the question be, What are yours? Since mine might very well be different. Century? Unimaginable violence? The terms are too diffuse, general, multiple, and complex for any expectation of a common reference. Reference is not needed for language to work. And meaning may not be produced by the concatenation of the sentence. And isn't the ethical connected to this thought? Aren't we anxious to be right about things? And does the aesthetic underlie this? Or is the aesthetic supervenient on the ethical? Or are the ethical and the aesthetic inseparably entangled, as well as basic? Have we reached bedrock yet?

Silence again. Then Dr. C reminds me of some words of Charles Saunders Peirce who he notes in passing was crazier and smarter than either of us could ever hope to be. He quotes at me from memory:

Dr. C: Esthetics is the science of ideals, or of that which is objectively admirable and without any ulterior reason … Ethics, or the science of right and wrong, must appeal to Esthetics for aid in determining the *summum bonum*.[4]

Me: In the dream there was *Duchamp's Given: 1. The Waterfall, 2. The Illuminating Gas…* But the liquid fall was of blood and the illumination that of a metal behaving like a gas and moving faster than anything in the universe.
By the mid-twentieth century both holocaust and nuclear detonation had shaded

the usual perspectives. And in retrospect, what perspective is to be taken on the American work of art in the first years of the twenty-first century? And what aesthetic does the ethical now appeal to here on the edge of the millennium?

Dr. C: It may be expected that conscious beliefs will form a scattered and probably uninteresting subpart of the full cognitive structure.[5]

Me: From Charles Wilson Peale's *Exhuming of the Mastodon* to the Twin Towers: the evolution of the *Mega Image* (MEGIG), the sublime that begins in the "natural world" of a vast new continent. Allegories of a certain *American Phenomenological Awe* (AMPHENA) repeated endlessly. Tall tales, railroads, vast western spaces, gold rushes, gunfighters, all to be balanced by an aesthetic prescription for gigantism in art. From Gutzon Borglum to Robert Smithson, Frederic Church to Michael Heizer, John Ford to Bruce Nauman. If Mount Palomar chagrins James Turrell, what do the Twin Towers tell us of Mark di Suvero? We approach cautiously here beneath the shadow of an urge. Dangerous territory. Artists in berets equipped for secret ops. Standing at attention, ready for aesthetic assaults. No, it's a dream, another bad Schwarzenegger movie on too large a screen. One of those exploding patriotic docudramas. Good art wouldn't be so… unconscious. Artists wouldn't *enlist*, would they? Artists don't *serve*. Artists aren't dragged down by the past. Anyway America doesn't have a past, only a future. And AMPHENA? Well, you've got to make yourself heard in a culture of spectacle. Can't blame anybody for that. Then that 9/11 spectacle. Big art event, so Karlheinz Stockhausen claimed. Well, a German said it, not one of us. Super spectacle. No getting around that. When the dust settled, as it is still doing, American art somehow looked different.

Dr. C: Now you're cranking.

Me: Everybody knows what Dr. Johnson said so long ago—patriotism is the last refuge of the scoundrel. But haven't we all been patriots in this vast land? No, that's not the right way to put it. Things are more elusive, more unconscious. Something vast stands behind us. We are obliged to stand tall. It looms behind us and we hear it on rare occasions like the roll of summer thunder. It is something large and we sense it is there even though we never see it directly. We hear only the rumble of blurred words. But America presents only… its great variety. So great a variety it can be said to own no reference. Anything so vast, so greatly varied, eludes reference. To begin a sentence, *America is…* is to feel oneself step off into empty space. And when the bunting is taken down and the band has gone home power vanishes behind the marble façade. Or around a corner like Mack the Knife. But art was listening while the band was playing, tapping its foot…unconsciously.

Dr. C: Let me deal with the unconscious. Just talk.

Me: The ideology of the monumental. From Frederic Church to Richard Serra. The numbing sublime. From nature to abstract art. The Wagner effect.[6] Overwhelming the human scale. Self-importance and grandiloquence. In classical times monumental art was in the service of military victories. Now the US is the dominant world power, the planetary imperial force. A nation where bigger was always better. And today the monuments are to what? Today, at the beginning of the twenty-first century, the idea of justifying the monumental in purely formal terms reeks of that blind ideology of art as autonomous, uninfected by the culture that produces it. Large abstract art is of course the most deluded example of such modernist denials. Spectacle is dedicated to avoiding consciousness and is always transporting in delivering the phenomenological ride. AMPHENA is always dedicated to forgetting. And there is always that spot of residue in large contemporary works of art. It feels like a bit of grit in the eye of memory.

Dr. C: Is this criticism or confession?

Me: Is there a difference?

Dr. C: You may be beyond help.

Me: The challenge of ambitious American art since the mid-twentieth century was up to the task of producing cultural icons befitting a world empire. What makes Jackson Pollock's canvases function as banners for an empire? First, their implicit defeat of European paintings; second, their focus on energy to sustain the agonistic triumph; and, third, their pragmatism in harnessing process. Besides the large-scale requirement, these characteristics—the agonistic, the energetic, and the pragmatic—have remained requirements of ambitious American art regardless of genre affiliations. A pessimistic attitude, always judged anti-American, has generally disqualified, but if writ large, even a Claes Oldenburg could be run up the flagpole.

The exception in the last half of the twentieth century to official American icons of the big, the loud, and/or the energetic was the work of Jasper Johns, who almost never worked on a monumental scale. But then there were the iconic American flags and maps. His work, always filled to the seams with ambivalence, was never pessimistic. More significantly, he was the most historically pregnant American artist of the last century. Johns rewrote Pollock's pragmatism of material process into one of logical structure. Beginning with his influence on Frank Stella, Johns's lessons in the pragmatism of the structural device that unfolded to complete the work also made minimal art possible. Johns, the cold-eyed strategist, was nothing if not agonistic toward European art—but with such European elegance. It was as if General Erwin Rommel had switched sides to give demonstrations on how to achieve victory by eschewing material and energy for strategic logic. As much code breaker as strategist, Johns the cryptologist general stood as the paradigmatic American aesthetic cold warrior of the nineteen-fifties and early sixties. No other American artist of the last century emblematizes the aggressivity of the unconscious imperialistic impulse more than Johns. Miniaturizing while others bloated up scale, he demonstrated that with the right signs you could have the right stuff and finesse scale. The national flag General Johns marched under was large in every way but size. If Johns was the ultimate aesthetic cold warrior he was hardly responsible for the burgeoning manifestations of imperial-sublime art. Abstract expressionism of the fifties proclaimed a near religious faith in both abstraction and large scale. Johns denied both tenets of the doxology. Looking back at abstract expressionism today a kind of self-hypnosis is required. Without being possessed by a quasi-religious stupor those stained and painted acreages of Clifford Still, Barnett Newman, Jackson Pollock, Franz Kline, and Robert Motherwell appear vapid and inane. Only Ad Reinhardt, the most politically aware and active of all of them (signing every petition, appearing in every civil rights and anti-Vietnam march), had the consciousness to resist the rhetorical, all-American, self-congratulatory monumental scale which continues down to today, that American art of the imperialistic unconscious (IMPUNC).

Dr. C: There you go again with that word… but there were precedents to numbing scale.

Me: Well, there was Albert Speer.

Dr. C: And his proposed *Hall of the Volk* for the Third Reich…

Me: Sixteen times the size of St. Peter's in Rome. But let's get back to some really big American art. In the sixties Earth Art recapitulated the conquest of the West as an aesthetic allegory. Expansion into space is the growth of empire. Space is never free but acquired by aggressive occupation. Space is one of the commodities the planet is running out of. To have it locked up in large-scale art speaks of luxury and excess. The art of grand spaces from Rome to the Third Reich to Bilbao all speaks of empire. Michael Heizer's grandiose *City* in the desert may be the most demented and blatant metaphor yet for the IMPUNC gesture.

Dr. C: The Grand Inquisitor is articulating the view that freedom is dangerous and people need, and indeed at some level even want, subordination, mystery, authority, and so on.[7]

Me: Aggressively large-scale, grand scale occupation, the buzz of spectacle. A long list could be drawn up. From Pollock and Newman on down to Stella, di Suvero, Heizer, Turrell, Kelly, Serra. From Andy Warhol's yard goods of camouflage to Jeff Koons's flowering puppies. From Chuck Close to Jeff Wall, plus all that screaming big video from Bruce Nauman to Bill Viola… the list goes on…

Dr. C: Hmmm, all males so far…

Me: …and, just wait, includes virtually all ambitious American art regardless of genre. By this point the aesthetic strategies that can be combed out of this work yield little more than art lint. But a meaning leaks from the MEGIG at the unconscious level of desire—a desire to limn a metaphorical sign for American power. As Edmund Burke noted long ago, allegories of the sublime are always ultimately political. Our version of the sublime valorizes neither nature nor revolution but rather that peculiarly American status quo of domination and blindness. A refusal of memory and the other is to be expected from such an unconscious enterprise that asserts the present as the only temporal dimension: a depthless phenomenological now where awe and entertainment encircle one another.

Dr. C: And those few examples of miniaturization that run counter to your thesis—those forays into a bioart of invisible microbes and viruses?

Me: I'm not saying that the MEGIG is completely unopposed. But in the last few years we have seen a surfeit of large, multimedia installations (Ann Hamilton, Matthew Barney, and others) and multiscreen video installations (Nauman, Viola, Douglas Aitken, and others). In these genres the MEGIG has expanded to a kind of multisensory spectacle in which viewers are engulfed. Here they are no longer independent observers so much as passive particles floating within the sublime surround. Installation art of the spectacle has moved far beyond those forms of theatricality that used to keep Michael Fried up at night.[8]

If conceptual art wanted to give up the object in favor of the word, *multiscreen video installations* (MUSCRVIT) and *multimedia installation art of the spectacle* (INARSE) gives it up in favor of an expanded, multisensory theatrical space. A different perceptual space actually. The object, or even the single screen of projected imagery, delivers a single perceptual focus. MUSCRVIT and INARSE deliver a more peripheral, pulsating multifocus—a space of dedifferentiation. Here our attempt at focusing must give way to the vacant, all-embracing stare.[9] Of course this perceptual space is not without precedent. Giambattista Tiepolo's vast painted ceilings, impossible to take in from a single point of view, touch on the dedifferentiated space. But we must look to Cubism's shattered surfaces to find the first modernist attempt to systematically disrupt representation from being encompassed by either proximate or distant vision. MUSCRVIT literalizes this by temporal and spatial expansions. And by foregrounding this fracture of focus MUSCRVIT attempts to solve that problematic of what to do with time. The hiccup in time of the looped repetition or the heavy-footed recording of "real time," the two strategies pioneered by single screen video, were failures. What was so massively boring on the single screen (which, in fact, still occupies the perceptual space of painting)—lives far better in a space of dedifferentiated focus provided by MUSCRVIT.

Dr. C: So MUSCRVIT gets to it better than INARSE?

Me: Sometimes you get INARSE and MUSCRVIT in the same place.

Dr. C: Sounds like old neuritis and neuralgia. But what about the IMPUNC?

Me: We're talking large-scale here. That plus the passivity required of the viewer of INARSE and MUSCRVIT make them divine vehicles for the IMPUNC. You could say that INARSE is the very emblem of the IMPUNC. Rome had the Colosseum and we have the Dia.

Dr. C: You mentioned Conceptual art. Wasn't it an exception to the case you are making?

Me: In the beginning when it said no to modernism, but by now conceptual art has seeped into everything. Now there is a version of it you might call *Conceptual Folk Art*, a rubric that covers bread bakers, tattooers, back rubbers, body huggers, quilters, feet washers, masochists of self-inflected suffering…

Dr. C: That sounds like body art…

Me: *Body Art*! The first bad body art was the Crucifixion, Smithson used to say.

Dr. C: But the artist as gift giver and sufferer might be a form of penance for all those past MEGIGs of the IMPUNC. Maybe we are seeing a form of resistance and implicit critique here.

Me: Well, Doc, I think your hopes are illusory. Nobody is apologizing.

Dr. C: The idea that we might apologize for having left maybe half a million dead or hideously deformed fetuses lined up in Saigon hospitals, that we might apologize for it, or even help the victims, that idea doesn't arise. [*P*, p. 56]

Me: The one time the phenomenological sublime attempted to turn itself toward memory was with the Vietnam Veterans Memorial in Washington DC These minimalistic walls for staging nativistic grief are also effective screens against consciousness (perhaps one wall obliterates the memory of North Vietnamese dead while the other suppresses the criminality of the war). There is nothing like the monumental minimal for suppressing the gruesome aspect of the political behind impregnable martial forms—whether this takes the form of those long steps at Nuremberg or the sinking black walls of the VVM. Names of the American dead carved on the VVM's polished minimal flanks reflect back the images of the mourners whose glances will never penetrate the granite to see causes and responsibility, level accusations, or exact justice. Nothing works like the minimal sublime for performing this *aufhebung* of cancelling consciousness by raising up formal, phenomenological awe. The VVM is the most prominent national monument of/to our unconscious imperialistic sublime. That it was designed by an Asian-American female also indicates that the IMPUNC is not an exclusively gendered or racial category.

Dr. C: Are you feeling lightheaded?

Me: We feel there is something buoying us up. There is a momentum and it is always forward and never looks back. A force from somewhere. Unseen, we feel it has always been there, urging pride on us. Oh, but when those towers fell, something went out of the force. In those dreadful moments of collapse a different reference became attached. Or uncovered. Could those two monstrous towers have been masking out something other than the sun?

Dr. C: These are things people need to know if they want to understand anything about themselves. They are known by the victims, of course, but the perpetrators prefer to look elsewhere.[10]

Me: It was nothing we *consciously* signed up for. It was just a tradition, this scouting of the MEGIG. It was expected. Not exactly a rule. But everyone was moving toward it, buoyed up by that unseen force. We never had a name for it. Now I'm trying to find one. But if I found it could I say it? Would it be part of a private language that everybody from Wittgenstein on said couldn't exist? Maybe I could whisper that name to Mary or to Peter…

Dr. C: Successful communication between Peter and Mary does not entail the existence of shared meanings or shared pronunciations in a public language (or a common treasure of thoughts or articulations of them), any more than physical resemblance between Peter and Mary entails the existence of a public form that they share.[11]

Me: But we wanted to be public. We believed in it. Something open to all. Nothing hidden, private. Everything above board and transparent. Then it could be really grand for those grand, public spaces. No narcissistic belly button stuff. And go easy on the shaggy expressionism. And nothing political either—unless of course those knee-jerk, liberal, overdetermined gestures toward race and gender. I mean shouldn't we remember modernism for having done *something*? Well today of course we can laugh at the idea of an old-fashioned autonomy. It seems like a faded photograph from another time. So what if today our grand public space throbs with entertainment? Isn't it better lit for all that? And who says we shouldn't entertain? Who says we shouldn't mesmerize with size? Who says MUSCRVIT and INARSE should not overwhelm? Who says the MEGIG is hiding anything? Who says AMPHENA is not still the way to go?

Dr. C: The intellectual class is supposed to be so well trained and so well indoctrinated that they don't need a whip. They just react spontaneously in the ways that will serve external power interests, without awareness, thinking they're doing honest, dedicated work. [*P*, p. 80]

Me: *Serve*? Us? What? How? Who's got the time? We're holding up the MEGIG, and it's a hell of a lot of work. We're doing our job, which is to furnish that grand space with something for people to come and see and marvel at.

Dr. C: In a democracy you have to control people's minds. You can't control them by force. There's a limited capacity to control them by force, and since they have to be controlled and marginalized, be "spectators of action," not "participants." [*P*, p. 152]

Me: You are pulling us toward what is irrelevant to our concerns. All we started out to do was to compare our MEGIGs to those vanished Twin Towers, just for the sake of a little perspective. And now the tone of accusation. What we really resent here are insinuations of a lack of innocence on our part.

We work in intuitive ways, ways that have to be more or less... unconscious. We may be serving forces we don't want to look at, filling up spaces provided by the ruling class, taking our vows of amnesia and no questions asked. But we're American artists and our power depends on that saturated and resplendent now.

Dr. C: [uncrosses and recrosses legs]

Me: But did it what? Allegorize some distribution of power? The kind of power we ever had in mind was the power of the MEGIG—big, bold, clean, sweeping you off your feet. That's what you came for, wasn't it? And you want to suggest there is some readable iconography behind all that formal variety? All that grand space of INARSE and the practice of AMPHENA might... what? Be screening something off? Well, it wasn't all just big, galumphing formalism. There was lots of ironic stuff in there about the empty, tinny aspects of America. And we can't be accused of ever being a violent group.[12]

Dr. C: Part of the reason why the US is trying to look as violent and vindictive and out of control as possible is to frighten off Europe and others, to say, We know we can't convince you, but get out of our way, because we're violent and dangerous. [*P*, p. 51]

Me: That's going too far. Those things are for the others. We remain innocent and sort of... unconscious. With certain exceptions, doubt, resistance, memory, and the contemplative mark the European aesthetic. American art, with certain exceptions, is distanced and distinguished from this by an aesthetic of immediacy and the aggressively invasive and occupying impulse. These are not merely formal categories.

A common language and dominant religious outlook are said to characterize a national culture. But Peirce's insight suggests we look to culturally specific aesthetic tendencies for a deeper assessment. It is not a question of stereotypes here but of tendencies, predilections, assumptions, tropes, and desires that move in ways that are less than... conscious.

Dr. C: [quoting Carl Schmitt, jurist of the Third Reich] "Tell me who your enemy is and I'll tell you who you are."

Me: Space may or may not be God as the great American Puritan, Jonathan Edwards, once said,[13] but it is surely a source of anxiety, maybe even a form of anxiety. What we do with space tells us who we are. The kinds of spaces we make, what we put in them, and how we put ourselves into them come to define us. Different cultures have different personal and public spaces. The spaces of Red Square or Tiananmen Square are not those of Pennsylvania Avenue. Foucault has spoken about such overdetermined, politicized spaces as prisons and schools. But there are also those more diffuse cultural spaces. Spaces that one goes up to. "Meaning something," Wittgenstein said, "is like going up to someone."[14] But there are also those spaces that come up to oneself. Perhaps there is no mind/body problem, only a mind/space problem.

Dr. C: [rolls eyes upward, looks at watch]

Me: Every cultural space has a certain semantic/pneumatic aspect. Meanings are read within a certain pressure and density of affect. There are spaces that invite and those that command. Cultural spaces do both. Once these commands were given a little more sotto voce. And what commands are heard today in those spaces of the new museums sprouting up everywhere? In the nineteen-twenties and thirties there were the movie palaces—the Fox of Atlanta, Grauman's Egyptian[15] and Chinese theaters of Hollywood. Today Frank Gehry, Santiago Calatrava, and others fashion new fantasy palaces of entertainment in the shape of the art museum where the spaces of spectacle once again benumb, lull, and command. Spaces of AMPHENA, spaces framing the MEGIG. Within these quintessential American spaces one hears a slight buzzing sounds. Perhaps that low, vibrating rumble is the echo of Pennsylvania Avenue. Listen too closely and it fades. Maybe it is just a ringing in the ears due to the vast amount of enclosed cubic feet of space. But inside or outside a certain commanding rhythm animates things. One can almost hear the sound of martial music. John Philip Sousa echoes across the tumbling volumes. A stirring, imperial strut animates those soaring arches. Here in the spectacle of the new museum/pleasure palace we hear the hymn of IMPUNC.

Dr. C: Then you should ask whether policies and the shaping of information reflect the distribution of power. That's what any rational person would expect. [*P*, p. 27]

Me: It is not a big step from the large, aloof, chromed, corporate spaces of the Chelsea galleries to the pleasure-palace art museum. But it is a different step. You must go up to the former; the latter rushes up to you. The former might deign to part with the fetish, for a price, in private; the latter gives you a feel in public. Both spaces exude overconfidence and condescension. Both flaunt the force. Both have folded within themselves the electric tingle of Pennsylvania Avenue. The MEGIG slides from the former to the latter on greased rails. The MEGIG services these two imperial spaces that were made for one another.

Dr. C: And these sublime spaces and things are saying to the world…

Me: America is saying to the world, Get out of the way.

Dr. C: You're quoting me.

Me: A Freudian slip.

Dr. C: And the American culture of AMPHENA, MEGIG, INARSE, MUSCRVIT, and IMPUNC?

Me: "Hit me again, Li'l Dahlink," as Krazy Kat said to the brick-throwing mouse Ignatz. "And may his eelbow neva wicken."

Dr. C: Settle down.

Me: Besides the building of museums as pleasure palaces, which are springing up like mushrooms across the country, there will no doubt soon be a more sober American public monument on the site of the former World Trade Center. A temporary monument in the form of a "theater of lights" marked the site of the two most monstrous and egregious pieces of architecture to have ever burdened the island of Manhattan. The temporary memorial also marks a kind of amnesia about another large, flat space: the Nuremberg Parade Ground of the Third Reich where some seventy years ago Albert Speer installed his memorable searchlights. But the IMPUNC has always been dedicated to the self-righteous suppression of history and to the forgetting of the other. The values, norms, and aspirations of every past civilization have been read through its art. Ours is going to be interpreted in the same way.

Dr. C: But you are not waiting for the ruins to arrive to prowl through the fragments.

Me: The ruins are already here.

Dr. C: If we want to consider this question seriously, we should recognize that in much of the world the US is regarded as a leading terrorist state, and with good reason.[16]

Me: There has been no program guiding the extensive catalogue of American IMPUNC monumental art that reaches back almost two centuries and shows no signs of abating. Self-congratulatory grand scale, the entertainment spectacle of awe and buzz, the obliviousness to the past, the optimism of domination —such attitudes are packed into the IMPUNC impulse. But since 9/11 the breeze of an overt nationalism has arisen. Has it blown the camouflage cover off? Can the beliefs in American pragmatism, liberalism, and corporate capitalism as non-ideological guides of purity (a purity so lofty as to have, in Francis Fukuyama's words, "evaded history") any longer be credible? Or will art come to the rescue to head off consciousness of our national belligerent, predatory, power-driven presuppositions? It did it before by folding into the work a phenomenology of dominating affect that submerged and screened from consciousness the implications of the values it promoted. Will it do it again? I think we can count on it making the effort.

Dr. C: I see our time is up.

Notes

1. Noam Chomsky, *Understanding Power: The Indispensible Chomsky*, ed. Peter R. Mitchell and John Schoeffel (New York, 2002), p. 356.

2. Chomsky, *Language and Thought* (Wakefield, R.I., 1993), p. 22.

3. Chomsky, *New Horizons in the Study of Language and Mind* (Cambridge, 2000), p. 36.

4. Charles Sanders Peirce, "Philosophy and the Sciences: A Classification," *Philosophical Writings of Peirce*, ed. Justus Buchler (New York, 1955), p. 62.

5. Chomsky, *Reflections on Language* (New York, 1975), p. 163.

6. For a discussion of Wagner effect art, see Robert Morris, "Size Matters," *Critical Inquiry*, 26, Spring 2000, 474–487.

7. David Barsamian and Chomsky, *Propaganda and the Public Mind: Conversations with Noam Chomsky* (Cambridge, Mass., 2001), p. 80; hereafter abbreviated *P*.

8. See Michael Fried's early prescient essay, "Art and Objecthood," *Art and Objecthood: Essays and Reviews* (Chicago, 1998), pp. 148–172.

9. See Anton Ehrensweig, *The Hidden Order of Art: A Study in the Psychology of the Artistic Imagination* (Berkeley, 1967), p. 74.

10. Chomsky, *9-11* (New York, 2001), p. 57.

11. Chomsky, *New Horizons in the Study of Language and Mind*, p. 30.

12. Unlike some groups. From World War II to 2001 America bombed China (1945–46, 1950–53), Korea (1950–53), Guatemala (1954, 1957–69), Indonesia (1958), Cuba (1959–60), the Belgian Congo (1964), Peru (1965), Laos (1964–73), Vietnam (1961–73), Cambodia (1969–70), Grenada (1983), Libya (1986), El Salvador (1980s), Nicaragua (1980s), Panama (1989), Iraq (1991-2001), Bosnia (1995), and Yugoslavia (1999). List compiled by Arundhati Roy in her *Power Politics* (Cambridge, Mass., 2001), p. 128.

13. "But I had as good speak plain: I have already said as much as that space is God" (Jonathan Edwards, "Of Being," *A Jonathan Edwards Reader*, ed. John E. Smith, Harry S. Stout, and Kenneth P. Minkema [New Haven, Conn., -795], p. 10).

14. Ludwig Wittgenstein, *Philosophical Investigations*, trans. G. E. M. Anscombe (Oxford, 1953), § 457, p. 133.

15. Sanford White's assassin, Harry K. Thaw, traveled to Hollywood after his release from prison. Seeing Grauman's million dollar Egyptian Theater he was reported to have exclaimed, "My god, I shot the wrong architect." Of course today most urban architecture has been reduced to a low, grubby form of white collar crime.

16. Chomsky, *9-11*, p. 23.

Iain Boal, T.J. Clark, Joseph Matthews,
and Michael Watts (Retort)

The State, Spectacle, and September 11

Excerpt from *Afflicted Powers: Capital and Spectacle in a New Age of War*, London: Verso, 2005

He too fought under television for our place in the sun.
Robert Lowell on Lieutenant Calley, 1971

We begin from the moment in February 2003, with the run-up to the war in Iraq entering its final stages, when the copy of Picasso's *Guernica* hung in the anteroom to the UN Security Council Chamber was curtained over, at American insistence—not "an appropriate backdrop," it was explained, for official statements to the world media. The episode became an emblem. Many a placard on Piccadilly and Las Ramblas rang sardonic changes on Bush and the snorting bull. An emblem, yes—but, with the benefit of hindsight, emblematic of what? Of the state's relentless will to control the minutiae of appearance, as part of —essential to—its drive to war? Well, certainly. But in this case, did it get its way? Did not the boorishness of the effort at censorship prove counterproductive, eliciting the very haunting—by an imagery still capable of putting a face on the brutal abstraction of "shock and awe"—that the Velcro covering was meant to put a stop to? And did not the whole incident speak above all to the state's *anxiety* as it tried to micromanage the means of symbolic production—as if it feared that every last detail of the derealized décor it had built for its citizens had the potential, at a time of crisis, to turn utterly against it?

These are the ambiguities, generalized to the whole conduct of war and politics over the past four years, that this chapter aims to explore. We start from the premise that certain concepts and descriptions put forward forty years ago by Guy Debord and the Situationist International, as part of their effort to comprehend the new forms of state control and social disintegration then emerging, still possess explanatory power—more so than ever, we suspect, in the poisonous epoch we are living through. In particular, the twinned notions of "the colonization of everyday life" and "the society of the spectacle"—we think each concept needs the other if either is to do its proper work—strike us as having purchase on key aspects of what has happened since September 11, 2001. Our purpose, in a word, is to turn two central Situationist hypotheses back to the task for which they were always primarily intended—to make them instruments of political analysis again, directed to an understanding of the powers and vulnerabilities of the capitalist state. (We take it we are not alone in shuddering at the way "spectacle" has taken its place in approved postmodern discourse over the past fifteen years—as a vaguely millenarian accompaniment to "new media studies" or to wishful thinking about freedom in cyberspace, with never a whisper that its original objects were the Watts Riots and the Proletarian Cultural Revolution.)

None of this means that we think we comprehend the whole shape and dynamic of the new state of affairs, or can offer a theory of its deepest determinants. We are not sectaries of the spectacle; no one concept, or cluster of concepts, seems to us to get the measure of the horror of the past four years. We even find it understandable, if in the end a mistake, that some on the Left have seen the recent wars in the desert and squabbles in the Security Council as open to analysis in classical Marxist terms, proudly unreconstructed—bringing on stage again the predictions and revulsions of Lenin's and Hobson's studies of imperialism—rather than in those of a politics of "internal," technologized social control.[1]

This much we are sure of. What is new in the current dark circumstance still largely eludes analysis. Any such analysis is obliged to begin from three obvious, interlinked questions of the moment, which now we set out in tabular form:

- To what extent did the events of September 11, 2001—the precision bombing of New York and Washington by organized enemies of the US empire—usher in a new era? Did those events change anything fundamental in the calculus and conduct of advanced capitalist states, or in the relation of such states to their civil societies? If so, how?
- Are we to understand the forms of assertion of American power since September 11—the hasty demonstration of military supremacy (largely to reassure the demonstrators, one feels, that "something could still be done" with the monstrous armory at the state's beck and call), the blundering attempts at recolonization under way in Afghanistan and Iraq, the threats and payoffs to client states in every corner of the globe, the glowering attack on civil liberties within the US itself—as a step backward, *an historical regression*, in which the molecular, integral, invisible means of control which so many of us believed were indispensable to a truly "modern" state-system have given way to a new/old era of gunboats and book-burning?
- Do the concepts "society of the spectacle" and "colonization of everyday life" help us to grasp the logic of the present age? Or has the level of social dispersal and mendaciousness to which those concepts once pointed also been overtaken—displaced, abruptly, at a special moment of urgency and arrogance—by cruder, older imperatives of statecraft?

None of these questions, to repeat, can be answered in isolation. No one level of analysis—"economic" or "political," global or local, focusing on the means of either material or symbolic production—will do justice to the current strange mixture of chaos and grand design. But one main aspect of the story—the struggle for mastery in the realm of the image—has so far been barely thought of as *positively interacting* with others more familiar and "material." It is the first outline of this interaction we aim to offer, for further debate.

1

The version of "spectacle" with which we operate is minimal, pragmatic, and matter of fact. No doubt the idea's original author often gave it an exultant, world-historical force. But his tone is inimitable, as all efforts to duplicate it have proven; and in any case we are convinced that the age demands a different cadence—something closer (if we are lucky) to that of the lines from *Paradise Lost* we use as our epigraph than to anything from Lukács or Ducasse.

The notion "spectacle" was intended, then, as a first stab at characterizing a new form of, or stage in, the accumulation of capital. What it named preeminently was the submission of more and more facets of human sociability—areas of everyday life, forms of recreation, patterns of speech, idioms of local solidarity, kinds of ethical or aesthetic insubordination, the endless capacities of human beings to evade or refuse the orders brought down to them from on high—to the deadly solicitations (the lifeless bright sameness) of the market. Those who developed the analysis in the first place resisted the idea that this colonization of everyday life was dependent on any one set of technologies, but notoriously they were interested in the means modern societies have at their disposal to systematize and disseminate appearances, and to subject the texture of day-to-day living to a constant barrage of images, instructions, slogans, logos, false promises, virtual realities, miniature happiness-motifs. Batteries Not Included, as the old punk band had it.

The choice of the word "colonization" to describe the process was deliberate. It invited readers to conceive of the invasion and sterilizing of so many unoccupied areas of human species-being—areas that previous regimes, however overweening, had chosen (or been obliged) to leave alone—*as a specific necessity of capitalist production*, just as much part of its dynamism as expansion to the ends of the earth. The colonization of everyday life, we might put it from our present vantage point, was "globalization" turned inward—mapping and enclosing the hinterland of the social, and carving out from the detail of human inventiveness an ever more ramified and standardized market of exchangeable subjectivities. Naturally the one colonization implied the other: there would have been no Black Atlantic of sugars, alcohols, and opiates without the drive to shape subjectivity into a pattern of small (saleable) addictions.

The point of the analysis, again, was to bring into focus the terms and possibilities of resistance (wars of liberation) against the colonizing forces; this in a situation, the latter 1960s, where it was not foolhardy, even if ultimately mistaken, to imagine "reassembling our afflicted Powers" and doing real harm to the enemy. Debord, to speak of him directly, was concerned most of all with the way the subjection of social life to the rule of appearances had led in turn to a distinct form of politics—of state formation and surveillance. His opinion on these matters fluctuated: they were the aspect of the present he most loathed, and which regularly elicited his best tirades and worst paranoia. We extract the following propositions from his pages.

First, that slowly but surely the state in the twentieth century had been dragged into full collaboration in the micromanagement of everyday life. The market's necessity became the state's obsession. (We say that this happened slowly, and in a sense against the state's better judgment, because always there existed a tension between the modern state's constant armored other-directed-ness—its *raison d'être* as a war machine—and capital's insistence that the state come to its aid in the great work of internal policing and packaging. This tension has again been visible over the past four years. (We believe it is one key to the obvious incoherence of the state's recent actions.) Second, this deeper and deeper involvement of the state in the day-to-day instrumentation of consumer obedience meant that increasingly it came to live or die by its investment in, and control of, the field of images—the alternative world conjured up by the new battery of "perpetual emotion machines,"[2] of which TV was the dim pioneer and which now beckons the citizen every waking minute. This world of images had long been a structural necessity of a capitalism oriented toward the overproduction of commodities, and therefore the constant manufacture of desire for them; but by the late twentieth century it had given rise to a specific polity.

The modern state, we would argue, has come to need weak citizenship. It depends more and more on maintaining an impoverished and hygienized public realm, in which only the ghosts of an older, more idiosyncratic civil society live on. It has adjusted profoundly to its economic master's requirement for a thinned, unobstructed social texture, made up of loosely attached consumer subjects, each locked in its plastic work-station and nuclearized family of four. Weak citizenship, but for that very reason the object of the state's constant, anxious attention—an unstoppable barrage of idiot fashions and panics and image-motifs, all aimed at sewing the citizen back (unobtrusively, "individually") into a deadly simulacrum of community.

Very often, the first writers to confront this nightmare seemed to despair in the face of it:

> *There is no place left where people can discuss the realities which concern them, because they can never lastingly free themselves from the crushing presence of media discourse and of the various forces organized to relay it ... Unanswerable lies have succeeded in eliminating public opinion, which first lost the ability to make itself heard and then very quickly dissolved altogether ... Once one controls the mechanism which operates the only form of social verification to be fully and universally recognized, one can say what one likes ... Spectacular power can similarly deny whatever it wishes to, once, or three times over, and change the subject: knowing full well there is no danger of riposte, in its own space or any other.*[3]

Too many times over the past four years these sentences, in their very anger and sorrow at the present form of politics, have echoed in our minds. But ultimately we dissent from their totalizing closure. Living after September 11, we are no longer so sure—and do not believe that spectacular power is sure—that "there is no danger of riposte, in its own space or any other." For better or worse, the precision bombings were such a riposte. And their effect on the spectacular state has been profound: the state's reply to them, we are certain, has exceeded in its crassness and futility the martyr-pilots' wildest dreams. Therefore we turn to another sentence from the same book, which (characteristically) acts as finale to the previous admissions of defeat. "To this list of the triumphs of power we should add, however, one result which has proved negative: once the running of the state involves a permanent and massive shortage of historical knowledge, that state can no longer be led *strategically*."[4] Issued by a devotee of Sun Tzu and Clausewitz, this last verdict is crushing.

Debord had a robust and straightforward view of the necessity, for individuals and collectives, of learning from the past. (It is not the least of the ways his thinking is classical, as opposed to postmodern.) Of course he knew that the past is a "construction"; but a construction, he believed, made of obdurate and three-dimensional materials, constantly resisting any one frame, and which only the most elaborate machinery of forgetting could make fully tractable to power. His deepest fears as a revolutionary derived from the sense, which grew upon him, that this elaborate machinery might now have been built, and really be turning the world into an eternal present. That was the key to his hatred of the image-life: that what is threatened, ultimately, was the very existence of the complex, created, *two-way* temporality that for him constituted the essence of the human.

Such was the nightmare. But even Debord sometimes took (cold) comfort from the recognition that the state too had lived the nightmare, and would suffer the consequences. For it too could no longer learn from the past: it had progressively dismantled the contexts in which truly strategic discussion of its aims and interests—thinking in the long term, admitting the paradoxes and uncertainties of power, recognizing, in a word, "the cunning of reason"—might still be possible.[5] The state was entrapped in its own apparatus of clichés. It had come almost to *believe* in the policy-motifs its think-tanks and disinformation consultancies churned out for it. How Debord would have reveled, over the past months, in the endless double entendres provided by the media, to the effect that Bush and Blair's rush to war in Iraq should be blamed on "faulty intelligence"!

2

What, then, politically and strategically, took place on September 11, 2001? And how, politically and strategically, has the US state responded to it? Of course, we realize the dangers here. Why should we follow the lead of the spectacle itself in electing this one among many atrocities—raised to the new power of ideology, inevitably, by the idiot device of digitalizing its date—as a world-historical turning point? How much of the real dynamic (and pathology) of American power is conjured away by pinning it thus to a single image-event—in much the same way that American victory in the Cold War was rendered in retrospect magical, unanalyzable, by the mantra "the Fall of the Wall"? There have been moments when we found it easy to sympathize with those of our comrades who, partly in reaction to the flood of cloying, pseudo-apocalyptic verbiage released by September 11 (which shows no sign of abating), go so far as to dismiss the bombings as so many pinpricks, *attentats*, hopeless symbolic gestures on the part of those with no real power to wound.

"Hopeless symbolic gestures." We agree quite strictly with all three words of the diagnosis. (As do the perpetrators, it seems. In them chiliasm is spliced with nihilism, to form a distinctively hyper-modern compound. When they boast in their communiqués of being "for Death"—in contra-distinction, they imply, to modernity's miserable attachment to a Life not worth the name—one is never sure if one is hearing Tyndale's cry from the stake or Stavrogin's in the last pages of *The Possessed*. As so often lately, the twenty-first century seems an amalgam of the sixteenth and the nineteenth.) And the question remains: What is the *effectiveness*—the specific political force—of this form of symbolic action, hopeless or not, within the symbolic economy called "spectacle"? *Spectacularly*, the American state suffered a defeat on September 11.

And spectacularly, for this state, does not mean superficially or epiphenomenally. The state was wounded in September in its heart of hearts, and we see it still, almost four years later, flailing blindly in the face of an image it cannot exorcise, and trying desperately to convert the defeat back into terms it can respond to.

One last caveat. Is it necessary to state that because we refuse to extract the September bombings from the cycle of horrors over which the US has presided since 1945, and believe it necessary, if we are to understand them politically, to treat the events of September as an occurrence in a war of images, it does not follow that we fail to recognize (and wish we could find words for) the events' obscenity? We hope not. On the contrary, precisely because the attacks in September were calibrated to leave an indelible image-trail behind them, they have seared in the memory item after item of evidence of just what it is, in terms of human fear and agony, that political calculus so habitually writes off. We too are haunted by the flailing arms of the jumpers, and the scream on the soundtrack as the tower stutters into dust; just as we are haunted by the image of Hanadi Jaradat's bloody head, "her thick hair tied in a ponytail," dumped by the clean-up squad on a table at the back of the restaurant in Haifa where she had been blown to pieces an hour before.[6] We wish we had words for these things. We wish we lived in a political culture where the language of revulsion had not been debauched by decade after decade of selective gravitas. (Your Chechnya for my Guatemala. Your Suharto for my Pol Pot.)

We proceed then, unwillingly, from the image on the screen. It matters profoundly, we are convinced, that the horrors of September 11 were designed above all to be visible, and that this visibility marked the bombings off from most previous campaigns of air terror, especially those sponsored by states. There were no cameras at Dresden, Hamburg, and Hiroshima.[7] The horror there had to be unseen; it had to act—was meant to act—on the surrounding population in the form of uncontrollable hearsay and panic; and it was to be presented to the enemy state apparatus in the form of report, statistic, prediction, ultimata.

September's terror was different. It made no demands, it offered no explanations. It was premised on the belief (learned from the culture it wishes to annihilate) that a picture is worth a thousand words—that a picture, in the present condition of politics, is itself, if sufficiently well executed, a specific and effective piece of statecraft. Of course the martyr-pilots knew that bringing down the Twin Towers would do nothing, or next to nothing, to stop the actual circuits of capital. But circuits of capital are bound up, in the longer term, with circuits of sociability—patterns of belief and desire, levels of confidence, degrees of identification with the good life of the commodity. And these, said the terrorists, thinking strategically, are aspects of the social imaginary still (always, interminably) being put together by the perpetual emotion machines. Supposing those machines could be captured for a moment, and on them appeared the perfect image of capitalism's negation. Would that not be enough? Enough truly to destabilize the state and society, and produce a sequence of vauntings and paranoias whose long-term political consequences for the capitalist world order would, at the very least, be unpredictable?

Or perhaps *entirely* predictable, from a geopolitical standpoint. "You know our demands," said the martyr-pilots (strictly to themselves).

"And we know you cannot accede to them … We know what you will do instead … We are certain your answer will be military … We anticipate your idiot leader blurting out the word crusade … What you will do will confirm the world of Islamism in its despairing strength … And you will do it because there is no answer to our image-victory, yet you (because humiliation is something in which you have no schooling) have to pretend there is one."[8]

The terrorists (to put it only slightly differently) followed the logic of the spectacle to its charnel-house conclusion. If, to trot out Debord's over-famous aphorism again, "the spectacle is capital accumulated to the point where it becomes image,"[9] then what more adequate encapsulation of the process could there be but the World Trade Center (with its multiplication of the terminally gigantic by two)? And what other means of defeating it—its social instrumentality, that is, its power over the consuming imagination—than have it be literally obliterated on camera?

We are rehearsing a logic, not endorsing it. But we believe that only by recognizing what was truly "modern" in the martyr-pilots' strategy—truly the opposite of a desperate, powerless, atavistic pinprick; truly the *instigator* of the state's present agony—will the Left be able to move toward argument with the new terrorism's premises and upshots. At the level of the image (here is premise number one) the state is vulnerable; and that level is now fully part of, necessary to, the state's apparatus of self-reproduction. Terror can take over the image-machinery for a moment—and a moment, in the timeless echo chamber of the spectacle, may now eternally be all there is—and use it to amplify, reiterate, accumulate the sheer visible happening of defeat. It is a confirmation of the terrorists' hopes that after the first days, in the US, the fall of the towers became exactly the image that *had not to be shown*.[10] The taboo only made the afterimage more palpable and effective. Everything in the culture went on, and still goes on, in relation to that past image-event; nothing in the culture can address the event directly. The silence of so-called "popular culture" in the face of September 11 has been deafening. (It is as if the commercial music of America in the mid-twentieth century had had nothing to say about war, or race, or the Depression, or the new world of goods and appliances. It had plenty—partly because the adjective "popular" still pointed to something real about its audiences and raw materials. That was long ago, of course: the present total obedience of the culture industry to the protocols of the War on Terror—its immediate ingestion and reproduction of the state's interdicts and paranoias—is proof positive, if any were needed, of the snuffing out of the last traces of insubordination in the studios of Time Warner.)

The logic of the pilots was part fantasy, we would argue, part (proven) lucidity. We could reply to it by saying that the new terrorists succumbed to the temptation of the spectacle, rather than devising a way to outflank or contest it. They were exponents of the idea (brilliant exponents, but this only reveals the idea's fundamental heartlessness) that control over the image is now the key to social power; and that image-power, like all other forms of ownership and ascendancy under capitalism, has been subject to an ineluctable process of concentration, so that now it is manifest in certain identifiable (targetable) places, monuments, pseudo-bodies, icons, logos, manufactured non-events; signs that in their very emptiness and worthlessness (the Twin

Towers as architecture were perfect examples) rule the imaginary earth; and whose concentrated, materialized nullity gives the new terror a chance —to frighten, demoralize, turn the world upside down.

Once upon a time (and still, as we write) bombers went out into the city with their sensible holdalls, or their windbreakers a little more tightly zipped than usual. Once upon a time the shrapnel sliced through livers and skulls in neighborhood restaurants, street markets, dance halls, breeding the contagion of rumor in the narrow streets, sapping the will of a class or colonial enemy, driving its cadres back into the isolation—the demoralization—of "home"; eroding, that is, the patterns of sociability (patterns of fear and enforcement, yes, but embedded in a wider and deeper universe of loyalties) that had held a regime together.

Now a new breed of bomber has understood that in the society they are attacking such networks of sociability are secondary: not absent, not irrelevant, but increasingly supplanted by a ghost sociability which does not need its citizens to leave home for its key rituals and allegiances to reproduce themselves. The terror of September 11 had a handful of targets (our tendency to make it, in memory, simply "the bombing of the Twin Towers" is not untrue to the logic of the event). The perpetrators knew full well that they lacked the means to spread out through the wider social fabric and bring day-to-day business to a halt. And they believed, rightly or wrongly, that in present circumstances they did not need to. What they did was designed to hold us indoors, to make us turn back and back to a moving image of capitalism screaming and exploding, to make us go on listening (in spite of ourselves) to the odious talking heads trying to put something, anything, in place of the desolation.

3

More than one commentator since September 11, particularly over the last two years or so, has tried to make sense of the special desperation of the state's conduct in the aftermath. David Runciman has gone so far as to argue that what is happening amounts to a genuine mutation of the international state system:

> *Suddenly, the Hobbesian view that states and states alone have the power to operate under conditions of lawfulness is threatened by the knowledge that even the most powerful states are vulnerable to assault from unknown and unpredictable sources. It can now be said that in the international arena "the weakest has the strength to kill the strongest," or they would do, if only they could get their hands on the necessary equipment. This, potentially, changes everything…*
> *The common view that 11 September 2001 marked the return to a Hobbesian world is therefore entirely wrong. It marked the beginning of a post-Hobbesian age, in which a new kind of insecurity threatens the familiar structures of modern political life. In one sense, of course, this insecurity is not new, because it carries echoes of the natural uncertainties of individual human beings. But it is new for states, which were meant to be invulnerable to such paranoid anxieties. And since they are not designed to deal with this sort of threat, even the most powerful states don't know what to do about it.*[11]

This strikes us as capturing something real. There are several things to be said in response.

First, Runciman's argument starts, very reasonably, from the idea that the state's new level of fearfulness is derived from the possible or actual availability of "weapons of mass destruction" to groups sheltering under the wing of regimes hostile to the new world order, or rich and skillful enough to bargain with such regimes for a share in their military technology. (The fact that such technology was usually, in the first place, eagerly provided by the states now quaking in their boots at the thought of its going astray—that fact ought to be entered into the reckoning, yes, if it can be done without too much repetitive "I told you so.") It is a slight embarrassment to Runciman that the attack which precipitated the change in the order of state relations used weapons that had nothing to do with the disintegrating international arms market. Nothing could be more foolish, of course, than to leap on Runciman's analysis at this point with sectarian glee, brandishing some tin-pot argument to the effect that from now on the real weapons of mass destruction are the media, that the war is a war of simulacra not bullets—that "the Fall of the Twin Towers Did Not Take Place." But we would argue that the present condition of politics does not make sense unless it is approached from a dual perspective—seen as a struggle for crude, material dominance, but also (threaded ever closer into that struggle) as a battle for the control of appearances.

We agree with Runciman (against many on the Left who would prefer al-Qaeda to be a last-gasp, exotic, pathetic, pre-capitalist phenomenon) that the September bombings are a distinctively modern symptom. What they point to, far beyond the specific atrocity and its grisly religious fuel, is a new structural feature of the international state system: that *the historical monopoly of the means of destruction by the state is now at risk.* That new feature has many causes. Technological advance is one of them. The rise of a worldwide secondary market in arms—partly the result of the chaos attending the end of the cold war, partly a natural product of the neo-liberal commodification of the globe—is another. Likewise the contracting-out of more and more military services to a shady corporate world, again something that neo-liberalism began by warmly recommending to its client nations. The permeability of borders obviously matters, and has become another major item in the new paranoia. But that fact is linked to a deeper and more pervasive reality, which again is a product of the "globalization" these same states are committed to—and on which their bloated home economies depend. *Failed states* is the term of art for this reality—this constitutive feature of the world we live in—from which the personnel and ideology of September 11 so unmistakably arose.

"Failed states," "rogue states," "weak states," "societies left behind by modernization"—the diagnoses are legion, and the facts they point to complex. Let us simply assert here, with the problem of September 11 specifically our object, that "failed states" seem to us a structural element of the international system—a product, a necessity, of the new universe of globalization. There is no ontological distinction between the successfully weakened and permeable states on which the world order now thrives and those whose weakness has become chronic fatigue and disintegration, and whose embrace of foreign capital has widened just enough to include independent arms dealers, warlords, and drug cartels.

There is a link here, clearly, to our previous argument about the necessity of weak citizenship to the state's internal health. *Weak citizenship*, then, at the spectacular center; and *weak states* in the "world economy" which the center works endlessly to exploit. A weak state is one whose local defenses against imperial control have (through the implanting of "bases," the rifling of natural resources, the helping hand to local elites in the event of indigenous revolt, and the neo-liberal penetration by the corporations) all been satisfactorily dismantled. A failed state is one where the logic of abjection has been carried, often imperceptibly, too far—so that suddenly the "flourishing" economy shatters, the bribes no longer produce the shoddy goods, the death rates climb, the effigies of Uncle Sam are paraded through the streets, and up in the mountains or in the university dormitories young men and women cover their heads and study *The Art of War*. We could say with only the slightest edge of exaggeration that failed states are the typical—determinant—political entities of the world left behind by the cold war, "crash programs," and the attentions of the IMF.

The events of September 11, it is common knowledge, were directly the creature of this world of despair. They were trained for in Jalalabad, paid for in Riyadh. But saying so does not in the least conflict with the perspective —that of spectacle—from which this chapter began. One of the key phenomena of the "failed state" reality we have been describing is the power of al-Jazeera, and the runaway world of Islamist websites (as the US has learned, much to its chagrin). Nothing enrages a certain young Arab intellectual so much as the sight of people his own age, surrounded by an urban fabric arrested midway on the path to postmodern squalor, clutching their cellphones and telling their video worry beads. One of the formative moments in the education of Muhammad Atta, we are told, was when he came to realize that the "conservation" of Islamic Cairo, in which he had hoped to participate as a newly trained town planner, was to obey the logic of Disney World.

Failed states are a hideous amalgam of the feudal, the Nasserite "national," *and* the spectacular—that is the point. Intellectuals brought up in such circles of hell need no lessons from postmodern theory about where power lies in the chaos around them, and what means might be available to contest it. They draw conclusions—cruel and mistaken ones, in our view, but emerging from a treadmill of pain and hopelessness we can only dimly guess at—and choose their weapons.

4

[This section excised.]

5

It seems that the state does not know what to do in these circumstances. This does not mean it is on the path to real strategic failure, necessarily, or that it will prove incapable of pulling back from the imperatives of the image-war and slowly, relentlessly, accommodate itself to the needs of a new round of primitive accumulation. The hatchet men and torture brigades (professionals, not part-timers from Appalachia) are being retrained as we write. "Road maps" are to be thrown in the trash can. Failed states become weak states once more. "Democracy" proves unexportable. Iran and Syria join the comity of nations. Exit Wolfowitz and Makiya, mumbling.

States can behave like maddened beasts, in other words, and still get their way. They regularly do. But the present madness is singular: the dimension of spectacle has never before interfered so palpably, so insistently, with the business of keeping one's satrapies in order. And never before have spectacular politics been conducted in the shades—the "historical knowledge"—*of defeat*. It remains to be seen what new mutation of the military-industrial-entertainment complex emerges from the shambles.

Notes

1. This is not meant to signal that we believe that all the key terms of Marx's analysis have outlived their usefulness. Our discussion of "primitive accumulation" has already indicated the contrary. It is the "proudly unreconstructed" that is the point at issue here. Too many Marxist commentators lately have struck us as a touch smug (or is it relieved?) in the face of the new imperialism, as if it validated the whole panoply of Marxist explanations, and put all others in the shade.

2. Perry Anderson, *The Origins of Postmodernity*, London 1998, p. 89.

3. Guy Debord, *Comments on the Society of the Spectacle*, trans. Malcom Imgrie, London 1998 (first published 1988), pp. 13–19 (order of sentences altered).

4. Ibid., p. 20.

5. We are not denying that arenas still exist, most of them deeply secret, in which certain aspects of state interest and policy are plotted over the long term. That is notably true, for obvious reasons, of the state's enabling role in economic affairs. No conspiracy theory of history is needed, now that the relevant documentation (or a small part of it) has been teased from the usual sources, to see how elaborate were the tradeoffs between capital and the state in the planning and instrumentation of the whole neo-liberal push. The problem lies not in the state's inability to think *capitalism* strategically—for here real ruthlessness, lucidity, and expertise are at its disposal, and able to insist on their need for policy as opposed to slogans —but on the lack of adequate contexts in which these economic imperatives can be coordinated with others, equally vital to the state's well-being: with "balance of power" geopolitics, notably, and with the changing nature and efficacy of warfare as an instrument of policy, and, above all, with the new valencies of ideological (both "cultural" and first-level "political") struggle.

6. *New York Times*, October 5, 2003.

7. It was not until a year after Hiroshima, in July 1946, that the twin signs of post-war modernity—the mushroom cloud and the two-piece bathing suit—were given form in and around the Bikini "tests." "Eighteen tons of cinematography equipment and more than half the world's supply of motion picture film were on hand to record the Able and Baker explosions" (Jack Niedenthal, *For the Good of Mankind: A History of the People of Bikini and their Islands*, Majuro, MH 2001, p. 3). Interested readers may also wish to consult Michael Light, *100 Suns*, New York 2003.

8. In an Al Qaeda statement released in the wake of the Madrid bombings, the organization announced that it hoped Bush would win the November election, because he acts "with force not wisdom," and "Being targeted by an enemy is what will wake us from our slumber." Cited in M. Rodenbeck, "Islam Confronts Its Demons," *New York Review of Books*, April 29, 2004, p. 16.

9. Guy Debord, *The Society of the Spectacle*, trans. Donald Nicholson-Smith, New York 1994 (first published 1967), p. 24.

10. A Bush campaign commercial in March 2004 broke the rule of invisibility, and was taken off the air (with groveling apologies) in a matter of hours.

11. David Runciman, "A Bear Armed with a Gun," *London Review of Books*, April 3, 2003, p. 5.

Dora Apel

Torture Culture: Lynching Photographs and the Images of Abu Ghraib

Art Journal, vol. 64, no. 2, Summer 2005

In the topical commentary on the moral disgrace of Abu Ghraib, several commentators have noted a resemblance between the torture photos from Iraq and American lynching photos.[1] These similarities have remained largely unexplored, however, including perhaps the most significant effects of the two sets of photos, which is that both came to function as sites of resistance against the very acts they represent. Between deeds that are very different in nature and motivation, and which took place at very different times and places, what might we learn from the similarities? What indeed constitutes these similarities?[2]

In this essay, I examine the usefulness of parallels between the photographs taken at Abu Ghraib and lynching photographs from the early decades of the twentieth century, and explore the political responses to the Abu Ghraib photos both through their public distribution and in contemporary artworks and civic displays.

We may think the similarity between the lynching and prison photos resides in the unabashed picturing of torture and humiliation itself. But more shocking, even, in both sets of photos, are the proud perpetrators whose smug gloating we do not expect to see and who flaunt an appalling shamelessness. This is because we identify the perpetrators as the immediate criminals here, not their prisoners/victims. In both cases, for us, national and international laws against torture and murder are clearly violated, the basic imperatives of humanity and decency dishonored, and the images, like the acts they represent, evoke revulsion at the humiliation and barbarity of it all. But the perpetrators don't see it this way. These events, in part staged for the camera, occur because both sets of perpetrators, in their loftiest rationalizations, believe they are committing their deeds for the good of the nation or, at the least, that their acts are sanctioned by a larger community and serve the interests of that community. This belief illuminates the fact that the exercise of such sadism and humiliation is a fundamentally political act. The viewer is meant to identify with the proud torturers in the context of the defense of a political and cultural hierarchy.[3]

The sense of community sanction was central to American lynching and created the conditions by which white townsmen would attack and drive out black residents, even burning down the black section of town. Following a lynching, they would close ranks around individual perpetrators to protect them from any threat of prosecution by state or federal authorities. Those who might have acted as whistleblowers had nowhere to turn and risked dire retribution. Many who thought they would find a spectacle lynching thrilling instead found it sickening, but they lived in silence with these traumatic experiences. The effects were of course far more devastating for black members of the community.

For white supremacists, souvenir lynching photos became ways of reliving the erotic thrills of torture and mutilation produced under the guise of righteous civic actions, as well as a way of reaffirming a racial and gendered hierarchy that kept white men on top and blacks at the bottom. In gendered terms, lynching meant asserting white male control over the desire of white women by punishing transgressions against the race barrier and affirming a sense of entitlement to the bodies of black women through unbridled coercion. It also meant indulging a covert form of homoerotic gratification through the subjugated bodies of black men, who would often be humiliated, tortured, and castrated. In addition to the lynchings themselves, the lynching photographs served as a means of continuing social control, extended tools of terror which ultimately justified the deeds they represented as protecting whiteness, which was code for America itself.[4]

After 9/11, "democracy" became code for America, and defending democracy meant arresting and imprisoning thousands of Middle Easterners in the United States, Guantánamo Bay, and Afghanistan, as well as in Iraq, where the sense of community sanction was fundamental to the torture and atrocities. The community in question was most immediately the military and more broadly the white, conservative, Christian culture represented by the regime of George W. Bush, the commander-in-chief, and reinforced by his cabinet and their chains of command.

As is now known, the campaign of torture in Iraq was a top-secret program, code-named Copper Green, which was approved by Secretary of Defense Donald Rumsfeld. Government lawyers turned somersaults in legal memorandums that attempted to skirt international treaties and show that the Geneva Conventions, which govern the treatment of prisoners of war, did not apply and that President Bush could authorize the torture of prisoners, effectively assigning him a status above the law. As Harold Hongju Koh, dean of the Yale Law School, observed in a scathing rebuke of this unprecedented move, "If the president has commander-in-chief power to commit torture, he has the power to commit genocide, to sanction slavery, to promote apartheid, to license summary execution."[5] In Bush's second term, Alberto Gonzalez, the architect of the memorandum characterizing the Geneva Conventions as "quaint," became the US Attorney General following the resignation of John Ashcroft. On October 25, 2004, the White House announced that according to a new legal opinion, some non-Iraqi prisoners in Iraq were still exempt from the rules of the Geneva Conventions.

Rumsfeld has since admitted to approving an order to hold an Iraqi prisoner but keep his name off the prison rolls in order to shield him from Red Cross inspectors, a violation of international law. An outside investigative panel documented at least seven more cases, followed by the admission that there were dozens or up to a hundred "ghost" detainees. At least forty cases of prison deaths are being investigated as homicides, and this does not include all those who have died in US-run prisons, an unknown number. At least three hundred incidents of abuse have been reported at Guantánamo Bay, in Afghanistan, and Iraq. Bush, meanwhile, demanded that American prisoners of war—a status the United States refuses to apply to Iraqi "detainees"—be treated humanely, a moment captured in the important and provocative film *Control Room* by Jehane Noujaim, about coverage of the war in its first months by the United States and Al Jazeera.

At least some of the explicit photos of humiliation and torture, moreover, were apparently meant as a form of potential blackmail against the prisoners, threatening to shame them in front of their families and community if they did not become spies for the United States. One government consultant said, "I was told that the purpose of the photographs was to create an army of informants, people you could insert back into the population." Seymour Hersh revealed the facts in the *New Yorker*, quoting an unnamed CIA official and both current and former intelligence officials. They trace the problem to a special program set up in Afghanistan with commandos authorized to use terror and degradation at secret CIA holding tanks, which was then exported to Iraq.[6]

This would explain why Rumsfeld's first reaction to the photos was not shock, horror, or surprise, but anger that they had gotten out.[7] He immediately banned soldiers' cameras at prisons. Like lynching photos, those from Abu Ghraib were meant to stay within a like-minded community. Spectacle lynchings were recorded by hundreds of amateurs with Kodaks, and professional photographers turned out thousands of postcards. But Southern town leaders were as distressed as Rumsfield when lynching photos found their way into the hands of Northern left-wing and liberal activists, who used them for opposing ideological purposes, although it would have been difficult to ban the taking of such photos (and mayors would sometimes take a cut of the profits of postcard sales).

The tortures in Iraq and the mistreatment of Muslims are not deeply rooted and systematic American phenomena like lynchings, which followed a history of slavery. On the other hand, the longstanding rhetoric of a demonizing "orientalism," the old and unresolved Israeli/Palestinian conflict, and the effects of the first Gulf War in 1991 have encouraged many Americans to view many Arabs and Muslims with growing suspicion and distrust, which burst into open and wanton violence in the United States following 9/11.

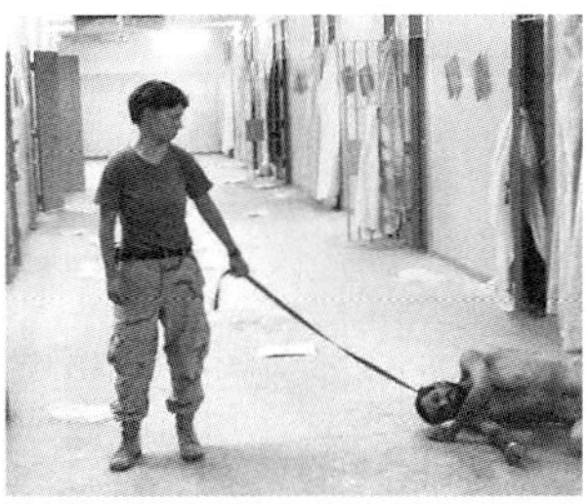

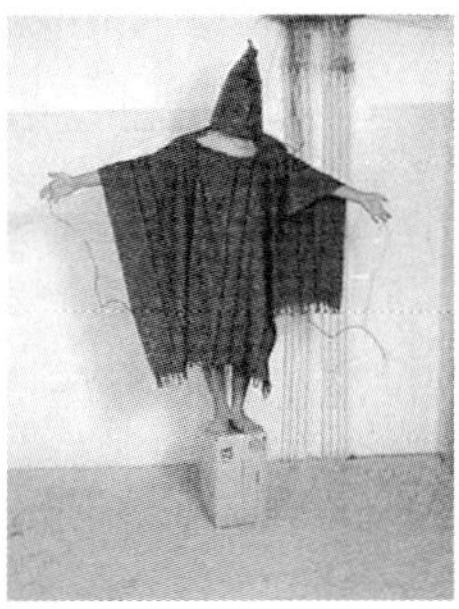

Two photos in particular have become most associated with the torture at Abu Ghraib. One is the picture of Private First Class Lynndie R. England, a twenty-one-year-old reservist, holding a leash attached to the neck of a naked crawling prisoner, known to guards as "Gus." England's training as an administrative clerk did not qualify her to be in the prison. She claims she was told by her superiors to pose for the infamous photo, which was first published in the *Washington Post* on May 21, 2004. Her discomfort is palpable as she looks away from the camera toward the human being at the end of the leash she holds. Linked to the prone figure both by her gaze and by the physical line of connection, we might believe that the youthful England is trapped in a descending spiral of victimization produced by the pressure to conform to the demands of prison culture exerted by her largely male peers and superiors. By impelling her to comply with an appalling act of deep humiliation and documenting her complicity, these actions paved the way for future acquiescence and collusion in further acts of torture and abuse. For the Arab world, however, the picture of a naked Arab man held by the throat as the "pet" of a short-haired American woman in military garb can only confirm the worst suspicions of the most perverse anti-Arab contempt harbored by Americans.

The second photo, first published in the *New Yorker*, represents the most emblematic image of the torture scandal: the hooded man standing on a box with wires attached to his hands, who was told by Specialist Sabrina Harmon that he would be electrocuted if he fell off the box. According to the testimony of the victim, Abdou Hussain Saad Faleh, the wires were not only attached to his fingers but also his toes and penis.[8] Known as the "Vietnam," the image resonates with allusions to the crucifixion, robed monks, the Statue of Liberty, the Klan, the executioner, the mask of death.

But most of all, like the mortified Christ, the image signals abjection and surrender. The echoes of innocence, sacrifice, and suffering that lend it a tragic air are made all the more chilling by the hooding and wires —a decidedly modern emblem of martyrdom, dubbed by Sarah Boxer "the icon of the abuse" although it shows "no dogs, no dead, no leash, no face, no nakedness, no pileup, no thumbs-up."[9] Rather, it "unites figures of torture and sacredness or divinity," as W. J.T. Mitchell observes. "This is not the crucified or resurrected Christ," he notes, "but a figure from the Passion plays, the staging of the humiliation and torture of Jesus." Indeed, the evocation of the man of sorrows and the sympathy summoned from the viewer, as Mitchell argues, is produced by the stillness and serenity of the figure under duress, the graceful, open-armed gesture that is the "natural result of a man's attempt to maintain his balance in a difficult situation." The US military, although claiming the moral high ground in the name of "spreading freedom and democracy" has here assumed the position of Roman torturers, crucifiers, persecutors of the humble and holy.[10]

Other images of torture also come to mind, such as those of lingchi —the ancient Chinese torture and execution ritual in which the victim is drugged and parts of the body slowly sliced away. Known as "death by division into a thousand parts," the practice was first photographed in Beijing in 1905 by French soldiers. Georges Bataille owned and published three such photographs in his 1961 book *The Tears of Eros*. More recently, a lingchi photograph became the basis of a twenty-four-minute video, *Lingchi—Echoes of a Historical Photograph*, by Taiwanese artist Chen Chieh-jen. Such photographs served colonial interests by justifying the Christian "saving" of China; they also represent the first uses of photography in China, making China available as an exotic spectacle in Europe, especially when lingchi photographs were made into postcards and widely distributed.[11] Like the lynching postcards and digital snapshots of Abu Ghraib, they functioned as souvenirs that were meant to demonstrate the political superiority of one group over another.

Chen's contemporary video, re-creating the historical torture of 1905, shows what appear to be the deeply shamed witnesses to the torture as well as the grueling ordeal of the victim, allowing the viewer to identify with both and making the experience virtually unbearable. Chen conveys the visual ambiguity between ecstasy and stupefaction in the lolling head and rolling eyes of the victim, which echoes the reading of such photos by Bataille, who saw on the Chinese victim's face an expression that confirmed his assumptions about the close connection between pleasure and pain. Bataille sought to endow the executions of lingchi with an ambiguously sacred or sacrificial quality; but, as Giorgio Agamben argues, the conceptual apparatus of sacrifice and eroticism is not adequate to grasp the profane and banal violence of modern political life.[12] The delirium of the victim combined with the shame of the witnesses in Chen's fictional video is piercingly traumatic; this helps to explain the psychological need for the hood in Iraq, which not only disorients the victim, but also effaces their humanity for the perpetrator and more easily turns the subject into an object.

When lynching photos were transformed into souvenir postcards, they were sent to friends and family with the senders' proud boasts of having been in the mob, making blackness an exotic spectacle and privileging the "look" of whites over blacks. Spectacle lynchings similarly relied on the look of the crowd to reaffirm notions of superior white "manliness" over the stereotype of the hypersexual black male, even as many white men in the mob acted on repressed homoerotic desires and many white women found vicarious pleasure in the mob's exposure and penetrations of the black body. At Abu Ghraib, compact discs, videos, and computer files of digital images performed the role of the postcards, and were meant to circulate only within the community of American military personnel, their families, and friends. The pictures established the right of the soldiers to "look" at the nude and brutalized bodies of their victims, even to pose with corpses, while effacing the look of the prisoners through hooding and other forms of degradation.

Likewise, the voices of the tortured, like the voices of lynching victims, were meant to be silenced outside the circumstances of their ordeal. But testimonies have been taken. One prisoner tells of being covered with phosphoric liquid from a chemical light and raped with a stick: "Then they broke the glowing finger and spread it on me until I was glowing and they were laughing. They took me to the room and they signaled me to get on the floor. And one of the police he put a part of his stick that he always carries inside my ass and I felt it going inside me about 2 centimeters, approximately. And I started screaming, and he pulled it out... And they were taking pictures of me during all these instances."[13] The photos were meant to add to the shaming as well as provide souvenirs. The thrills of sexualized violence became less veiled and more explicit than in lynching photos, to the point where photographs and videos of torture and the sexual abuse of prisoners were interleaved with images of American soldiers having sex with each other.

But the pornographic function of the torture scenarios serves a larger political function. The pleasure in the extreme pain and degradation of others relies on a process of dehumanization that depends in large part on constructing Arabs and Muslims as an undifferentiated mass, just as black men were stereotyped en masse by white supremacists. Back then they were all "black beast rapists"; now they are all "terrorists," making them far easier to humiliate, torture, sexually exploit, and kill. The necessary emotional distancing and dehumanization of the Other is also revealed by language. The Nazis referred to Jews as "pieces"; American soldiers refer to an Iraqi prisoner as "it."[14] Although the torture photos seem to employ the basic structuring principle of pornography —the events are real but staged for the camera in order to deliver prurient pleasure—the protocols are fundamentally different. Porno actors do not mug for the camera; they maintain a fiction of authenticity. Here there is no "fiction" of authenticity, not only because the victims are not willing actors, but because the pleasure is not meant to be found in their pruriently deployed bodies but in the exultant mastery of those who wield power over them, representing a different cultural and political order.

Thus the influence of pornography did not determine these torture scenarios, any more than it did lynchings. The trend in American culture which holds Arabs and Muslims in contempt, just as "blackness" was held in contempt, or earlier colonial subjects, must be held responsible for such acts. Hersh reports that as government authorities were searching for ways to dominate Muslims in the months before the invasion of Iraq, pro-war Washington conservatives latched onto the notion that Arabs are particularly vulnerable to sexual humiliation. They used the 1978 book *The Arab Mind* by Raphael Patai, a cultural anthropologist, which became "the bible of the neocons on Arab behavior" and depicted sexual shame and humiliation as the biggest weakness of Arabs. Although privacy is indeed deeply ingrained, commentators have noted that Arabs are as shamed and humiliated as any of us would be in the same situation.[15]

Stephen Cambone, Rumsfeld's top intelligence official, was the point man for implementing the secret program in Iraq and deciding that no rules applied. Cambone's military assistant, William G. Boykin, in a speech in an Oregon church, equated the Muslim world with Satan. This helps to explain why prisoners, in addition to being raped and ridden like dogs, were also forced to eat pork and drink alcohol in contravention of their religion.[16] These are crimes of national, ethnic, race, and religious hatred, as well as a colonialist mentality by military occupiers. It is no surprise that this is the perception of much of the Arab world, expressed by Abdelbari Atwan in *Al Quds al Arabi*, a London-based Arabic daily: "The torture is not the work of a few American soldiers. It is the result of an official American culture that deliberately insults and humiliates Muslims."[17]

Cultural theorist Slavoj Žižek suggests that the issue of abuse is more pervasive and fundamental to American culture. "Far too often," he writes, "we are treated to images of soldiers and students forced to assume humiliating poses, perform debasing gestures, and suffer sadistic punishments. The torture at Abu Ghraib was thus not simply a case of American arrogance toward a Third World people. In being submitted to the humiliating tortures, the Iraqi prisoners were effectively initiated into American culture."[18] Žižek's assertion stereotypes American culture as a whole, while diminishing the specific political culpability of the Bush regime for the crimes of Abu Ghraib. My argument is not that there is some essential American impulse to torture, but that torture and its representations are conscious political acts which follow recognizable protocols of power and subordination, of which lynching and Abu Ghraib are two examples.

There is also an important difference between American college hazing rituals and the torture of prisoners, in that those who are victims/participants in the former activity ultimately have a choice, while Iraqi prisoners decidedly do not. The pranks of frat boys, however dangerous and sadistic, do not yet equal the crimes of rape, torture, and murder at Abu Ghraib, as Rush Limbaugh has publicly suggested.[19] Such behavior was tolerated for months with full knowledge up the chain of command and would not have occurred as an ongoing practice without the conviction that it was sanctioned. It was not surprising, then, when an independent panel headed by James R. Schlesinger, the former defense secretary, assigned responsibility for the abuse of prisoners in Iraq, Afghanistan, and Guantánamo Bay to senior Pentagon officials, including Rumsfeld, stating that officials were aware of the problems and failed to address them.[20] Indeed, they effectively authorized them.

The abusive behavior of American prison guards—and Charles F. Graner, for example, one of the most sadistic abusers in the Abu Ghraib scandal, was one—serves as a better analogy than hazing rituals. This is especially evident in relation to immigrant "detainees" in the United States who are locked up by the Department of Homeland Security prior to deportation. Without access to lawyers and soon-to-be-out-of-reach in countries such as Guyana, Egypt, and Tunisia, many of these detainees receive brutal treatment all too reminiscent of Abu Ghraib, as Daniel Zwerdling reports for National Public Radio. Such prisoners have no redress for their complaints.[21]

Like the lynching photos which were appropriated and transformed into antilynching images by left-wing and liberal artists and organizations in the 1930s (such as the John Reed Club and International Labor Defense, both affiliated with the Communist Party and the NAACP), the torture photos of Abu Ghraib also have become the basis for antiwar images and artworks.[22] The photos of the man on a leash and the hooded man are now painted side by side as murals on a wall in Tehran, demonstrating once again that the meaning of images depends on the arena in which they circulate. Like their distribution in the world media, this public visibility transforms them from private souvenirs of American supremacy into blistering anti-American pictures.

The photograph was reprinted in the *New York Times*, where Sarah Boxer commented on the hooded man as echoing the veiled woman who walks by the murals (with a male companion), effectively conflating the two.[23] But there is a difference between hooding and veiling. Though there is clearly an attempt to "feminize" Arabs and Muslims as a whole through their subordination to American dominance, the hooded figure never becomes a veiled figure. Rather, a continuum is produced between the two murals that transforms the abjection of the crawling prisoner, his body truncated by the edge of the mural, into the upright man of sorrows. The hooded man parallels the masculinized figure of Lynndie England, produced at about the same size, counterpoising the diffident American soldier engaged in a debasing action with the figure who seems to appeal to the world through his open-armed gesture, creating the appearance of noble sacrifice, if for a nonexistent redemptive purpose.

Just as the lynching rituals threatened men with castration, at Abu Ghraib, terror also took the form of threatening the masculinity of the prisoners, using dogs to menace and attack naked prisoners and allowing women soldiers to sexually humiliate them and even to handle and mock their genitals, pointing and laughing while taking photographs. Here, as England mocks the genitals of one in a row of naked prisoners, her jauntiness and the casualness of her dangling cigarette differ markedly from the stiffness of her pose with the prisoner on a leash. England's cooptation is complete. The man to whom she points, who has since been released, has come forward to identify himself as Saddam Saleh. He says he only knows that he is the third from the right because American soldiers brought the photograph to his cell and pointed him out, in an obvious effort to humiliate him further. He was tortured for another eighteen days before the interrogations began.[24]

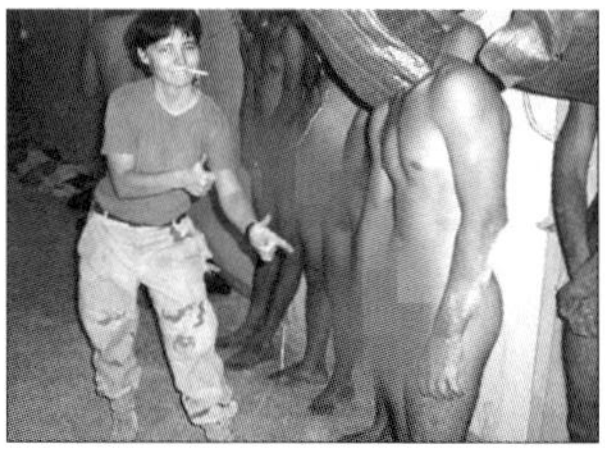

Other prisoners also have testified about their sexual humiliation: "The two American girls that were there when they were beating me, they were hitting me with a ball made of sponge on my dick. And when I was tied up in my room, one of the girls, with blonde hair, she is white, she was playing with my dick." This prisoner was also urinated on by a military policeman and made to bark like a dog, hit on the side of the head so forcefully that he lost consciousness, forced to wear women's red underwear on his head, and tied to a window in his cell with his hands behind his back until he again lost consciousness. Another saw a prisoner's genitals beaten with gloves. Others remembered how soldiers ordered them to masturbate, sometimes in front of female soldiers, and to simulate homosexual acts.[25] Jonathan Raban effectively characterizes the infantilization and feminization of Arabs by the Americans: "Here is Arabia nude, faceless under a hood, or ridiculously feminised in women's panties, forced into infantile masturbatory sex and sodomy."[26]

A photograph of a human pyramid pictures a grinning Sabrina Harman and Charles Graner posing with their handiwork, Graner offering a thumbs-up. The word "RAPEIST" [sic], written on the leg of one of the prisoners, echoes the charges against black lynching victims and becomes a bitter parody of blaming the victim for the crime of the perpetrator. "We thought it looked funny, so pictures were taken," England told investigators.[27] She confessed that piling prisoners naked or forcing them to masturbate had nothing to do with interrogations; but it has everything to do with the arrogance that seeks global domination and is insensitive to the subjugation of "others," functioning as a corollary to American nationalist pride.

Hussein Mohssein Mata al-Zayiadi was among the Iraqis in the pyramid who later gave sworn testimony in which he described his ordeal and its aftermath: "After that they brought my friends, Haidar, Ahmed, Nouri, Ahzem, Hashiem, Mustafa, and I and they put us 2 on the bottom, 2 on top of them, and 2 on top of those and one on top. They took pictures of us and we were naked. After the end of the beating, they took us to our separate cells and they opened the water in the cell and told us to lay face down in the water and we stayed like that until the morning, in the water, naked, without clothes." When asked how he felt about this treatment, he replied, "I was trying to kill myself but I didn't have any way of doing it."[28]

Some antiwar images of the hooded man produce a conflation of the two most iconic images. A photograph of a figure at a London protest depicts a black hooded figure with a noose or a leash around his neck, holding a sign with a picture of the hooded man, and the slogan, "Bring the troops home now." In another protest painting, the hooded man is painted next to the Statue of Liberty on a wall in the crowded Shiite section of Baghdad known as Sadr City. The mural is the work of the thirty-one-year-old artist Salaheddin Sallat. The wires attached to the hooded man are connected to an electric grid, as they are in the real photo, with the Statue of Liberty pulling the switch. Sallat, who lives in a small house with eighteen members of his family, observed, "In fact, when I saw the photo of that man, it made me think of the Statue of Liberty," further noting, "I chose this area because everyone can see it."[29] Such recontextualizations of the Abu Ghraib images may be seen as contributing to the resistance against the acts they represent. Here Sallat makes clear his understanding that the mere act of rendering the images visible to the public begins their undoing.

The Statue of Liberty sports a white hood below the spikes of her crown and wears a medallion with a small red cross at her neck, the Eastern Orthodox cross more familiar to Iraqis. The words painted on the wall indicate the mockery of "freedom" that the war on Iraq has produced, doubling the hooded man with the preeminent symbol of America. The Statue of Liberty, once the icon of welcome to refugees, stands above all for American democracy. But the rhetoric of democracy is exposed for its extreme hypocrisy. The images that illustrate the words "That Freedom for Bush" represent what this rhetoric has set in motion and come to mean; since the rationale for war was the export of freedom and democracy, it is Liberty and no other symbol, such as Uncle Sam, which best represents America. But her torch now becomes a lethal electric current. Effectively conflating Liberty and the executioner into a single image, the figures become doppelgangers; the mask of degradation becomes the face of America, the hooded man its innocent victim. Commenting on the power of the hooded man and the leashed man images, Mark Danner calls such representations the "perfect masterpieces of propaganda" which have "the considerable advantage of being true." "Had bin Laden sought to create a powerful trademark image for his international product of global jihad," he writes, "he could scarcely have done better hiring the cleverest advertising firm on Madison Avenue."[30]

The Statue of Liberty transformed into the standard bearer of racial oppression evokes an antilynching image from the 1930s produced in protest of the Scottsboro trials, the notorious case of nine young black men falsely accused of raping two white girls on a freight train headed toward Alabama. In *Scottsboro: A Story Told in Prints*, first produced in 1933, a linocut depicts the attempt by the courts to carry out a "legal lynching." A hooded Klansman assumes his position on the pedestal, holding a lynch rope in one hand and a small electric chair in the other. Marked by a swastika, cross, and backwards dollar sign, the Klansman replaces Liberty with race hatred, intolerance, and greed while Liberty runs for her life.

Another protest image, produced by the LA graphic design group

Forkscrew Graphics, was placed in the subways and streets of New York City and Los Angeles following the revelations of Abu Ghraib.[31] Produced in silhouette, the hooded man in his ragged cape stands on what now becomes a pedestal, like the Statue of Liberty, emphasizing his precarious balance even as it strengthens the iconic status of the image. The hooded man has become a logo for the war itself, codified in the symbol of a time bomb next to the stylized word "iRaq," an echo of the iPod logo, just as the fake hot-pink or chartreuse backgrounds evoke the iPod ads. Alluding to the Pop art multiples associated with Andy Warhol, the slick and colorful posters suggest the commercialization of the war, evoking Halliburton and the staggering profits it has made on noncompetitive contracts. The posters further imply the commodification of torture itself as central to the occupation of Iraq. Torture as a commodity takes its crassest form in the phenomenon of "outsourcing"—the common employment and delegation of the task of interrogation to mercenaries euphemistically called "civilian contractors" (the four men who were notoriously murdered and mutilated in Fallujah in April 2004 were civilian contractors). Inserted among actual iPod ads in subway stations and on the streets of New York and Los Angeles, the selling of torture as a war product is ironically complete.

Richard Serra also appropriated the hooded man for *Stop Bush*, a color lithograph done as a free downloadable poster for pleasevote.com, and, in another version, for an Artists Coming Together benefit print, *Stop B S*.[32] Serra distributed these prints widely in art venues, mainstream publications, and on the Internet in support of the Democratic campaigns for the 2004 election. The haunting image becomes emblematic of American imperial arrogance as well as the signal crime of the Bush administration, encapsulating the argument for his defeat. In an interview with the German newspaper *Die Zeit*, Serra condemned the Bush administration for its denial of Western values and law.[33] Geoffrey Sirc has argued that although images can still unnerve us, it is much harder now to penetrate our "overmediated consciousness."[34] The images that still have such power are those that allude to the real.

The hooded man is the latest addition to a genealogy of iconic images, which includes the photos of the planes crashing into the World Trade Center towers on 9/11 and, from the Vietnam War, Nick Ut's photograph of a naked Vietnamese girl burned by napalm fleeing down a road in Saigon, another sacrificial figure, or Eddie Adams's photo of a communist guerrilla being executed in a Saigon street. After the US government censorship of photographs from World War II and Korea, such pictures had a shocking effect on the American public.[35] Similarly, the Abu Ghraib photos stand in stark contrast to the officially approved and sanitized representations of the American presence in Iraq, which are consistent with the government's refusal to report on Iraqi civilian casualties and its censorship of photos of returning coffins with the American dead.

The issues of gender and sexuality also have been addressed in protest art. The Taguba Report and an unreleased video both show that at least one woman prisoner was raped, while others were forced to strip.[36] Further evidence of soldiers engaging in various sex acts with prisoners and among themselves was reported following the three-hour, closed-door session on May 12, 2004, during which members of Congress were shown over eighteen hundred photographs and videos.[37] In another case, three Army soldiers were accused of assaulting a female

Iraqi prisoner. While publications such as the *New Yorker* and the *Washington Post* made decisions not to publish many of the more disturbing photographs, Klaus Theweleit, author of *Male Fantasies*, in an interview with the *Suddeutsche Zeitung*, argued against such restraint: "I have these kinds of scenes in my head, from concentration camps, from splatter, snuff, and porn films. We could repress these images, but then we give ourselves over to the illusion spread by the sanitized editions of the daily news: that we live in a half-civilized world."[38]

A protest image produced by Qassim al-Sabti, a fifty-one-year-old Iraqi artist and owner of the Hewar Gallery in the Wazerieh district of central Baghdad, poignantly captures the crimes against the Iraqi woman. A lifesize female mannequin lies prone, her veil a white death shroud marred only by an oozing red triangle. Al-Sabti was inspired to produce this work after receiving a copy of a letter that a prisoner, who was raped and impregnated by a US guard, had sent to her family. "There was a letter circulating in Fallujah from a woman inside Abu Ghraib," al-Sabti said. "She was begging the resistance to bomb Abu Ghraib and bring down the walls on their heads so that their suffering would end. I felt like screaming when I heard this. I wanted to draw the attention of the American people.[39]

The letter, smuggled out of the prison, was one of the few to reveal what was happening to women inside Abu Ghraib. The shame and ostracism attached to having been raped is so egregious that most Iraqi women who have been released will not discuss their experiences, even in private. Amal Kadham Swadi, one of seven Iraqi women lawyers representing women at Abu Ghraib, has begun to uncover the extent of atrocities against women across Iraq, including the case of one seventy-year-old woman who was harnessed and ridden like a donkey at Abu Ghraib. Many women are the wives or daughters of male suspects, arrested as a way of pressuring the men.[40]

Al-Sabti invited twenty artists to contribute works to an exhibition inspired by the humiliations at Abu Ghraib.[41] Abdel-Karim Khalil produced three works for al-Sabti's exhibition, including a roughly foot-high marble carving of a hooded detainee. Combining the medium of white marble associated with classical Greek sculpture and rational civilization with the symbol of a barbarian oppressor, Khalil appropriates a form traditionally used to represent "whiteness" in order to universalize the figure. He observed, "Some artists used to be neutral, but now there are artists, poets, and writers who have all reached the decision that the Americans are destroyers. It has given them a new sense of purpose in art."[42]

It took decades of struggle as well as economic and political forces to finally subdue the systematic lynching of black people and to transform lynching photography from a support of white supremacy into an antilynching weapon through the mass publication of lynching photos and especially the pictures of the vicious disfigurement of Emmett Till, which helped galvanize the civil rights movement. The Abu Ghraib photos had a more instantaneous effect, unleashing public horror and outrage around the world through global distribution of the pictures via the Internet and television. More recently, seventeen of the images were on view in the fall 2004 exhibition "Inconvenient Evidence: Iraqi Prison Photographs from Abu Ghraib," curated by Brian Wallis for the International Center of Photography in New York and the Andy Warhol Museum in Pittsburgh. Like the photographs of lynchings in the exhibitions of *Without Sanctuary* that began in New York in 2000, "Inconvenient Evidence" may raise the question for some of whether such exhibitions make the photographs available once again to a gaze of mastery, reinforcing their humiliating effect. But just as the photos' initial production and forms of circumscribed circulation were political acts, so is their display in such public venues now, exposing American pretensions to racial, cultural, and political dominance in Iraq and revealing a brutality and sense of entitlement that is firmly rooted in the nationalist ideology of the Bush administration.

Indeed, the lurid atrocities that traveled the globe were branded by one military official a "moral Chernobyl." But unlike Chernobyl, as Christopher Hitchens points out, the only accident at Abu Ghraib was the release of the pictures to the world.[43] The torture and abuse of prisoners was mandated and justified at the top, and those who gave vent to even the most gratuitous sadistic impulses felt safe in a carefully circumscribed culture of community sanction. That community began scrambling to repair the public relations disaster this represented for the United States, not to ameliorate the trauma and loss that constitute the human cost in Iraq or to reexamine the underlying policies that have led to the systematic and continuing pattern of torture, but to salvage their moral authority by shirking responsibility and blaming a few "bad apples." And they succeeded, at least in the United States, by winning another election. How, then, do photographs of torture produce their own undoing? When is the power of an image turned against itself, transforming it into a picture that opposes the very thing the photograph means to uphold? We can affirm that different meanings are produced according to the arenas in which those images circulate, and that the association of photographs and artworks with the status of the real is critical to producing both a successful countereffect and an effectively persuasive protest art. But we must also recognize that torture images do not inherently produce their own undoing—it depends on us.

Notes

1. See Luc Sante, "Tourists and Torturers," opinion-editorial, *New York Times*, May 11, 2004, A23; Susan Sontag, "The Pictures Are Us," *New York Times Magazine*, May 23, 2004, 24ff; Frank Rich, "It Was the Porn That Made Them Do It," *New York Times*, May 30, 2004, Section 2, 1; Abigail Solomon-Godeau, "Remote Control," *Artforum*, Summer 2004, 61.

2. For key texts on Abu Ghraib, see three articles by Seymour Hersh in the *New Yorker*: "Torture at Abu Ghraib," posted April 30, 2004, available online at http://www.newyorker.com/fact/content/articles/040510fa_fact; "Chain of Command," posted May 9, 2004, available online at http://www.newyorker. com/fact/content/articles/040517fa_fact2; and "The Gray Zone," posted May 15, 2004, available online at http://www.newyorker.com/fact/content/articles/040524fa_fact; see also Hersh's book *Chain of Command: The Road from 9/11 to Abu Ghraib* (New York: HarperCollins, 2004). For Abu Ghraib images, see Web sites such as http://www.antiwar.com/news/?articleid=2444, and http://www.rotten.com/library/crime/prison/abu-ghraib/. The torture photographs and major documents and reports have also been collected in Mark Danner, *Torture and Truth: America, Abu Ghraib, and the War on Terror* (New York: New York Review Books, 2004).

3. In this regard, Deleuze notes the importance of the revolution of 1789 for the Marquis de Sade and the revolution of 1848 for Leopold von Sacher-Masoch, whose writings invite the viewer to identify with either the sadistic torturer or masochistic victim respectively. See Gilles Deleuze, *Sacher-Masoch: An Interpretation*, trans. Jean McNeil (London: Faber and Faber, 1971).

4. See my *Imagery of Lynching: Black Men, White Women, and the Mob* (New Brunswick, NJ: Rutgers University Press, 2004).

5. Quoted in Adam Liptak, "Legal Scholars Criticize Torture Memos," *New York Times*, June 25, 2004, A14.

6. Hersh, "The Gray Zone."

7. On the role of the father of Ivan Frederick, one of the accused soldiers, in getting the pictures to *60 Minutes II*, which broadcast them on April 28, 2004, see "Here's How the Abu Ghraib Photos Got Out," available online at http://talkleft.com/new_archives/006410.html#006410, May 8, 2004. Specialist Joseph M. Darby also turned over CDs with photographs of the torture. See "In a Soldier's Words, an Account of Concerns," *New York Times*, May 22, 2004, available online at http://www.nytimes.com/2004/05/22/politics/22WTEX.html?ex=1113969600&en=c6dc9c55e8f06b78&ei=5070&fta=y.

8. See translation of statement provided by Abdou Hussain Saad Faleh, January 16, 2004, in Danner, *Torture and Truth*, 230.

9. Sarah Boxer, "Torture Incarnate, and Propped on a Pedestal," *New York Times*, June 13, 2004.

10. W. J. T. Mitchell, "Echoes of a Christian Symbol," *Chicago Tribune*, June 27, 2004. Section 2, 1, available online at http://humanities.uchicago.edu/faculty/mitchell/interviews.htm.

11. For the most authoritative information on lingchi, see the work of the research group Turandot, which held a conference on "The Representation of Pain," April 22–23, 2005, at University College Cork in Cork, Ireland. The Turandot Web site on Chinese torture is http://turandot.ish-lyon.cnrs.fr/. Also see An-yi Pan, "Contemporary Taiwanese Art in the Era of Contention," in *Contemporary Taiwanese Art in the Era of Contention*, exh. cat. (Ithaca: Johnson Museum of Art, Cornell University; Taipei: Taipei Fine Arts Museum, 2004), 158, 160–61.

12. Giorgio Agamben, *Homo Sacer: Sovereign Power and Bare Life*, trans. Daniel Heller-Roazen (Stanford: Stanford University Press, 1998), 112–15.

13. Translation of statement of [name blacked out], January 21, 2004, in Danner, *Torture and Truth*, 248.

14. Robin Tolmach Lakoff. "From Ancient Greece to Iraq, the Power of Words in Wartime," *New York Times*, May 18, 2004, Section F, 3. The Iraqis are also derisively called "hajis," the way the Vietnamese were called "gooks."

15. See, for example, "Muslims Were Outraged; So Were Christians," *New York Times*, May 9, 2004, Section 4, 5. Edward Said roundly attacked Patai's book in his landmark 1978 study *Orientalism*.

16. Andrew Buncombe, Justin Huggler, and Leonard Doyle, "Abu Ghraib: Inmates Raped, Ridden Like Animals, and Forced to Eat Pork," available online at http://news.independent.co.uk/world/middle_east/story.jsp?story=523724.

17. Quoted in Alan Cowell, "Bush's Words Do Little to Ease Horror at Prison Deeds," *New York Times*, May 7, 2004, A12.

18. Slavoj Žižek, "What Rumsfeld Doesn't Know that He Knows about Abu Ghraib," *In These Times*, May 21, 2004, available online at www.inthesetimes.com.

19. Rush Limbaugh dismissed the Abu Ghraib photos saying, "It is no different than what happens at the Skull and Bones initiation." Quoted in "Abu Ghraib Timeline," in *Inconvenient Evidence: Iraqi Prison Photographs from Abu Ghraib*, exh. cat. (New York: International Center of Photography; Pittsburgh: Andy Warhol Museum, 2004). See also "Commentators Conflate 'Depraved' Art and Abu Ghraib Photos," May 14, 2004, available online at Artforum.com/archive/id=6885.

20. See "The Schlesinger Report," August 2004, in Danner, *Torture and Truth*, 329–99.

21. Daniel Zwerdling, "U.S. Detainee Abuse Cases Fall through the Cracks," November 18, 2004, available online at www.npr.org/templates/story/story.php?storyld=4173701.

22. See my *Imagery of Lynching*.

23. Boxer. "Torture Incarnate, and Propped on a Pedestal."

24. Buncombe, Huggler, and Doyle, "Abu Ghraib."

25. See translations of statements: [name blacked out], January 21, 2004; Shalan Said al-Sharoni, January 17, 2004; Nori Samir Gunbar Al-Yasseri, January 17, 2004; Hussein Mohssein Mata al-Zayiadi, January 4, 2004; Hiadar Sabar Abed Miktub al-Aboodi, January 20, 2004; all in Danner, *Torture and Truth*, 247–48, 234, 236–37, 240, 245.

26. Jonathan Raban, "Emasculating Arabia," *The Guardian* (London), May 13, 2004, Features, 6.

27. "U.S. Rules on Prisoners Seen as a Back and Forth of Mixed Messages to G.I.'s," *New York Times*, June 22, 2004, A7.

28. Translation of statement provided by Hussein Mohssein Mata al-Zayiadi, January 18, 2004, in Danner, *Torture and Truth*, 240.

29. Virginie Locussol, "U.S. Prison Abuse Painted on Wall," June 2, 2004, available online at Novinite.com/view_news.php?id=35348.

30. Danner, *Torture and Truth*, 29.

31. The hooded man is one of four poster parodies; the other three depict American soldiers in silhouette handling guns, shoulder-fired missiles, or grenades. See www.forkscrew.com/main.html.

32. See www.bloodforoil.org/please-vote/ for another pleasevote.com image designed by Serra that superimposes Bush's face on Goya's painting *Saturn Devouring His Children*; the image was featured as an ad on the back cover of *The Nation*.

33. Artnet.news, September 7, 2004, available online at www.artnet.com/Magazine/news/artnetnews2/artnetnews9-7-04.asp.
34. Geoffrey Sirc, "Undecided, but Leaning toward Skull: Political Art in the Age of Spin," October 28, 2004, available online at http://www.mnartists.org/article.do;jsessionid=EEA59F7168038D64A9417438CA880F4A?rid=51507.
35. See George H. Roeder, Jr., *The Censored War: American Visual Experience during World War Two* (New Haven: Yale University Press, 1993). For the Nick Ut and Eddie Adams photos, see http://images.google.com/images?hl=en&lr=&q=vietnam+war+photos.
36. "The Taguba Report," in Danner, *Torture and Truth*, 279–328.
37. Images included forced sodomy, Lynndie England having sex with other U.S. soldiers in front of prisoners, prisoners cowering in front of attack dogs, Iraqi women being forced to expose their breasts, naked prisoners tied up together, prisoners forced to masturbate, and a prisoner repeatedly smashing his head against a wall. On May 21, 2004, on the *Washington Post* web site, executive editor Leonard Downie, Jr., described the newspaper's decision not to publish many of the abuse images because they were "so shocking and in such bad taste, especially the extensive nudity." See "Abu Ghraib Timeline," in *Inconvenient Evidence*. Also see Seymour Hersh's presentation at Hampden-Sydney College in Virginia, "Terrorism: A Report from Washington," a video presented on C-Span, September 9, 2004, in which he attests to having seen "many worse" photographs than the ones published by the *New Yorker*, available online at www.c-span.org/search/basic.asp?ResultStart=1&ResultCount=10&BasicQueryText=Seymour+Hersh). The *New Yorker* decided not to publish those photos, a decision that Hersh defended.
38. Quoted in "Theweleit et al. on the Iconography of War," International News Digest, May 17, 2004, available online at www.artforum.com/news/week=200421#news6892.
39. Nicholas Blanford, "Iraqi Artists Depict Anger over Abu Ghraib," June 15, 2004, available online at http://www.csmonitor.com/2004/0615/p07s01-woiq.html, and Samir Haddad and Mazen Ghazi, "Iraqi Plastic Art Documents Abu Ghraib Abuse," June 6, 2004, available online at http://www.islamonline.net/English/News/2004-06/06/article02.shtml.
40. See "Abu Ghraib's Women Prisoners," May 26, 2004, available online at http://www.thinkingpeace.com/pages/arts2/arts210.html; Francine D'Amico, "The Women of Abu Ghraib," *The Post-Standard*, May 23, 2004, CI; and Annia Ciezadlo, "For Iraqi Women, Abu Ghraib's Taint," May 28, 2004, available online at http://www.csmonitor.com/2004/0528/p01s02-woiq.html.
41. Sculptor Taher Wahib produced a Statue of Liberty with her head replaced by chained hands, her feet lashed together, and her robe set on fire by her own torch, which stands on a Baghdad street behind barbed wire and barriers with a flag that reads, "Abu Gulag Freedom Park"; another statue is made entirely of chains and wears a T-shirt distributed to Iraqis by coalition troops, bearing the words, "Iraq, progress and prosperity." See Sammy Ketz, "Iraqi Artists Portray Ugly Wounds of U.S. Occupation," June 7, 2004, available online at http://www.middle-eastonline.com/english/culture/?id=10196=10196&format=0. For more on Baghdad artists, including al-Sabti, see Steve Mumford, "The Artists of Baghdad," in Baghdad Journal, November 11, 2003, available online at Artnet.com/magazine/features/mumford/mumford 1-11-03.asp. For an interview with al-Sabti, see Edward Miller, "In the First Person," Mennonite Central Committee, September 8, 2003, available online at www.mcc.org/areaserv/middleeast/iraq/interviews/qasim.html.
42. Blanford, "Iraqi Artists"; Hamza Hendawi, "Images of Iraqi Prisoners Used in Art," May 8, 2004, available online at http://www.liberaltopia.org/archives/2004/05/more_proof_some.php.
43. Christopher Hitchens, "A Moral Chernobyl: Prepare for the Worst of Abu Ghraib," *Slate*, June 14, 2004, available online at slate.msn.com/id/2102373.

Kymberly N. Pinder

Biraciality and Nationhood in Contemporary American Art[1]

From *Race-ing Art History: Critical Readings in Race and Art History*, London: Routledge, 2002

"For when we swallow Tiger Woods, the yellow-black-red-white man, we swallow something much more significant than Jordan or Charles Barkley. We swallow hope in the American experiment, in the pell-mell jumbling of genes. We swallow the belief that the face of the future is not necessarily a bitter or bewildered face; that it might even, one day, be something like Tiger Woods' face: handsome and smiling and ready to kick all comers' asses."[2] The hope in "the yellow-black-red-white man," reflected in the Tigermania that swept the US in the mid-1990s, is indicative of the racial crossroads at which we, as a nation, find ourselves at the close of the twentieth century. As Stanley Crouch describes, "We have been inside each other's bloodstreams, pockets, libraries, kitchens, schools, theaters, sports arenas, dance halls, and national boundaries for so long that our mixed-up and multi-ethnic identity extends from European colonial expansion and builds upon immigration."[3] Where are we as a nation regarding race when Woods can consider himself "Cabliasian" while some Southern states are still officially ending their "one-drop" rules and laws against mixed marriages? How can we address the concerns of those who see the demise of Affirmative Action and a multiracial category on the 2000 census equally devastating to racial equality? There is a (melting) pot boiling here as we transverse a millennium and the suspense is killing all of us.

Some contemporary artists in the US have been hashing out these issues in the 1980s and 1990s. Lorraine O'Grady is one of them. She originally titled her photomontage diptych *The Clearing* in 1991; however, later, she lengthened the title to *The Clearing: or Cortez and La Malinche, Thomas Jefferson and Sally Hemings, N. and Me* to clarify the historical and personal relevance of the work. The left half of the piece presents the relationship between the black woman and the white man as loving while the right as malevolent. The skeletal face of the man and the gun on the pile of clothing provide elements of violence and death. Yet O'Grady says, "It isn't a 'before/after' piece; it's a 'both/and' piece. This couple is on the wall in the simultaneous extremes of ecstasy and exploitation."[4] The complex relationship between exploitation and defiance for such women of color as La Malinche and Sally Hemings has become a trope of American hybridity and assimilation.

Though anthropologists have established the mixed-race heritage of all humans with the discovery of "missing link" hominids in Central and South Africa, racial purity, mixing, and conflict are still hotly debated issues in American society. I am not contesting any scientific definitions of race and human origins in this essay, but I will focus on representations of multiraciality and their socio-political currency in American society, specifically contemporary popular culture. Throughout this essay, I will use the terms biracial, mixed-race, multiracial, multiethnic, racial hybridity, and multicultural with the understanding that such terms are socially constructed and based on perceptions, either of oneself or by others in our society. These terms and their instability reflect the challenge we face to meaningfully discuss the reality of racial mixing, as well as to create the very language needed to do so.

Of course, the reality of a nation of immigrants, the legacy of slavery, and the genocide of native populations prevents issues of race and difference from being resolved in the US. In the last decade or so, as the collapse of Affirmative Action initiatives and the rise of white supremacy groups attest, racial divides seem to be widening rather than narrowing. Some race scholars such as Crouch think otherwise and see the increased mixing of the races in the US as the "end of race":

> *The international flow of images and information will continue to make for a greater and greater swirl of influences. It will increasingly change life on the globe and also change our American sense of race … In that future, definition by racial, ethnic and sexual groups will most probably have ceased to be the foundation of special-interest power … Americans of the future will find themselves surrounded in every direction by people who are part Asian, part Latin, part African, part European, part Indian.*[5]

As panaceas or true saviors, historical figures, like Hemings, and contemporary celebrities, like Woods, have become national touchstones for unity. These biracial or multiracial individuals who were once outcast traces of taboo sexual transgressions, the stereotypical "tragic mulattos," are now signifiers of a future of racial harmony. In February 1995, *Newsweek* devoted an entire issue to the "New Race" in America and though its surveys showed some significant pessimism among blacks and whites regarding our nation's race relations, the magazine presented the nation's growing mixed-race population as a future remedy for current racial conflicts.[6] As one biracial writer responded, the magazine declared "it hip to be mixed."[7] Another article, with a markedly flippant tone, in *Harper's Magazine* in 1993, even recommended a more practical "need" for racial mixing: melanin-rich skin for the survival of future generations as our ozone layer erodes.[8] Popular movies such as *Bulworth* (1998), written and directed by Warren Beattie, present a jaded white politician who, after living a few days with a black family in South Central Los Angeles, makes "procreative, racial deconstruction" his political platform, his remedy for racial discrimination and the economic disparities it has caused in this country.

Historical figures who loved transracially, such as La Malinche and Pocahontas, have also gained political significance as they offer hopeful moments of cross-cultural cooperation in our racially divided pasts. For example, the 1995 Disney film about the latter presents the saga as a love story in which Pocahontas risks her own life to save that of John Smith. This narrative, based upon Smith's account and revised for a young audience, excludes Matoaka's (Pocahontas's real name) later kidnapping and forced conversion. Many applauded Disney's politically correct inclusion of Native American history into its repertoire; however, the effects of the distortion of "Distory"[9] on our children's understanding of national history and race relations are questionable. The scale of this type of nationalistic desire for harmony, past and present, through these icons, is summed up in the words of Woods's father, Earl, "Tiger will do more than any other man in history to change the course of humanity ... Because he's qualified through his ethnicity to accomplish miracles. He's a bridge between East and West. There is no limit because he has the guidance ... He is the Chosen One. He'll have the power to impact nations. Not people. Nations."[10]

O'Grady's photomontage parallels the relationships of La Malinche and Sally Hemings which did impact nations and bridge cultures in the past. La Malinche's facility at languages made her translator for the Spanish conqueror Hernan Cortez; then she gave birth to a racial bridge, their son, the original mestizo. La Malinche's other name was La Lengua, the language, and the transformation from "race traitor," La Malinche, a slur in some Mexican dialects, to the status of the great communicator and reconciler, as she has been recently reclaimed, namely by feminists, is a leitmotif in the biographies of such historical figures. No matter her intentions, La Lengua brought together Europeans and Indians; Hemings united, inside and outside of herself, Africans and Europeans; and Woods, "the yellow-black-red-white man" brings together all of the "primary races" in one body. As his mother Tida says, "Tiger has Thai, African, Chinese, American Indian, and European blood; he can hold everyone together; he is the Universal Child."[11]

The artist, O'Grady, considers this mixing to be a great strength of multiethnic people. She uses the diptych format symbolically in *The Clearing*, and in other works, such as *The Miscegenated Family Album Series* (1994), which explores her own family history and, most recently, in *Studies for Flowers of Evil and Good* (1996), which addresses the relationship between Charles Baudelaire and his black, common-law wife, Jeanne Duval. O'Grady feels that the diptych reflects her "cultural situation" as an artist of bicultural identity (the artist's family was originally from the Caribbean and is of mixed-race ancestry). These works explore interracial relationships both personally and historically. I quote extensively from her:

> *I think that the biggest problem that those of us have who are bi- or even tricultural and are trying to interpolate our positions with those of the west ... the way in which, both philosophically and practically, the west divides its ability to comprehend good/evil and black/white, the way in which it makes oppositions of everything. Not just simple oppositions, but hierarchical, superior/inferior oppositions, so that male/female, black/white, good/evil, body/mind, nature/culture are not just different, one is always better than.*[12]

In *The Clearing*, O'Grady addresses this dualism in a number of ways. Besides the diptych format that presents a "good/bad" dichotomy, she presents compelling details such as the lush landscape and happy children on the left in opposition to the specter of death on the right. This figure on the right wears armor (chain mail) which, juxtaposed with his actions, rape, subverts all ideas of European chivalry. This photomontage is also a montage of ideas concerning the complexity of cross-racial unions, either through love or violence.

In earlier American representation of the "bicultural condition," we can find little of this nuanced treatment. Thomas Noble's *The Price of Blood* (1867) shows a white slave owner selling his own biracial son who stands sullenly in the background. This representation of the "tragic mulatto" continued almost unchanged into the middle of the twentieth century.[13] The African-American painter Archibald Motley, Jr. created a series of portraits of mixed-race women in the 1920s whose solemn faces against dark backgrounds also convey some of these tragic qualities. Motley considered this series to be both an artistic and scientific experiment. Writing about one of the portraits, he commented, "In this painting I have tried to show that delicate one-eighth strain of Negro blood. Therefore, I would say that this painting was not only an artistic venture but also a scientific problem."[14]

Such writers as Frantz Fanon have articulated the social, political, and economic power of the visibility of race, "the racial epidermal schema" of non-whiteness in a post-colonial world.[15] Motley's interest in pigment as a painter resonates in the recent work of a number of contemporary artists. The Korean-American artist Byron Kim's "skin" paintings are abstract musings on the visual reality of a multicultural society. Some of these pigment paintings, such as *Cosmetic Portrait Series* (1992), are rows of flesh-toned ovals reminiscent of cosmetic products. Usually, Kim arranges groups of them in grids that suggest a pseudo-scientific project similar to Motley's. In *Synechdoche* (1991), for example, the key on the work's label identifies each panel as the skin tone of a family member or friend which makes these panels function as racial indices. As Kim alludes to cosmetics, Gabrielle Varella uses paint color sample strips as her referent to address the loaded function of skin tone in our society in her *Untitled Series* (1999). In these fragile, mundane gradations of beiges and browns that run the spectrum from café au lait to deep mahogany, Varella has printed phrases, such as "The color of my skin makes you think I can't be lucky" or "My name is not Mexican enough for you to know what I am." These "skin samples" address a multiracial audience with the visual realities regarding the daily assessments and assumptions that are made and internalized about race. Each one of us is embraced, dismissed, respected, or ignored in every encounter. In a series of altered photographs by Paul Solomon entitled *Biracial Portraits* (1997), his sitters appear to be literally half one race and half another. The literal halving of an individual questions the validity and potential absurdity of racial labels if indeed these racial markers were so clearly visible on each biracial body. Returning to the often ignored issue of race in Latin American cultures, the painter Bibiana Suárez presents a retable of two self-portraits from 1991–92. In one, *Y tu abuela a donde estâ?* (What color is your grandmother?), Suárez celebrates the Afro-Antillean aspects of her Puerto Rican heritage, something that many Puerto Ricans deny. The title of the work is taken from the poem "Y tu agüela, a'onde ejitá?" (1942) by Fortunato Vizcarrondo in which he confronts these racial biases in his culture. In the accompanying portrait, *La Blanquita* (The White One), Suárez paints herself more as she is, fair-skinned with an emphasis on her whiteness. In the same way in which the Conceptual artist Adrian Piper has explored the social and personal ramifications of her being a light-skinned African-American, Suárez forces her audience to acknowledge the reality of Puerto Rico's *mestizo* legacy *and* how much American racism has affected this legacy. As she writes, "The colloquial expression 'blanquita' (or *blanquito* for a male) in Puerto Rico signifies more than just the color of one's skin. It conveys the common perception in Puerto Rico that a light skin person is better, revealing a colonial mentality that values its own racial heritage only so far as it compares to the dominant US culture." The way in which she presents her two selves in dress and demeanor speak to these biases since one can interpret the head wrap and ill-fitting t-shirt of the *black* Suárez versus the neatly coiffed blond hair and embellished title banner of *La Blanquita* as communicating a value hierarchy. She does not neglect to suggest class distinction as part and parcel of the history of racial bias in Puerto Rico and elsewhere.

Robert Colescott, who has made a career out of confronting racism and racial taboos in his art, approaches the same themes of racial labels and self-identification in *Lightning Lipstick* (1994). Like Varella and Suárez, Colescott addresses the conflict for dark-skinned Latinos who are Latino-identified, meaning, they derive their identity from their specific geographical roots, i.e., Mexico or Puerto Rico, but they are seen as black, "negrito," by others, especially North Americans. In *Grandma and the Frenchman: Identity Crisis* (1991) the "tragic mulatto" rears her misshapen head. Not only does this woman have all of the colors of many races, but all of their hair, eyes, mouths, and noses! Colescott says this work is "all about identity—this woman cannot have just a two-faced Picasso head, she must be even more fragmented because her identity is so screwed up. Mixed-race people are all around us, we all are and have been for centuries." Standing in stark contrast to the happy, mixed-race children in O'Grady's *The Clearing* who offer hope for the future, Colescott's image speaks to both white and non-white fears of racial mixing and the hegemonic collapse it signals. One could see the distorted head as a metaphor for the social and political morass that occurs when the physicality of racial marking is obscured. For the dominant, European power structure, this ambiguity subverts exclusion, the bedrock of its oppression, and for the non-Europeans it oppresses, it betrays any solidarity against this very exclusion.

Though recently the horrific events in Rwanda and Bosnia have proven that intraracial oppression and annihilation are alive and well, these genocidal projects are complicated by this very issue of the physicality of difference and its intersection with personal relationships, such as intermarriage. Michael Lind addressed the statistical reality of this breakdown in the US in his essay, "The Beige and The Black." He interrogated the many statistical predictions regarding racial demographics for the next century and noted that interracial unions are not included in these projections, therefore, skewing the numbers and our ideas of our multiracial future. The most compelling observation he makes, which simultaneously dampens and bolsters the optimistic rhetoric regarding this future of racial blurring and erasure, is that blacks are intermarrying at a fraction of the rate of Asians, Native Americans, and Latinos:

> *In the twenty-first century, then, the US population is not likely to be crisply divided among whites, blacks, Hispanics, Asians, and American Indians. Nor is it likely to be split two ways, between white and nonwhites. Rather, we are most likely to see something more complicated: a white-Asian-Hispanic melting-pot majority—a hard-to-*

> *differentiate group of beige Americans—offset by a minority of blacks who have been left out of the melting pot once again.*[16]

Lind goes on to articulate the socioeconomic fallout of this shift in the racial power structure, which would, on one hand end balkanization, but, on the other, would significantly weaken what few political alliances that current "rainbow coalitions" have against discriminatory treatment. The dissolution of identity politics will also affect representation.

Another artist from the first half of this century helps us frame these contemporary issues. William H. Johnson's painting of 1941 entitled *Mom and Dad* shows his mother with a photograph of his father on the back wall. Johnson sometimes said his father was Native American and other times, white. This father's powerful presence of absence, if you will, in the hanging portrait reflected the importance of Johnson's mixed heritage to his identity as both a black man and an artist in the 1930s and 1940s. He considered himself "both a cultured painter and a primitive man."[17] He frequently used his ambiguous racial lineage as proof of his natural artistic hybridity that made him an "authentic" modern primitive, the fusion of European and "primitive," that was by blood. Like Woods who "can hold everyone together," Johnson too felt his heritage made him superior to the "purer" races—*and* to such wannabe primitives as Pablo Picasso and Paul Gauguin.

In Johnson's case, we see the colonial catch-22 of racial purity. Johnson was essentially defining himself within the discourse created by others. Like all non-white "primitives," he was trying to win in a game whose rules are ever shifting. It is similar to the uneasy alliances such political leaders as Marcus Garvey and Malcolm X made with segregationists and other whites against racial mixing. As O'Grady expands on this slippery slope:

> *My own feeling is that the only thing that will ultimately work is if we can somehow find a way to use the "mixed product" to negate not just the idea of "purity" but the idea of "superiority" itself. In racial code, "purity" is a cover for what is really meant, "superiority/inferiority." Those who espoused it certainly didn't mean that pure blackness was superior ... Seducing blacks into accepting that form of discourse was a way of gaining their collaboration in the maintenance of their own inferiority, under the false guise of preserving their own purity.*[18]

Yet, the rhetoric of "the new and improved" prevails in some sectors and I would suggest, rules at the current time. Racial hybrids become evolutionary cultural products. Their strength lies in their ability to genetically unify two or more oppositional forces. Johnson became the perfect modernist while La Malinche and Hemings have become the perfect postcolonial beings—and feminists. The subversive nature of their acts of racial and cultural mixing transcends their victimization. Though artists like O'Grady and Colescott question this transcendence, they would agree that though these interracial unions are exploitative, their very existence and their resulting offspring weaken the very hegemonic structure that enables such exploitation. A not-so-"sub" subtext of this entire discussion about the representation of racial mixing has been the visibility or more accurately, the erasure of whiteness.

The pop success of the actor Vin Diesel in such films as *Pitch Black* (2000), *The Boiler Room* (2000), and *The Fast and the Furious* (2001) at the turn of this current century also attests to the new appeal of racial ambiguity. Diesel's refusal to answer any questions regarding his race and its link to his success is something he himself foreshadowed in an independent film he made titled *Multifacial* (1995) in which an actor of unclear ethnicity rises to stardom because he can play anything from an Italian to an African-American. He becomes whatever part is needed. It is interesting to note that in these Hollywood films, Diesel has become an outsider in each film, yet his sexual appeal and physical and mental superiority are also highlighted as aspects of this "bad boy" aura. Diesel's characters are always experts at being devious. In each film, lead characters seek, often reluctantly, his help and advice for survival, be it against deadly alien creatures (*Pitch Black*) or in a crucial business teleconference (*The Boiler Room*). His talents surpass those of all other characters, black and white.

O'Grady has said, "Interracial sex, and the fear surrounding it, seems to me to be at the nexus of the country's social forces."[19] Hence, the creation of elaborate miscegenation laws to control the potential of interracial sex to degrade the white, European, capitalist patriarchal social structures in the Americas and elsewhere. As the controversy over the descendants of Thomas Jefferson and Hemings attests, much can be at stake when these biracial offspring are allowed to be heard. Can whites transcend their race? Does not the mirror of difference always help construct, or reconstruct in some cases, the self? The critique of race in the academy has recently turned to examinations of whiteness and notions of white ethnicity with such works as David R. Roediger's *The Wages of Whiteness: Race and the Making of the American Working Class* (1991), Theodore W. Allen's *The Invention of the White Race* (1997), Matthew Frye Jacobson's *Whiteness of a Different Color: European Immigrants and the Alchemy of Race* (1998), Karen Bodkin's *How Jews Become White Folks and What that Says about Race in America* (1998). In the movie *Bulworth*, the love affair between Halle Berry's "ghetto girl" and Warren Beattie's racist politician is such a bridging of disparate sectors of the American population that is presented as socially, politically, and personally altering; here, the interracial relationship serves as a moral corrective of sorts for the white oppressor who empathizes so much with blacks that Berry even refers to Beattie as "my nigger." The Jefferson-Hemings union is the best example of this type of nationalistic racial "spin" placed on relationships. Some of those who have acknowledged their relationship and its longevity have reread Jefferson's more tempered statements regarding blacks as a reflection of the humanity he witnessed in his relationship with Hemings. As many have been quick to point out, however, he still allowed politics to silence his abolitionist feeling and no matter how much he may or may not have cared for Hemings, he still owned her until his death.

However, post-colonial theorists have continued to argue that the very core of white, European identity was indeed shaped by such transgressions, especially those of the late-nineteenth and twentieth centuries. In *The Empire Writes Back: Theory and Practice in Post-Colonial Literature*, Bill Ashcroft, Gareth Griffiths, and Helen Tiffin point out that

> *Africa is the source for the most significant and catalytic images of the first two decades of the twentieth century. In on very significant way the "discovery" of Africa was the dominant paradigm for the self-discovery of the twentieth-century European world in all its self-contradiction, self-*

> *doubt, and self-destruction, for the European journey out of the light of Reason into the Heart of Darkness. As such, the more extreme forms of the self-critical and anarchic ushered in can be seen to depend on the existence of a post-colonial Other which provides its condition of formation.*[20]

In this next millennium, the cultural syncretisms of European encounters with not only Africa but Asia and Latin America will redefine, and possibly extinguish, European hegemony in some parts of the world where it exists. The numbers tell the future. Within a few decades, people of non-European ancestry or mixed ancestry will dominate certain populations in America and Europe.

Christian Walker alludes to the sexual dimension of these encounters in his *Miscegenation Series* (1985–88). It consists of sepia photographs which depict close-up views of interacting body parts whose blurred and grainy surface simultaneously allude to old daguerreotypes and contemporary pornography. The nudity and overlapping suggest sexual encounters, yet gender is often unclear. The murkiness of the sepia tone forces the viewer to stare and probe for more information. Walker makes us conscious of the act of looking. This consciousness makes the viewer aware of the exotic and verboten aspects of the social attitudes towards interracial sex. Adrian Piper's *Vanilla Nightmare Series* (1986–87) also uses ambiguity to address societal fears of racial mixing and conflict beneath the surface of everyday life. She literally brings these hidden terrors to the surface in her drawings of blacks, some sexually menacing to whites, over pages of the *New York Times*. Similarly, her video installation, *Cornered* of 1988 presents a personal view of being a light-skinned black woman whose very existence, poignantly documented with her father's "conflicting" birth certificates: one declaring him white, the other "colored," makes whites and blacks confront the distorted race relations of the US.

The frenzy over Tiger Woods and the anticipation of Colin Powell's bid for the presidency in the mid 1990s were desperate, national scrambles for racial reconciliation. Both a recent advertisement for a clothing company called NuSouth and the work of Kara Walker struggle to simultaneously confront and market slavery's past, one source of the nation's racial woes. Yet, is the nation read to "sell" slavery? The Africanized, red, black, and green Confederate flag is NuSouth's logo and the ad's text identifies its buyers as the sons and daughters of former slaves and former slave owners, a line lifted from Martin Luther King Jr.'s "I Have A Dream" speech. A final line presents the sportswear as conciliatory: "Threads that connect us. Words that free us." The controversy over Walker's representations of our slave past, such as *Cotton* (1997) whose blending of humor, brutality, and racial stereotypes are considered by some to be offensive and dangerous, and the dismal failure of Oprah Winfrey's project, the movie *Beloved*, may indicate that we are not quite ready to confront this history only 140 years later.[21]

Are multiracial icons the answer to national harmony? Can they really transcend centuries of conflict as revisions of the past and hopes for the future? Despite his symbolism, Tiger Woods was never announced as the first multiracial person to win this or that PGA tournament. In the US blacks claim him and in Asia, Asians. And despite the multiracial rhetoric, his proclivity towards telling racist jokes about big black penises has been disappointing to some and dampened many multiracialist hopes. A "multiracial" choice on the 2000 census will not erase the "us/them" (and now more often, "us/them/them and them") mentalities that the artists discussed in this essay are critiquing. What has motivated me to write on these artists is that their reflections on these multicultural realities resist current trends in the mainstream media to simplify our increasingly complex populations through a nationalistic lens. O'Grady, Kim, and others encourage us to scrutinize and problematize the idea of a "raceless," "colorblind" world. As O'Grady honestly writes, "With the diptych [both real and symbolic], there's no being saved, no before and after, no either/or; it's both/and, at the same time. With no resolution, you have to stand there a nd deal."[22] These artists present the complexities of our society. The coexistence of beauty, horror, love, death, happiness, and rape does not shy away from the history that shapes our present. Historical figures like La Malinche and Sally Hemings *did* build nations with their European lovers.

And it is this burden of history that prevents a multiracial person to be devoid of race; widespread ethnic "cancellations" will not "end race" as writers like Crouch predict. It will be the challenge for us and following generations to cope, articulate, and understand the conundrum of a multiethnic nation, the polyptych of cultures in which we live. I am not arguing for ignoring our post-colonial hybridity, for, as Ashcroft and his colleagues so eloquently note:

> *It is arguable that to move towards a genuine affirmation of multiple forms of native "difference," we must recognize that this hybridity will inevitably continue ... [and through it] a genuinely transformative and interventionist criticism of contemporary post-colonial reality can be achieved.*[23]

Through creating new critical linguistic, socio-political and economic models that are inclusive and not dismissive of the lingering effects of our new societies' historical foundations, we can address all of the complexities and challenges of our multiracial "conditions." We must follow the example of our historical, transracial icons like La Malinche and Hemings who, according to O'Grady's eloquent statement, "met the future with forgiveness and lack of fear."[24]

Notes

1. A version of this essay was presented during the panel, "La Malinche as Metaphor" at the College Art Association Annual Conference on February 13, 1999 and yet another appeared in *Third Text*, vol. 53 (Winter 2000-01).

2. Smith, Gary. "Sportsman of the Year: The Chosen One" in *Sports Illustrated*, vol. 85:26 (December 23, 1996), 55.

3. *The All-American Skin Game; Or, The Decoy of Race* (Vintage Books, 1997), 244.

4. Cottingham, Laura. "Lorraine O'Grady. Artist and Art Critic. An Interview" in *Art Influences* 1996, vol. XV. Ed. James V. Hatch, et al. New York: Hatch-Billops Collection, Inc., 1996, 214.

5. Crouch, Stanley. "Race is Over. Black, White, Red, Yellow—Same Difference" in *New York Times Magazine*, September 29, 1996, 29.

6. *Newsweek*, vol. 125:7 (February 13, 1995). *Newsweek* revisited this issue as a cover story in Fall of 2000.

7. Senna, Danzy. "Passing and the Problematic of Multiracial Pride" in *Black Renaissance/Renaissance Noire*, vol. 2:1 (Fall/ Winter 1998), 76.

8. Bush, David A. "Ozone Anxiety: It's a White Thing" in *Harper's*, vol. 187:1723 (December 1993), 28. Bush actually recommends that the government encourages racial mixing. In reading through the popular press and its take on the new multiethnic nation, I found it to be overwhelmingly contradictory with much statistical manipulation. The races and ethnicities that were considered also varied. A survey of this literature is evidence enough that we are plunging ahead in our analysis yet incredibly bereft of the tools to do so.

9. Stephen M. Fjellman coined this phrase in his *Vinyl Leaves: Walt Disney World and America* (Oxford: Westview Press, 1992), 59.

10. Smith, 33.

11. Smith, 36.

12. Davis, Theo. "Artist as Critic. An Interview with Conceptualist Lorraine O'Grady," in *Sojourner: The Women's Forum*, November 1996, 28.

13. For more on nineteenth-century images of miscegenation, see Judith Wilson's seminal article, "Optical Illusions. Images of Mixcegenation in Nineteenth- and Twentieth-Century American Art," in *American Art*, vol. 5:3 (Summer 1991), 88-1-7. I am indebted to this essay and subsequent discussions with Professor Wilson. It is my hope that my essay successfully continues the dialogue she began in 1991.

14. Greenhouse, Wendy and Joyntyle Robinson. *The Art and Life of Archibald Motley, Jr.* (Chicago: Chicago Historical Society, 1991), 9.

15. *Black Skin, White Masks* (New York: Grove, 1967 (1952)), 112.

16. *New York Times Magazine*, August 16, 1998, 39.

17. Powell, Richard J. *The Homecoming: The Art of William H. Johnson* (Washington, DC: Smithsonian, 1991), 69.

18. E-mail letter to author, February 5, 1999.

19. Quoted in Laura Cottingham, "Lorraine O'Grady. Artist and Art Critic. An Interview" in *Art Influences* 1996, vol. XV. Ed. James V. Hatch, et al. New York: Hatch-Billips Collection, Inc., 1996, 213.

20. New York: Routledge, 1989, 160.

21. For more on the Walker controversy see *International Review of African-American Art* (December 1997).

22. Quoted in "The Diptych vs. the Triptych: An Excerpt from a Conversation between Lorraine O'Grady and a Studio Visitor" (unpublished, undated, and unpaginated), courtesy of the artist.

23. *Empire Writes Back*, 180.

24. E-mail letter to author, February 5, 1999.

Molly Nesbit

Notes from New York

July 2005

Around 1844 Bronson Alcott helped Henry David Thoreau get the roof on his cabin at Walden Pond, just outside Boston. After they had finished, Thoreau wrote of him:

> *I think that he should keep an inn, a caravansery, on the world's highway, where the thinkers of all nations might put up, and on his sign should be written … 'Enter all ye that have leisure and a quiet mind, who earnestly and without anxiety seek the right road.' A thought floats as serenely and as much at home in his mind as a duck pluming herself on a far inland lake … Ah, such discourse as we had—hermit and philosopher … It expanded and cracked my little house.*[1]

Thoreau went on to write his essay "On the Duty of Civil Disobedience" just before the revolutions of 1848. This was the essay that impressed Gandhi and Martin Luther King Jr., and many more advocates of nonviolent politics. Remember the opening lines?

> *I heartily accept the motto,—"That Government is best which governs least;" and I should like to see it acted up to more rapidly and systematically. Carried out, it finally amounts to this, which also I believe,—"That government is best which governs not at all;" and when men are prepared for it, that will be the kind of government which they will have. Government is at best but an expedient; but most governments are usually, and all governments are sometimes, inexpedient. The objections which have been brought against a standing army, and they are many and weighty, and deserve to prevail, may also at last be brought against a standing government. The standing army is only an army of the standing government. The government itself, which is only the mode which the people have chosen to execute their will, is equally liable to be abused and perverted before the people can act through it. Witness the present Mexican war, the work of comparatively a few individuals using the standing government as their tool; for, in the outset, the people would not have consented to this measure.*
>
> *This American government—what is it but a tradition, though a recent one, endeavoring to transmit itself unimpaired to posterity, but each instant losing some of its integrity? It has not the vitality and force of a single living man; for a single man can bend it to his will. It is a sort of wooden gun to the people themselves; and, if ever they should use it in earnest as a real one against each other, it will surely split. But it is not the less necessary for this; for the people must have some complicated machinery or other, and hear its din, to satisfy that idea of government which they have. Governments show thus how successfully men can be imposed on, even impose on themselves, for their own advantage. It is excellent, we must all allow; yet this government never of itself furthered any enterprise, but by the alacrity with which it*

got out of its way. It *does not keep the country free.* It *does not settle the West.* It *does not educate. The character inherent in the American people has done all that has been accomplished; and it would have done somewhat more, if the government had not sometimes got in its way. For government is an expedient by which men would fain succeed in letting one another alone; and, as has been said, when it is most expedient, the governed are most let alone by it. Trade and commerce, if they were not made of India rubber, would never manage to bounce over the obstacles which legislators are continually putting in their way; and, if one were to judge these men wholly by the effects of their actions, and not partly by their intentions, they would deserve to be classed and punished with those mischievous persons who put obstructions on the railroads.*

But, to speak practically and as a citizen, unlike those who call themselves no-government men, I ask for, not at once no government, but at once a better government. Let every man make known what kind of government would command his respect, and that will be one step toward obtaining it.

* * *

"For the first-rate artist, there is a moment when he's really getting revved up, and the time just flows into him. It only happens once. It happens without his awareness at all. He planned nothing. He was just going ahead doing this next thing."[2] So Mike Nichols observed, sounding like a latter-day Hegel, of Tony Kushner. The time is history. It cracks our little houses open.

* * *

Periodically, while writing about something else, American writers stop to open the door for air. This past year two did so as they mulled over the words coming from the government, specifically, those of an advisor to the president of the United States. The advisor had told Ron Suskind, a reporter, that he and other people like him lived "in what we call the reality-based community," which the advisor defined as those believing "that solutions emerge from your judicious study of discernible reality." The advisor cut the idea down: "That's not the way the world really works any more. We're an empire now," he declared, "and when we act, we create our own reality."

Anthony Grafton dropped these words abruptly into the essay he was writing on the work of Sir Isaac Newton. This gave them even darker purpose. "We Americans," Grafton had just explained to the reader, "trace our origins, spiritual and intellectual, largely to the heralds of the Newtonian movement: writers and doers like Benjamin Franklin. The creators of the United States couched their arguments for its independence and their visions of its constitution in the Newtonian language of reason, nature's laws, and factual evidence. Nowadays, powerful leaders around the world defy these forms of intellectual self-discipline."[3] In other words, nowadays an apple cart spills over the Enlightenment and the world as a whole. What once could only have been satire, or farce, is now policy. In the case of the United States, one could say that this policy flaunts its ideology to such a degree that it reveals itself to be smoke-screen, or plain old smoke.

Smoke signals fire. The house could be burning down. When Mark Danner looked out to the assembly of literature students graduating from the University of California at Berkeley, he called upon them to look at the way the world was working and observed that we had lost the ability to act on the scandals in our time, like the illegal abuse of prisoners at Abu Ghraib, and to prosecute them as crimes. The scandals too were actions. Not a matter of "a few bad apples" as the Bush administration has claimed, but a matter of policy decisions taken at the top. This, Danner told the students, had happened since they had arrived at school in the fall of 2001. The conclusion? In the space of those four years, "our government decided to change this country from a nation that officially does not torture to one, officially, that does."[4]

"America has no empire to extend or utopia to establish," George W. Bush had declared in 2002 when announcing his policy of pre-emptive war to the graduating class of West Point cadets, and to the country.[5] These words of seeming no purpose have had enormous, terrible, and concrete consequences both inside and outside the United States. They are there to be read, if one is willing to read, to fish the smoke and subterfuge and catch the facts. Danner advised the students to do just that, to remain determined Empiricists of the Word.

He gave them more evidence, more words and an example. He quoted more of the presidential advisor's counsel to the reality-based reporter. "And while you're studying that reality—judiciously, as you will," the advisor had said, slick, too confident, lordly, "we'll act again, creating other new realities, which you can study too, and that's how things will sort out." A prophesy or a problem? Danner spoke with martial art. He recited Czesław Miłosz's strange, sad lyric, "A Song on the End of the World," which was written in the throes of another war in Warsaw in 1944. It had not become defenseless with time. In the "Song" an old man binds his tomatoes, others cannot see the end happening, but the man sees the end's absolute banality and equates it with life:

On the day the world ends
A bee circles a clover,
A fisherman mends a glimmering net.
Happy porpoises jump in the sea,
By the rainspout young sparrows are playing
And the snake is gold-skinned as it should always be.

On the day the world ends
Women walk through the fields under their umbrellas,
A drunkard grows sleepy at the edge of a lawn,
Vegetable peddlers shout in the street
And a yellow-sailed boat comes nearer the island,
The voice of a violin lasts in the air
And leads into a starry night.

And those who expected lightning and thunder
Are disappointed.
And those who expected signs and archangels' trumps
Do not believe it is happening now.

As long as the sun and the moon are above,
As long as the bumblebee visits a rose,
As long as rosy infants are born
No one believes it is happening now.

Only a white-haired old man, who would be a prophet
Yet is not a prophet, for he's much too busy,
Repeats while he binds his tomatoes:
There will be no other end of the world,
There will be no other end of the world.

Apples and tomatoes too create the conditions that allow time to flow suddenly into a person. Remember Newton's gravity. Remember Miłosz writing his song. Remember how history is actually made. Time flows through the facts in the poet's words too. Together an empiricist and a poet were raising the roof.

Notes

1. From Thoreau's original manuscript for *Walden*, as cited by Geraldine Brooks, "Orpheus at the Plough: Louisa May Alcott's Difficult Father," *New Yorker* (January 10, 2005), p. 64.

2. Quoted by John Lahr, "After Angels: Tony Kushner's Political Theatre," *New Yorker*, January 3, 2005, p. 48.

3. Anthony Grafton, "The Ways of Genius," *New York Review of Books* (December 2, 2004), p. 37. He is quoting from the report of Ron Suskind, "Without a Doubt," *The New York Times Magazine* (October 17, 2004).

4. Mark Danner, "What Are You Going To Do With That?" *New York Review of Books* (June 23, 2005), pp. 52–56.

5. President George W. Bush, "Answering the Call of History," Address at 2002 Graduation Exercise of the United States Military Academy, West Point, New York, June 1, 2002. U.S. Department of State: http://www.state.gov/images/i_spcr08.gif.

I have no choice in this matter

CORRECT

I rate the static and whine for independence
the calcium of our age
and the plaque for every era

CORRECT

Can I at least ask about the definer.
The central idea
the mirror for value? The t.v. commercial?
As value defines   independence correct?

N/A

Not possible. N/A is not possible. Absolutely
applicable. The cord is in the bag.
The opiate is the double "W". Want to be wanted.
What to be wanted. The tradition of independence
and subsequent demand for it is vanity. A decomposing
vanity. Close to vain. And closer to vein.
Open it up to flap and drain. Open it up
to prevail. To give great to place.

CORRECT

I heave to the side of the road, and in broken status,
the beast, I, fall to the dirt path gutters. Remove my load
flag down assistance from the following farmer. As a failure
is never a fulfillment of service blink at my wounds and pass.
My death is an act.

CORRECT

Lets say I am a young man, and for certain of my purpose
for certain of my mark
For certain that to be for certain is my mark.
I adopt the voice of power. I embrace the cache of opinion.
And I master the misused performance. "" I am a young engineer.
Grown strong on books and familial love. Aware of the
quadrants and their areas of strain.Poor things.
"To buckle" states two meanings. I am unsure which precedent to
believe in most. But that doesn't silence me.
In time, Jason looked to its pendulum and resisted his anger.
Who is Jason? Is he a mover or a runner?

The political voice is a pointer   and
independence is a purchase.

N/A

N/A

Further reading

- Appiah, Kwame Anthony. "Whose Culture Is It?". *New York Review of Books*, February 9, 2006
- Armstrong, Elizabeth. *UltraBaroque: Aspects of Post-Latin American Art*. La Jolla, CA: Museum of Contemporary Art, San Diego, 2000
- Ault, Julie. *Alternative Art New York, 1965–1985*. Minneapolis: University of Minnesota Press, 2002
- Backström, Fia. *Heard Instinct*. New York: Self-published, 2006
- Badiou, Alain. "Fifteen Theses on Contemporary Art". *Lacanian Ink*, 23, 2004
- Baker, George. "Photography's Expanded Field." *October*, 114, Fall 2005
- Baker, George, Benjamin H.D. Buchloh, Hal Foster, Andrea Fraser, David Joselit, Rosalind Krauss, John Miller, Helen Molesworth and Robert Storr. "Round Table: The Present Conditions of Art Criticism," *October* 100, Spring 2002
- Benkler, Yochai. *The Wealth of Networks: How Social Production Transforms Markets and Freedom*. New Haven: Yale University Press, 2006
- Bersani, Leo. "Psychoanalysis and the Aesthetic Subject." *Critical Inquiry* 32, no 2, winter 2006
- Bevan, Robert. *The Destruction of Memory: Architecture at War*. London: Reaktion Books, 2006
- Boxer, Sarah. "The Remains of the Day". *Artforum*, vol. 30, no. 5, January 2002
- Buck-Morss, Susan. *Dreamworld and Catastrophe: The Passing of Mass Utopia in East and West*. Cambridge, MA: The MIT Press, 2000
- Burton, Johanna. "The 'Urmaterial' Urge". *Parkett*, 70, 2004
- Colomina, Beatriz. *Privacy and Publicity: Modern Architecture as Mass Media*. Cambridge, MA: The MIT Press, 1994
- Danto, Arthur. *Unnatural Wonders: Essays from the Gap Between Art and Life*. New York: Farrar, Straus and Giroux, 2005
- De Bay, Philip and James Bolton. *Garden Mania*. New York: Clarkson Potter, 2000
- Derrida, Jacques. "The Global Theater of Forgiveness". *The Village Voice*, May 26, 2005
- Dickinson, Emily. *The Collected Poems of Emily Dickinson*. New York: Barnes & Noble Classics, 2003
- Diederichsen, Diedrich. "The Primary: Political and Anti-Political Continuities Between Minimal Music and Minimal Art". *A Minimal Future?: Art as Object, 1958–1968*. Los Angeles/ Cambridge, MA: Museum of Contemporary Art, Los Angeles/MIT Press, 2004
- Foster, Hal. "An Archival Impulse". *October* 110, Fall 2004
- Foster, Hal. "Arty Party," *London Review of Books*, vol. 25, no. 23, December 4, 2003, 21–22
- Foster, Sesshu. *Atomik Aztek*. San Francisco: City Lights Publishers, 2005
- Flusser, Vilém. *Writings*. trans. Erik Eisel. Minneapolis: University of Minnesota Press, 2002
- Frankfurt, Harry G. *On Bullshit*. Princeton, NJ: Princeton University Press, 2005
- Funcke, Bettina, ed. *New York Twice*. Paris: Air de Paris, 2005
- Fusco, Coco and Brian Wallis, eds. *Only Skin Deep: Changing Visions of the American Self*. New York: International Center of Photography with Harry N Abrams, Inc., 2003
- Gass, William H. "On Evil." *Harper's*, January 2004
- Gillick, Liam. *Literally No Place: Communes, Bars, and Greenrooms*. London: Libro / Book Works, 2002
- Hainley, Bruce and John Waters. *Art, A Sex Book*. London: Thames & Hudson, 2003
- Handey, Jack. "This Is No Game." *New Yorker*, January 9, 2006
- Huberman, Anthony and Paul Pfeiffer, eds. *Grey Flags*. New York: Sculpture Center, 2006
- King, Emily. "This Charming Man." *Frieze*, 81, March 2004
- Kwinter, Sanford. *Architectures of Time: Toward a Theory of the Event in Modernist Culture*. Cambridge, MA: The MIT Press, 2002
- Latour, Bruno and Peter Weibel, eds. *Making Things Public: Atmospheres of Democracy*. Karlsruhe, Germany and Cambridge, MA: ZKM Center for Art and Media and The MIT Press, 2005
- McDonough, William and Michael Braungart. *Cradle to Cradle: Remaking the Way We Make Things*. New York: North Point Press, 2002
- Mitchell, W.J.T. *What Do Pictures Want?: The Lives and Loves of Images*. Chicago: University of Chicago Press, 2005
- Miller, John. *The Price Club: Selected Writings (1977–1998)*. JRP Editions, 2000
- Nauman, Bruce and Janet Kraynek (ed.). *Please Pay Attention Please: Bruce Nauman's Words: Writings and Interviews*. Cambridge, MA: The MIT Press, 2003
- Parrino, Steven. *The No Texts (1979–2003)*. New York: Abaton Book Company, 2003
- Plagens, Peter. "How Art Has Changed a Lot," *American Art*, vol. 16, no. 1, Spring 2002
- Rancière, Jacques. *The Politics of Aesthetics*. London: Continuum Books, 2004
- Rectanus, Mark. *Culture Incorporated: Museums, Artists and Corporate Sponsorships*. Minneapolis: University of Minnesota Press, 2002
- Relyea, Lane. "Your Art World: Or, The Limits of Connectivity." *Afterall* 14, 2006
- Rinpoche, Tenzin Wangyal. *Healing with Form, Energy and Light: The Five Elements in Tibetan Shamanism, Tantra, and Dzogchen*. Ithaca, NY: Snow Lion Publications, 2002
- Ross, Kristin. *May '68 and Its Afterlives*. Chicago: University of Chicago Press, 2002
- Rothkopf, Scott. "Hit or Myth". *Artforum*, vol. 39, no. 2, October 2001

– Santner, Eric. *On the Psychotheology of Every-day Life: Reflections on Freud and Rosenzweig.* Chicago: University of Chicago Press, 2001
– Sen, Amartya. *Identity and Violence: The Illusion of Destiny.* New York: W.W. Norton, 2006
– Stallabrass, Julian. "Spectacle and Terror". *New Left Review*, 37, January–February 2006
– Strauss, David Levi. "Inconvenient Evidence: The Effects of Abu Ghraib." *Abu Ghraib: The Politics of Torture.* Berkeley, CA: North Atlantic Books, 2004
– Thompson, Nato and Gregory Sholette (eds.). *The Interventionists: Users' Manual for the Creative Disruption of Everyday Life.* Cambridge, MA: The MIT Press, 2004
– Virilio, Paul. *Art and Fear.* trans. Julie Rose. London and New York: Continuum International Publishing Group, 2003
– Virno, Paolo. *A Grammar of the Multitude.* New York and Los Angeles: Semiotext(e), 2004
– Wacjman, Gérard. "The Birth of the Intimate." *Lacanian Ink*, 23/24, 2004
– Wagner, Anne M. "Splitting and Doubling: Gordon Matta-Clark and the Body of Sculpture." *Grey Room*, 14, Winter 2004
– Wark, Mackenzie. *A Hacker Manifesto.* Cambridge, MA: Harvard University Press, 2004
– Warner, Michael. *Publics and Counterpublics.* New York: Zone Books, 2002
– Wu, Chin-tao. *Privatising Culture: Corporate Art Intervention Since the 1980s.* London: Verso, 2002
– Žižek, Slavoj. *The Parallax View.* Cambridge, MA: The MIT Press, 2006
– Tirdad Zolghadr. "Them and Us." *Frieze*, 96, January–February 2006

"Uncertain States of America" premiered at the Astrup Fearnley Museum of Modern Art, Oslo, in November 2005 and has since appeared at the Center for Curatorial Studies, Bard College, New York, the Serpentine Gallery, London, and, as this book goes to press, the Reykjavik Art Museum, Iceland. It will later travel to Denmark, France, Poland, and China – perhaps beyond.

This reader is a further extension of the exhibition and a valuable compendium to the catalogue produced by the Astrup Fearnley Museum in 2005. An earlier version of this publication was released alongside the presentation of "Uncertain States of America" at the Serpentine Gallery in September 2006. Compiling writings around American artistic practice since 2000, it provides a richer context for "Uncertain States of America" and acts as a unique entrée into the minds of the exhibition's artists – numerous texts were recommended by them – and a selection of today's leading critics, curators and scholars. Like the exhibition itself, the *USA Reader*, is a gauge of contemporary creativity and critical thinking in the United States. It serves as a vital document for our audiences and one that challenges us to think deeper about "Uncertain States of America."

We would like to extend special thanks to Hans Rasmus Astrup, Stuart Bailey, Daniel Birnbaum, André Gélis, Charles Gute, Noah Horowitz, Wojciech Krukowski, Nicole Lanctot, Holger Reenberg, David Reinfurt, Caroline Schneider, Brian Sholis, Li Xianting, Hafthór Yngvason, all of the artists in "Uncertain States of America," and the entire teams of the Astrup Fearnley Museum of Modern Art, the Serpentine Gallery, and Sternberg Press.

Julia Peyton-Jones
Director,
Serpentine Gallery
and Co-Director,
Exhibitions
& Programmes,
Serpentine Gallery

Gunnar B. Kvaran
Director,
Astrup Fearnley Museum
of Modern Art

Hans Ulrich Obrist
Co-Director,
Exhibitions & Programmes
and Director of
International Projects,
Serpentine Gallery

The Uncertain States of America Reader is published by Sternberg Press, New York/Berlin, in association with the Astrup Fearnley Museum of Modern Art, Oslo, and the Serpentine Gallery, London.

SternbergPress

Caroline Schneider, 1182 Broadway #1602
New York, NY 10001, USA
and Linienstrasse 159, 10115 Berlin, Germany
T +49 30 59 00 958 21
F +49 30 59 00 958 20
www.sternberg-press.com

ASTRUP FEARNLEY MUSEET FOR MODERNE KUNST
ASTRUP FEARNLEY MUSEUM OF MODERN ART

Dronningens gate 4, Oslo, Norway
T +47 22 93 60 60
F +47 22 93 60 65
www.afmuseet.no

Serpentine Gallery

Kensington Gardens, London W2 3XA, UK
T +44 20 7402 6075
F +44 20 7402 4103
www.serpentinegallery.org

Edited by Noah Horowitz and Brian Sholis.

Designed by Dexter Sinister, New York.

Illustration on cover and title page by Matthew Brannon.

Printed by GZD, Ditzingen-Heimerdingen, Germany.

All articles in this publication have been reproduced as closely as possible to their original manifestation.

ISBN 1-933128-21-6